20th Century Boomer

JAMES ARTEMUS

Copyright © 2023 James Artemus

All rights reserved.

No part of this book may be reproduced, stored in a retrieval system, or transmitted, in any form or by any means, electronic, mechanical, photocopying, recording, or otherwise, without prior written permission from the publisher, except for brief quotations embodied in critical reviews and certain other noncommercial uses permitted by copyright law.

ISBN: 978-1-963017-15-1 (Paperback)

ISBN: 978-1-963017-16-8 (Hardcover)

Printed in the United States of America

For Dad

Willis Howard

Thanks to my wife, Janine, and daughter, Lanie, for their love, patience, and support throughout the process of writing this book.

Special thanks to Michael Nesmith who's autobiography "Infinite Tuesday" inspired me to write "20th Century Boomer"

Contents

Introduction 1
Part One (The 60s) 11
   And So It Begins 12
   Ask Not What You Can Do for Yourself…. 16
   A Tale of Time and Place 23
   The Big Bang 27
   Why Should I Cut My Hair? 34
   Lone Star President 41
   The Long Shadow of War 46
   Fantasy and Adventure 61
   Up Up, and Away… 68
   The First Time We Fall in Love 70
   "Eddie" 75
   The Race of 68 77
   The Birth of a Phobia 80
   Your Ballroom Days are Over 83
   George and "The Duke" 88
   All They Wanted Was to Be Free 92
   Everything Must Pass 96
Part Two (The 70s) 99
   Change is in the Air 100
   The More Things Change… 104
   Let it Be 107
   It All Goes Down on the Playground 109

- The Same as it Ever Was 121
- The Teacher and the Student 125
- The Heart of a Champion 132
- The Middle School Blues 140
- The Art of Sneaking 144
- This is the End…. Or is It? 150
- 200 Hundred Years and Counting 154
- The Final Frontier 156
- The Second Time We Fall in Love 159
- The Long and Short of It 163
- Life, Love, and the High School Ecosystem 167
- This is Captain America Falling… 170
- Disco Boys v.s. The Rockers 173
- Gallons of Trouble 182
- The Sweet Success of Failure 184

Part Three (The 80s) 185
- Into the Breach 186
- Do You Believe in Miracles? 190
- A Mountain of Trouble 195
- The King is Dead and so is the Walrus 198
- The Sage Recommends Psychedelics 203
- Acting Presidential 207
- Challenging Times 210
- Marginal Utility 214
- The Dating Slump Phenomenon 216
- And Then I Saw Her Face… 220
- I Want My MTV 224

    Big City Lights 228
    And Now for Act II… 233
    Big News Heard Around "My World" 235
    Awareness Born From Crumbling Rock 239
    The Soviet Union has a "Meltdown" 243
    Meanwhile, Back at the Ranch… 246
    School is Out… Forever 251
    The Actor and His Final Scene 253
    Meet the New Act... Same as the Old Act 257
    There's No Place Like Home 259
    And the Wall Came Crumbling Down 262
    Wagon Train to the Northern Plains 265

Part Four (The 90s) 270
    A New Beginning… Same Problems 271
    A View Like None Other 275
    Desert Storm 278
    Cold War Put into the Deep Freeze 282
    Hero's Are People Too... 285
    Left Turn After a Right 293
    Smell's Like the Death of Rock'n Roll 296
    The Colonel and I 301
    The Juice is On the Loose 306
    Good Times… Bad Times 313
    One Bill at a Time 320
    Love As a Wrecking Ball Part One 324
    Love As a Wrecking Ball Part Two 335
    I Want to Be Like Mike 343

Only the Lonely 350

What the Hell Bill? 358

A Distant Ship's Smoke on the Horizon 361

And So the Curtain Falls 366

Part Five The Truth as I See It… Though I Could Be Wrong ... 369

    How Different Could The Same Be? 370

    Just Think of It 373

    The Dimming Light of Religious Dogma 379

    When You Are Swimming in a Sewer, it's Hard Not To Be Covered in Shit 385

    Propinquity Where Have You Gone? 391

    There Once Was a Note… 400

Introduction

Since my early twenties, I always felt I had a least one book in me. I recall telling my father many years ago of my goal and my wish to pursue this endeavor. With a rather curious look on his face, he inquired about my motivation to engage in such a grand effort. I told him my reasoning was simple. It would be a taste of immortality. The way I figured the result of writing a book would mean somewhere, someplace, someone might just pick it up and read my thoughts. Long after I had turned to dust, my thoughts would still exist in perpetuity. Like I said, "A taste of immortality."

I began this sojourn decades ago in the late eighties with a novel I was developing titled "The Road." At that time, and for years later, I never considered writing anything but fiction. I have a reasonably good imagination with decent writing skills, so it seemed quite natural to me to venture into the world of fiction as my writing endeavor.

The novel was based on a man waking up on a desolate road in the middle of a vast barren land afflicted with a severe case of amnesia. Time had been so badly refracted and perverted to the point he no longer had any concept of the past, present, or future. Throughout his journey on the road, pieces of his memory would reignite, enlightening him to an actual past life he had once lived. Along the way, he would meet interesting people and engage in intriguing scenarios providing him clues about who he once was. As the pieces of his past began to materialize, he also gained insight into what his future might hold and what would be his destiny at the end of his long journey.

Ultimately the story would be rooted in the fundamental aspects of spirituality. It was to be built around the idea that striving for spiritual illumination eventually leads to redemption. The cost of suffering and sacrifice that would have to be endured to gain this enlightenment was where the core of the story would be told.

Of course, at the time, I had no idea in the "real world," I would take a similar journey for myself, as I suppose we all must do at some level. The novel was filled with similar scenarios I would actually face later in my own life... it was like I was creating my own future reality in the pages of fiction I was writing. In the end, it would be the adventures in my own life that would take me away from the fiction I was creating on paper. I never finished the novel. It sits somewhere in a cluttered corner of junk in an old three-ring binder, along with many other items from my life I never bother to look at anymore but don't have the heart to throw away.

The core of that story is still worth telling, and it still has merit in the sense we all have our own similar stories to tell. Our lives are filled with personal experiences of pleasure, suffering, and sacrifice, and if we are fortunate, we also have stories of illumination and redemption. The life of the solitary man wandering upon the road did matter, and his story was worth telling, perhaps as much as any other, though he may have forgotten the reason why.

I can't say what "illumination" or "redemption" may look like for anyone else but myself. All of us have eyes through which we see the world, and we all have our own established beliefs that guide us through this life. Some people worship money, power, or "things" while some worship themselves, claiming they worship God. Still, there are others who have no interest in any of those things and possess an entirely different set of values and beliefs. The truth is, what you value or worship will likely dictate how you live life and measure your own success.

None of us are free from the bonds of our own belief systems or personal perceptions of the world surrounding us. All of us are grounded in this physical reality we call our lives. What we have learned, lived, and observed forms our conscious awareness of our own existence. It is our experiences throughout our lives that ultimately define in the end what "existence" means to us and whether we believe it continues after we drop our physical bodies.

Our lives are filled with varying forms of stark and subtle contrasts, which ultimately allow us to comprehend any existence at all. Without these contrasts, we would exist in a world, not unlike the fabled character "Tommy" in the Who's rock opera of the same name. We would be deaf, dumb, and blind to all experiences living an existence without substance... nothing to define and nothing to understand.

This leads me to the explanation of why I chose to write this book and why I chose to write of "reality" instead of fiction. We often live our lives facing the stress and pressures of daily living without pondering how we got where we are. We simply accept our present circumstances, often never pondering what beliefs and attitudes were formed through our previous experiences. We know we are on this road we call our lives, but we sometimes forget it was built by us. This, of course, leads to the next obvious question "If we built the road, can we change its course?" Sometimes it feels like we are helpless to its twist and turns and we may even foresee a final destination that is unpleasant to us.

The truth is there is always time to change the course we are on. However, if we chose to change course, would we know what direction to take it? Have we lived, learned and observed enough through the years to finally know the direction we want to proceed? Reflecting on our past experiences and the development of our belief systems (based on those experiences) will provide us the knowledge of how we got where we are today. This is the starting point for real change... understanding our past to reshape our future.

Our attitudes that direct our actions throughout our lives are formed by fundamental beliefs garnered through our own personal experiences and observations. They build upon one another, supporting our beliefs and creating a cycle of self-fulfilling prophecy. In a very true sense, we create our own reality because we form it through our own psyche and play out the drama to meet the expectations of our own conscious and subconscious beliefs.

This book was written with the idea to address the past of those individuals of the "Baby Boomer" generation. To be more specific, attention is focused on those who came from the late stages of this generation. I was born in 1961, and this is where the story begins. I am by no means a voracious reader but from my perspective, there are few books that address this "late stage" Boomer generation who today are now experiencing life in their sixties. In a blink of an eye, we have grown from wide-eyed kids to mature and hopefully wise adults.

This is my story, to be certain, but it is also "our story," as we all experienced most of the events that will be addressed in this book. By choice, I took the recounting of our history to the new millennium and no further. The new millennium and beyond are for another time and perhaps another author to explore.... we shall see.

For the reader, the past events and experiences I discuss in this book will likely appear in their memory differently than my descriptions of them. Though hopefully rooted in historical accuracy, the fact remains the recounting of events covered in this book is from the hand and the mind of its author. Ultimately we all view life from our own lens based on our own beliefs and attitudes.

My hope is through the recalling of some of the major events of the 20th century, the reader will once again be placed "in the moment." The past will once again become a moment experienced in the present. More importantly, I hope the reader will look through the lens of their own past and recall how they felt in that moment and not how it appears to them decades later.

My desire is to have the reader drift back to the feelings they held at the time these events were actually occurring and assess the emotions they felt. In addition, the experiences I share of my personal life hopefully will spur thoughts of the reader's own similar experiences, thus providing an opportunity to examine the emotions tied with these events as well. In the end, many of these experiences have contributed to our current beliefs and attitudes toward interpersonal relationships, society and life itself.

If I am successful, the reader will take every personal experience I share or event I observed and reflect on their own feelings about *their* past. The reader will drift back to a time they have mostly ignored because the present now demands their full attention. It will be a journey back in time to explore feelings and moments that have mostly been forgotten even though, at a minimum, they are still quite active at a sub-conscious level.

One very poignant point I hope to make is that all of us have a story worth telling. You don't have to be a successful entertainer, sports figure or fighter pilot to have experiences worth sharing. The simple fact is life is filled with complex and intriguing scenarios surrounded by randomness and unpredictability. The very nature of this existence does not allow us to predict future events effectively. All of us are at the mercy of a future that, for the most part, is unknown, and all of us are faced with scenarios that require us to react and respond the best we can at the moment. God has equipped us all with problem-solving abilities, but how we engage in our life experiences and resolve the issues confronting us will vary greatly from person to person.

By the very nature of human beings' capacity to problem solve, combined with a sense of personal ego, the complexity of our species is unrivaled. Though similarities certainly do exist between us, none can reach into the mind of another and supplant the sense of "self" we all possess. While asleep, my dreams are uniquely *mine*. I *create* my dreams just as I *create* my waking existence, and no other participant can step into the theater of my consciousness as it is my drama and mine alone.

Each one of us has our own "theater of the mind" and, with it, a story worth telling if, for no other reason, every life is distinctly unique. We must never lose sight of our own unique place in this drama we call existence. I hope by sharing my story, the reader will take time to appreciate their own unique life journey and recognize the value of sharing those experiences with others. There is always something to learn and appreciate in listening to the experiences of another.

All of us see our past from a unique and individualistic perspective. The memories created based on previous experiences can impact us in the present as well. Often we unconsciously apply knowledge garnered from past events to address current scenarios. From a strictly philosophical perspective, the "present" is the only relevant moment in time. The past is simply just imagery we conjure up, as is the future. Neither the past nor the future can be experienced. They can only be imagined. However, reflection upon the past does provide us with a road map to how we ended up where we currently are. More importantly, through the examination of the past, we can determine what experiences and choices were made that delivered us to this exact moment we live in the present.

It is one thing to recount our experiences and choices we made, but it is quite another thing to come to some level of understanding of why we believe what we believe. Therefore it is not enough to just reflect on the past. Where the real value lies is upon the discovery of how our past experiences molded the person we are today.

Everything in life is in constant motion... from the swirling microscopic molecules that form our existence to the vast universe, which is ever-expanding. Life is constantly changing, which means we are changing as well, whether we wish to or not. The question is... will we be in control of those changes and guide our future life path, or will we helplessly submit to outside forces? The truth is we have control of our reality even if our senses often tell us a different story. It begins and ends with our mental approach to this existence and how we want to perceive the challenges it presents to us. It is in our hands, or rather in our minds, to determine the road we are on.

Much like the hero in my unfinished novel, I believe we live this life often lost in a haze of incomplete memories and forgotten actions that have led us to this present moment. The protagonist in my novel appears utterly lost on a path he has no idea how he landed upon. The truth is he has always been in charge of creating his own reality, even though he believes that is not the case. In the end, of course, our hero finds redemption through his own reckoning of his past. He reclaims his present existence and sets a new direction for his future. He does this by finally realizing that all along, he has been responsible for the creation of his own experiences.

A few words about the construction of this book: it made sense to take a linear approach to my story, addressing each decade in its proper sequence. There are five parts to this book, with the first four parts dedicated to recounting the last forty years of the twentieth century. The fifth part is an amalgamation of thoughts and suppositions I have developed based on six decades of personal observations.

Throughout the book, you will notice an obvious theme... I am human. To tell my story with any degree of accuracy, I am compelled to expose all aspects of my character. Throughout the pages, you will note I can be petty, bitter, unfair, and unapologetically hypocritical. At times I will display unwarranted arrogance and blatant bias. However, at other times, I will demonstrate self-sacrifice, loyalty, and a strong belief in a divine being.

In the end, I am not unlike most people who are simply trying to do their best and make sense of their existence. To be human is to be imperfect, and being imperfect is our fate. To seek something greater beyond our imperfection requires faith. I am simply a person just trying to make good in this life while trying to come to some conclusions about what all of this means in the end. In other words... I'm just your average guy.

That being said, I do hope after reading this book, you will have reconciled your part in all of the events and personal experiences that, at one time or another, entered into your conscious thoughts. I am no sage and certainly have not been a receptor of divine grace from a higher source. That being said, at times, I will humbly submit my own personal philosophies and share a few pieces of wisdom I may have garnered through the years. Whether they are "right" or "wrong" is for you to determine or, for that matter, decide if they hold any usefulness to you at all. In the end, my experiences and conclusions are all I have to offer.

This is not a "self-help book" by any means, but perhaps it could be. It is not a book of enlightenment or a path to redemption.... but then again, who knows what it may provide? It is strictly up to you to decide through self-reflection upon the stories I impart and the experiences I share. Ultimately it will be what you choose to make it. It can simply be a vessel used to journey back in time and reminisce about the "old days," or it may possibly provide some insight into why you ended up on the road you are currently on. Whatever the final disposition is, like everything else in life, it will depend on your mental approach to it.

We all have created the road on which we travel, but is it the one we had wished for ourselves? Reflection may provide us with part of the answer as to whether we are happy with the path we have set for ourselves or perhaps need to change its course. Here's hoping your journey in the pages that follow leads to some level of reconciliation of the past with the present, and through this exercise, you will discover a path toward further illumination in the future.

20th Century Boomer

Part One
(The 60s)

And So It Begins

I was born on September 20th, 1961, in Cheyenne, Wyoming. It was unseasonably cool that late summer day, the temperature only reaching 59 degrees. Then again, Cheyenne, the state capitol of Wyoming, sits at an impressive elevation of 6100 feet where the summers are short, and the winters are long. My dad once told me that the only good thing that came out of Cheyenne was me. He hated the place, he hated the cold, and he hated the wind.

My father was raised in the panhandle of Oklahoma and Northern Texas. My mother, a German refugee from World War II, grew up in Amarillo, Texas, after arriving from Germany at the tender age of nine. They would marry in 1957 in Amarillo with just a few family members in attendance. In the two years that followed, my mother gave birth to my two older sisters, Kelly and Kathy.

Just prior to my birth in 1961, my father had relocated his young family to a town much further north than he had ever lived. As I mentioned, Cheyenne was a town he did not care for. However, a job promotion coupled with growing family needs drove him far from his childhood homeland. This predicament was not so much by choice but by practicality. He was the "breadwinner," as was common for most families back in those days. Therefore, he bore the full financial responsibility for its survival.

Much to my father's delight, we moved away from Cheyenne when I was only four. Though my memories are limited, I am proud to say I was born there and, through the years, have visited it often. It is, after all, the place of my birth, and my dad did claim I was the best thing to come out of that windy old cowboy town, so what's not to like about it?

My memories of life in Cheyenne are really just snapshots with very little fluidity to them. Petting a puppy through the neighbor's fence, pushing a toy lawn mower, and hitting my head on the corner of a white stool are mere frozen images burned into my memory. However, I do recall asking my parents each night if there was a monster lying beneath my bed, with them always assuring me there was no monster lying in wait to devour me. I usually was able to sleep after their assurance, but my fears would return the next day, and I would need their validation each night I would be safe. At that age, the most pressing issues, I suppose, were safety, being fed, and being kept warm, and my parents made sure these primal needs were satisfied. That's about all I remember regarding those very early years of life, but from that time on, my memories still remain surprisingly clear to me.

Anyway, I'm not that pretentious to believe my story and what I have observed, lived and learned since 1961 is remarkable in any way. However, it is to me. It is my life and my memories, and it is the only story I can tell with any level of accuracy and with limited scrutiny because it is my story and none other.

Speaking of memories, they're a funny thing, aren't they? How many times in your life have you reminisced with an old friend only to find their recollection of the same event is different than yours? In fact, isn't it so that, at times, their recollection is radically different than your own? Why is that?

What occurs in the mind that changes our perception of not only long-ago events but events that have just occurred? Why is it that two people can witness the exact same event, but their perceptions of the event may be far different? Just what exactly is occurring in the mind that precipitates such a variance of perception from one person to another?

It is a strange phenomenon. We often just shrug our shoulders and give little thought or reasoning for its occurrence, but what is actually going on in the mind that can create such variances of perception between individuals? Is it possible we all are individually responsible for creating our own realities, and if so, what does that mean in terms of our own lives? It is indeed a subject worth pursuing later in this book.

In any case, what I will share in the following pages is my story as perceived by my own conscious thoughts. Is it accurate? Well, my mind tells me it is and in the end, what else matters but our own perception of the world we find ourselves immersed in?

As mentioned, I was born in 1961, near the beginning of a new decade, and what a decade it turned out to be! The 50s, on the surface, was a time of unbounded hope for the future given to us by the blood spilled on the battlefields, primarily in Europe and the Pacific. The carnage that arose from the 1930s and 40s would reach its pinnacle in 1945 with the dropping of the Atomic bombs upon Nagasaki and Hiroshima, Japan.

A tired, beaten down, and war-torn world was ready to heal. America, in particular, had emerged from the war as a newly arrived "superpower." It was indeed a time to celebrate, procreate and begin living anew with the promise of a bright future. The baby boomer generation was born under this new promise for the future, and I was born in the latter stages of this great boom. I had known no war or strife in the world in which I was born, but before my first memories were formed, things had already changed.

Emerging out of the jungles in Southeast Asia, and soon after the war in the Korean Peninsula, there was trouble brewing. The face of war is never far away from showing itself, and as a young child, I would not avoid its reach. It would soon consume me and impact me for the rest of my life.

War is dogged in its determination to destroy lives or, at the very least, infect our memories with the chaos and horror it brings.

Unfortunately, war is a part of the human condition, and likely not a single one of us has avoided being touched on the shoulder by it. It reminds us all of the imperfection and the potential brutality of our species. It is always with us, either blatantly or haunting us in the dark shadows and recesses of our minds.

What is it in us that, throughout time, has compelled our species to pray upon one another? Why has humankind turned upon itself time and time again and continues to do so to this day? We have killed in the name of God for land, pride, power and greed. Long after the smoke of fierce battles ceases to linger in the air, we mourn our wounded and dead. We regret the destruction we have reigned and sincerely talk about never letting it happen again, and yet nothing ever changes.

This I can say with absolute certainty... the flawed human characteristic that drives us to pray upon ourselves is still alive and well to this very day. Its dark presence has been lurking over my shoulder my entire life.

Ask Not What You Can Do for Yourself....

John F. Kennedy

In 1960 America voted in a young, dynamic President who seemed to "fit like a glove" for the times the country was bounding optimistically towards. John F. Kennedy, a WW2 hero, was no doubt a charismatic leader who had been bred from a prominent American family. He represented a youthful and dynamic approach toward leadership at a time when the country was looking for just such a leader.

Kennedy was a powerful orator who had the ability and potential to bring out the best in our country. At 43, he was one of the youngest Presidents in American history, and he carried the promise of a new decade, envisioning almost unimaginable possibilities for a country that had reached a new pinnacle of strength and success.

Along with his lovely wife and young children at his side, the description of "Camelot" was often used to describe his residency at the White House, and for a brief moment in time, it was. The American public was indeed enamored by this compelling young couple. The youth and exuberance the first family brought to the nation were unparalleled, and with the age of television reaching new heights, they enjoyed unprecedented exposure.

Just beneath the surface of this new and exciting decade, however, trouble lay in wait. The cold war had taken a strong foothold upon American awareness, and the specter of mass destruction (the end of everything through nuclear holocaust), for the first time, had entered the consciousness of humankind. Such is life when you think about it. For every "good," there is a "bad," and for every positive, there is a negative. We have daylight that relents to night and night back to the day. There is matter, and there is anti-matter, and there is peace and violence. I could continue on, but you see my point.

John F. Kennedy and Family

It would clearly appear there is an "opposite" to almost every fundamental aspect of our existence. Spirituality is even filled with this "rule of opposites," for many spiritualists believe in a heaven and, of course, the opposite being a hell. Is there a reason the world in which we exist is filled with this phenomenon? This will be explored in later chapters, but for now, it is enough to accept that "dualism" cannot be dismissed or ignored. It is a rule that plays a large part in our physical reality as well as our mental one.

The fact is we require this duality in life, for without it, there would be no ability to differentiate any of our experiences. Without the opposite to contrast, there would be only "one experience" available to us. We would be no better off than a deaf, dumb, and blind individual who, in many ways, lives a mono-chromatic existence.... but I digress. Back to the story of our 35th President.

John F. Kennedy was given the mantle by the American people to lead our country into a new decade filled with great promise and hope. The "Russian Bear," however, was certainly a threat to our way of life, and it demanded America's immediate attention. After World War II, the Soviet Union had also grown into "superpower" status and had geopolitical intentions which were in no way congruent with the United States' vision for the future.

In the same sense, an athlete pushes his opponent to put forth their very best effort. This budding competition between the two countries pushed America towards further advancement of its technology, science, and military prowess. Indeed the threat of the Soviet Union forced our country to "step up its game."

Perhaps there is no better representation of this fierce competition between the two superpowers than the "Space Race." The starting gun was literally shot in the air with the successful launch of the Russian satellite "Sputnik" in 1957. By the late summer of 1962, Kennedy made it known to our country and to the world of his bold aspirations for the United States space program. Kennedy, in his now-famous speech, "We choose to go to the moon," pronounced that the United States would land a man on the moon before the end of the decade.

There is no doubt the Cold War hit a new level of fierce competition in the 60s, spreading fear and paranoia throughout the country and the world. The Soviet Union had taken a foothold in Cuba, propping up Fidel Castro and his budding communist regime. In addition, the Soviet Unions' not so subtle involvement in the brewing conflict in Vietnam would eventually draw America into a war that would cost a generation its innocence in the jungles of South East Asia.

The "Domino Theory," propagated initially by President Dwight Eisenhower in 1954, laid the foundation for American involvement in Vietnam. The theory, simply stated, presented the proposition that if one country fell to communism, the neighboring country could then fall, thus creating a "domino effect" of countries yielding to regimes supporting communist idealism.

Kennedy embraced this theory and fanned the flames, which would eventually lead to an all-out war in Vietnam. One thing I have learned through these many years is the critical nature of American foreign policy and the impact it can have on its people and, for that matter, the entire world. Kennedy's willingness to support a war to defend a corrupt and crippled Vietnamese government would be his biggest mistake as President and would cause severe damage to the psyche of an entire generation of Americans, which still persists to this day.

In November 1963, before any of my memories had yet been formed, Kennedy was assassinated in Dallas, Texas. To this day, there is still much discussion of this event and "conspiracy theories" run rampant. A shroud of mystery that surrounds this assassination may continue to linger on for decades, but what is not a mystery is the devastation our country felt upon hearing the news of our fallen President. "Camelot" had come to a horrible end in the back seat of a Lincoln Continental convertible. It was a shocking end to a time of promise, which had primarily been part of the American psyche since the end of World War ll, and it would no doubt signal the beginning of a very tumultuous decade to come.

Kennedy, armed with his charm and charisma, had sparked the imagination of the American people. He had painted an exciting picture of what we could have become and what we were capable of accomplishing. He was the perfect leader at the perfect time, and suddenly without warning, he was gone.

As for myself, I remember none of this, but I did grow up in the aftermath of his assassination and felt the shock waves for years to come. I began my school years in 1966 at the newly renamed "John F. Kennedy Elementary." His influence and the societal grief which followed his death were simply inescapable. Kennedy's assassination would be the first of four in the decade of the sixties. Malcolm X, an African American Nationalist and religious leader, Martin Luther King Jr., a Baptist minister and prominent civil rights leader and Robert Kennedy, a Democratic candidate for President, would follow.

On April 4th, 1968, Martin Luther King Jr. was shot down in Memphis, Tennessee, and just two months later, on June 5th,

Kennedy was gunned down in Los Angeles, California. At the age of six, I distinctly remember these two events. For some reason, which I have never been able to explain, I was drawn to the news at a very young age. At 5:30 in the evening, Monday through Friday, you would most likely find me watching Walter Cronkite on "CBS News" with my mother. Looking back, this was a bad idea, and I had wished my mother had sent me off to do something else during that time, but nonetheless, my little brain was absorbing the news of the sixties daily.

I didn't really understand what Martin Luther King stood for at the time of his death, but I knew he was an important figure and that his death was big news. I could see and feel the sadness emanating from the chaotic scenes projecting from the family tv set. Only much later in life would I learn and understand what King had meant to this country, and though I may have been taught about him in school, it was cursory at best. Since the days of my public education, his importance in the Civil Rights movement and his value as a great American figure in history has been rightfully cemented into our culture.

Martin Luther King and Robert Kennedy

Robert Kennedy was at an entirely different level in terms of my awareness of him if, for no other reason, the school I went to was named after his brother! As previously mentioned, the impact of the assassination of John Kennedy sent shock waves rippling outward throughout the decade of the sixties. Thankfully it's not often an American president is shot and killed in public view; however, when it happens, the impact it will have is indeed palatable for an extended duration of time.

Robert Kennedy had entered late into the presidential Democratic primary race of 1968, but it didn't take long for him to build up steam in the race. He was no doubt quickly becoming a force in the party with a win in the California primary the night of his assassination.

Obviously, I had no political ideology at the age of six, but what I noticed about Robert Kennedy and what gripped me, much like his brother before had done with the American public, was his ability to reach people through his natural charisma. Aside from my father, Robert Kennedy was the first hero in my life. I greatly admired him and wanted to be just like the young politician. I would watch him on tv and then go to the mirror and comb my hair exactly like his. No, I wasn't enamored by the "Monkees." I had no desire to have my hair, just like Davy Jones. I wanted to be like Robert Kennedy. My family knew this, and my older sisters would tease me about my hair and my desire to look like him.

I was shocked when I heard the news about the assassination of Robert Kennedy shortly after midnight on June 5th, 1968. It felt like a gut punch to my soul. I was young true enough, but I felt the pain of that moment as much or perhaps more as an adult. Still, he was not pronounced dead at the time and, in fact, would live for another 26 hours. I held out hope the entire day he would live and prayed that the good lord would save him.

On the morning of June 6th, while riding in the car with my mother and sisters, the news came over the radio of his death. God did not answer my prayer. I tucked my head down and brushed my hair straight over my forehead, symbolically marking the end of my adoration of Robert Kennedy. I pressed my face into the corner of the backseat and silently cried. Not a word was uttered by my sisters or mother. My sisters would never tease me again about wanting to emulate Robert Kennedy, and I would never wear my hair like his again... my hero was dead.

Much the same way certain smells can instantly bring back a moment in life or a person you once knew into clear focus, I still feel the sadness of that moment. Our minds have the ability to not only hold onto memories in a factual sense but also to continue to carry along the deep feelings assigned to our more intense observations. What is it in the mind that can so quickly attach emotions to these sensory recollections? Is the brain, a three-pound piece of fleshy grey matter, responsible for all of these incredible, almost instantaneous activities? Is this three-pound mass of flesh truly accountable for mental actions that occur faster than the speed of light? Materialists would say it is so, but does that really make sense? Is it possible something else is in play here? We shall explore this later, but for now, let's leave the door open for further conjugation on the subject.

A Tale of Time and Place

The sixties were defined through my eyes by many things that occurred during that tumultuous period… some good, some bad, but always filled with a sense of wonder. It was the summer of my youth, and though dark clouds such as Vietnam bellowed over the horizon at times, there was also a world of true amazement. I was learning about life and my place in the world, and the lessons learned during that first decade of my life I would carry with me throughout the many decades that would follow. One of those important lessons was learning to say goodbye and move on.

By 1965 my father got the break he desperately needed and had found a way out of Cheyenne. His company offered him two options: move to Baltimore, Maryland (corporate headquarters) or move west to Salem, Oregon. My father had never been to either state, but he knew he had no desire to move his family back east to a large city. It was an easy choice for him, and we packed up our things and headed to the Pacific Northwest in the summer of 1965. It would be the first of many moves I would make throughout my life and the only one I have little recollection of. It certainly did not carry the drama or pain of other moves I would make later in life.

It was in Salem where my life's adventures truly began. Cheyenne is relegated to mere photo images in my brain, lacking any fluidity. Just snapshots, really, fragmented memories and moments. Salem is where I "cut my teeth" in my youth. It is where my memories become fluid, like watching a movie. Salem is the place where I became aware life was larger than just our family home and that other families and neighborhoods existed just like ours.

I made my first friends in Salem, and I still remember those days with great fondness. It is where my memories intersect with my current reality and bend the splintering fragments of time contrasting with" what was" and will sadly never be again. I was growing and learning what life was about in 1965 as my universe began to expand to a new cosmic level comprised of an actual neighborhood! We all start out life in a tight circle of closely related and mostly controlled experiences. Our concentric circle remains primarily closed off from outside variables and experiences through design and because of our own intellectual limitations.

We know our mom and dad, our siblings, and perhaps grandma and grandpa as well. We know where the bathroom is in our house, and we know where we sleep and eat. Eventually, the circle expands out into our neighborhood and, with the advent of television, out into worlds that exist far beyond the streets where we learn to ride our bikes. We begin to realize safety is a relative term depending on who you are with and where you are at, and it is not just a "given." Safety is earned through the understanding of circumstances and the law of "cause and effect." Maintaining safety is of prime importance throughout life, but when young, the variables are more "black and white," not colored by the intellect weighing all the potential outcomes or risk factors.

I knew if I came home ten minutes late from the park across the street, I would be in trouble. I also knew if I took candy from a stranger at the park, that could mean *big trouble*. What "big trouble" really looked liked or meant, I wasn't sure, but my parents made it clear it was nothing I wanted any part of.

Speaking of "ten minutes late," time was also much different when I was young. Ten minutes standing in the corner after getting in trouble could feel like an hour, just as being granted an additional half hour to play at the park felt like a reprieve from the Governor. I still remember standing in the corner as if I was frozen in time, not thinking in the least of the indiscretions that led me to my predicament, rather wondering if time had actually stopped.

The truth is time is nothing more than a man-made nomenclature and one in which we have all become enchained by which there is no escape. Everything has been "time-stamped" even though, in reality, time flows like an endless river. We abide by the rules of this self-created manifestation, never pondering we have enchained our very existence to the rhythm of the clock. We measure *everything* through time. Minutes flow into hours.. hours into days... days into months etc. We gauge our remaining life span based on how many projected birthdays we have left. Estimates of the length of our entire life experience are built from actuary tables established by life insurance companies. We have *sold out* to time, and as our master, it controls us until our very last breath.

However, at age six, time is endless in this sense; our mortality is a concept not even worth considering at such a young age. We are primarily concerned with the present and not so much the past or the future, focusing only on what is actually occurring at the moment. When did we lose that outlook regarding life? What stole the concept of *living in the moment* from us? After all, the past cannot be changed, and the future cannot be fully controlled. It is only this moment, *the here and now*, which we can truly be certain of… just as certain as this moment has now moved into the past.

The only "time" that is not illusionary is the present moment. The future or the past must *be imagined* in order to exist at all. You cannot "live" in the past. However, you can imagine the past. You cannot "live" in the future, but you can imagine the future as well. It is only through the ability of recollection coupled with imagery that the past or the future can be experienced at all. The present is the only real moment that exists in our physical reality, and it is what binds us together in this common state of mind.

As a child, time moved much slower for me than it does now as an aging adult. Just as hunger feels differently to a starving man than to a man who has just happened to miss his lunch, as is the case with most things in life, time is based on relativity. Time, as a child, appeared to march at a consistent but arduous pace. It took what seemed forever for the school year to end. The short days and long nights of the Pacific Northwest, often filled with clouds and rain, seemed intolerably slow. Now at my age, not only do months run together as if they were thrown into a particle accelerator, the years become one endless river, at times completely indiscernible from one to the other.

The Big Bang

The "Big Bang" is the prevailing scientific theory that explains how our universe was created. Its premise is that from an extremely dense form of energy and matter, the universe was born through a cataclysmic explosion that spewed matter, gases, and energy outward in an expansive manner that continues to this day. However, this is not the "Big Bang" I will be discussing or that I observed in the decade of the sixties.

The "Big Bang" that occurred in the sixties had nothing to do with science but everything to do with the arts. The original explosion of this artistic event expanded and grew throughout the years and has impacted multiple generations in its wake. I am, of course, speaking of 'The Beatles'.

The Beatles story can be traced back to the early sixties when four lads (John, Paul, George, and Ringo) honed their skills in nightclubs throughout Europe. However, the "Big Bang" occurred with their arrival in America, and it would strongly resonate in the decades that followed.

Early Beatles

The Beatle's sound was fresh and exciting and fundamentally was an interpretation of American blues reconstituted from a British perspective. They were not the only ones from England to revive American blues with a fresh, youthful sound. The Rolling Stones, the Who, and the Kinks were all bands from England that took this uniquely American art form and presented a fresh new interpretation of it. History would label this artistic renaissance as the "British Invasion," and it would change the face of rock 'n roll forever. Legends of the 50s, such as Elvis Presley and Little

Richard, prominent influences during the early years of rock 'n roll, now found themselves challenged by these youthful British bands. However, none of these bands did so with the veracity, charisma, and talent of the Beatles. They alone would produce worldwide manic excitement in 1964.

What are the odds that four young men born in a war-torn industrial harbor city, Liverpool, England, would somehow come together in the midst of such destruction to produce some of the greatest popular music ever created? Liverpool was certainly not "the hub" of artistic expression in Europe in the early sixties. Yet John, Paul, George, and Ringo did arise from the ashes of World War II to not only greatly impact and forever change popular music but also help lead a cultural revolution that was felt throughout the world.

Something I have learned is that "timing" and "placement" can be critically important not only in my life but also when it comes to world events. Don't ask me why this is. Perhaps it's some level of karmic influence coupled with the congruency of random variables all locking together in perfect sequence and just at the perfect time. This is an absolute truth in life that randomness plays a greater part in all aspects of life than we would care to believe.

In fact, it is the randomness of DNA sequences in all living things which, for no apparent reason, break away from the established DNA chain to create a new sequence that promotes species evolution. This new sequence will either survive and replicate only if it is determined to be beneficial to the survival, or it will cease to continue if it provides no apparent benefit. To ignore the power of randomness in our world is to ignore the very essence of our physical reality.

The Beatles were certainly not a DNA sequence, but they were an important link in music history that did fundamentally change the course of music. The randomness of these four individuals joining forces to combine their artistic skill sets and unique musical influences in such an unlikely environment as Liverpool at the perfect time in world history is truly a wonder.

By 1964 the Beatles had already taken England by storm, but America had yet to be impacted by the force of this band. America was still very much in a deep swoon over the assassination of its president just three months earlier when the Beatles arrived at Kennedy Airport in New York on February 7th, 1964. "Beatlemania" had arrived on its shores, and popular music would never be the same. The Beatles were met by 3,000 screaming fans as they stepped off the plane and onto the tarmac at Kennedy Airport. Dressed in their trademark suits, "Beatle Boots," and fashionably new "mop-top" hairstyles, the Beatles, who themselves were stunned to see such a raucous crowd waiting for them, smiled gleefully and waved to the adoring American fans. A love affair had begun.

Beatles Arrive in America

Two days later, the Beatles would perform on "The Ed Sullivan Show," America's premiere variety entertainment show at the time. Ed Sullivan launched many entertainment careers and hosted memorable breakthrough performances of the 50s and 60s, including Elvis Presley, the Rolling Stones, the Supremes, the Jackson Five, and the Beach Boys, to name a few, but none would have the impact the Beatles did on that fateful February Sunday evening.

It must have been difficult to even hear the Beatles 'music that evening for those who actually attended the show. The roar of screaming, adoring young fans, primarily young girls, was deafening and would be a precursor of what was to come. Through the chaos, it was clear to anyone watching on tv that the Beatles' style, charisma, and charm were truly something special.

That night nearly 40 percent of all American tv households watched the Beatles perform on "The Ed Sullivan Show." Like ripples in a pond, the impact and influence of that performance would resonate beyond anyone's imagination, and it would shape popular music for decades to come. The "Big Bang" from that evening inspired thousands of kids to pick up guitars and begin learning to write and sing their own songs.

Prior to the Beatles, most entertainers performed songs written and composed by other artists. It was specifically the writing team of John Lennon and Paul McCartney that changed all the preconceived notions about how popular music would be presented to its audience. No longer would artists be chained to performing songs written and composed by "someone else." Lennon and McCartney decided that they would create and perform their own music without the help of outside writers. It would be entirely upon them, along with their fellow bandmates, to write and perform most everything on the records they were to make.

This decision to be the "alpha and omega" of their music profoundly changed the music industry, and it led to the belief, misguided or not, that anyone with writing and singing skills could become a star. Suddenly, thanks to the Beatles and, in particular, their performance on the "Ed Sullivan Show," thousands of young aspirants would try to find their way to stardom by means of their own songwriting talents with guitar in hand.

Many famous artists since have noted the Beatles' performance on the "Ed Sullivan Show" was so exciting and filled with indescribable magic that they knew exactly what they wanted to do with their lives after watching them perform that evening. They wanted to be rock stars! Artists such as Bruce Springsteen, Tom Petty, Gene Simmons (Kiss), Nancy Wilson (Heart), Micheal Nesmith (The Monkees), Joe Perry (Aerosmith), and many others have all spoken of the great impact the Beatles performance on Ed Sullivan had on them. Nothing would ever be quite the same after they witnessed the "Fab Four" perform that evening.

The music of the Beatles and their magnetic persona was only part of the story, though. They led a cultural revolution during the sixties in music, art, fashion and political awareness. They incorporated "psychedelia" into their music, integrating drug-induced mind-altering ideations into their sound, lyrics and dress. They promoted peace and love unabashedly and denounced violence and war, and an entire generation followed their lead. It became quite clear their influence went well beyond the screaming girls and fainting fans who had once attended their concerts.

As for me, I have no recollection of the "Big Bang" created by the Beatles. However, I was bathed in its immediate after-glow, and my first memories of my own existence included the sound and image of the Beatles. I do not know what life is like without the Beatles. They have always been a part of my consciousness and continue to be so to this day.

I have such sweet and happy memories of my youth, and the soundtrack of those memories invariably leads to the Beatles. They were so prevalent on tv and radio they could not be avoided if one tried. There were Beatles cartoons, movies, paraphernalia, and, of course, music that permeated the radio airwaves. I have one profound memory that lingers with me, like the fresh smell of an early June morning. I was walking on a neighborhood street with a warm summer wind caressing my face. My little red transistor AM radio was pressed against my ear, and as I walked, the Beatles'

"Penny Lane" was playing its sweet melody... filling my senses with happiness.

I have never forgotten that moment as it signifies something more than a "moment in time" or a "particular place." It is a symbolic memory for me that has no rival. I was young, life was fresh, and I didn't have a care in the world. The music that filled my brain at that moment made me feel so alive, but more than that, I was truly happy. Looking back, perhaps it was the last time I would ever feel that way, or at the very least, the last time I could remember such free-flowing happiness.

Of course, nothing lasts forever. My perception of life would soon change thanks to images flowing from the family tv set. Vietnam would soon impact me in ways I could have never imagined. And the Beatles? Well, as is almost always the case… fame led to money which led to power which led to arrogance which led to defiance, which led to conflict, which led to indifference which led to resentment, which led to the Beatles' demise.

In May of 1970, the Beatles released their last album titled, "Let It Be." The title track seemed to me to be the perfect swan song to end their story and, in a sense, also end the decade of the sixties. Nothing would ever be the same as time's relentless march would move onward without the Beatles. As George Harrison once wrote, "All things must pass." However in a little over five years, from the moment of the Big Bang in February 1964 to the Beatles' self-destruction in September of 1969, the Beatles racked up twenty songs that reached Billboard #1. They currently have record sales of nearly 300 million, far outdistancing any other performers. Whether the Beatles' record sales will ever be surpassed is certainly in question, as to this day, they sell exceptionally well. In fact, their greatest hits release, "Beatles 1," became the worldwide best-selling album of the millennium's first decade.

The Beatles' musical dominance has never been in question, and it appears it never will be. They were the greatest musical act of the 20 century.... end of the story. Thankfully I was a part of this exceptional phenomenon called "Beatlemania." It truly is one of the highlights of my life. If you weren't there, I can't explain it to you with any level of depth. It was unlike anything I have ever observed or been a part of... it was supernatural.

Why Should I Cut My Hair?

At the beginning of the decade, the fashion and hairstyles of both men and women, though somewhat modified, still primarily reflected the fashions of the 50s. This would soon change as the generation gap between the culture of the youth and their conservative predecessors was about to unfold into clear lines of demarcation.

The look of the first lady, Jacqueline Kennedy, influenced much of the style of dress for women in the early sixties. It was an elegant but conservative style of dress that lacked variance in color and fashionable whim. As for men, short hair and the "standard" men's attire still reigned supreme, consisting of plain and sedated fashions with little imagination integrated into its style. However, all of this was about to change.

The Mini Skirt

In the mid-sixties, the fashion and music of the "London Scene" began to find their way across the pond to America. By 1965 the mini skirt became a popular fashion for women, and the Beatles' historic arrival on American shores in 1964 brought not only their stylistic suits and "Beatle boots" but also longer hairstyles for men as well. Another rock group, The Who, sported London's "Mod Scene" consisting of bold, colorful shirt designs coupled with lean-fitting pants, which brought even more style to the look of young men's clothes.

The Who

Enamored with the fashion and music coming from England and with more disposable income than ever before, American youth began to spend their hard-earned dollars on clothing and music. They strutted their new fashions and hairstyles not only as a means to attract the opposite sex but also as a way to separate themselves from their parental counterparts. A new counterculture was being born, fueled by pop/rock stars who modeled not only alternative fashion but also oppositional behavior. Lines were clearly being drawn, more so than in any other decade, separating the American teenager from the distinctly patriarchal conservative approach of their parents.

It became "cool" to arrogantly oppose and smugly mock the "old ways." The music being created, and specifically the song lyrics being written, not only reflected defiance but also inspired the rebellious attitude of teenagers. Lyrics such as "I hope I die before I get old" and "The old get old, and the young get stronger" provided oppositional anthems to outdated parental viewpoints and lifestyles.

As the sixties proceeded into the later stages of the decade, fashions took another turn. Once again, with the pop/rock genre leading the way, teenagers changed their fashions to match the evolving music scene. The groundbreaking album "Sgt.Peppers Lonely Hearts Club Band" by the Beatles was an astounding musical achievement and an artistic triumph right down to the artwork of the album cover. The explosion of color and

bizarreness of the album cover alone could have stood independently as an expressive and culturally relevant piece of art. However, it would be what was carved into the black vinyl of the record that would cement the Beatles forever as a cultural phenomenon influencing music, art, fashion and a "state of mind" for an entire generation.

Sgt. Peppers Album Cover

The album, inspired by the Beach Boys "Pet Sounds," not only sent the general public into the realm of new sonic exploration but also absolutely devastated, while in the same breath, greatly inspired contemporary artists in the music industry. "Sgt. Peppers" set a new industry standard expanding the boundaries of popular music. The Beatles introduced musical instruments not heard before in rock 'n roll and inter-mixed them with clever mind-expanding lyrics.

Inspired by Indian sitar artist Ravi Shankar, George Harrison continued to explore the use of the sitar in his songwriting, integrating "Eastern music" and, ultimately, clothing fashion into the Beatles' universe of influence. Hints of this "Eastern influence" could be found in their previous album "Revolver" in songs such as "Tomorrow Never Knows" and "She Said She Said," but it was Sgt. Peppers blew the lid off of musical exploration with the introduction of a multitude of different types of instruments, including the sitar that created a new genre of music titled "Psychedelia."

The Beatles continued to push the envelope of "popular music" with their next album, "Magical Mystery Tour," coupled with a bizarre, disjointed film of the same name. Lyrics such as "Sitting on a corn flake waiting for the van to come" and "Yellow matter custard dripping from a dead dogs eye" from the song "I am the Walrus" were intellectually indiscernible and yet "very cool" and driven, believed by many, by the use of the psychedelic drug LSD.

LSD or "Acid" grew in popularity throughout the sixties. Marijuana, a long part of the underground culture of the 50s, was now becoming more widely accepted and used. The expanded use of marijuana, coupled with an exploration into psychedelic drugs, took many young Americans into a new experiential thought-expanding world that invariably created more questions than answers.

At the same time, thanks once again to influential pop/ rock stars such as the Beatles, Indian spirituality and mysticism became the popular subject matter for a disillusioned youth looking for answers that their parents had very little understanding of, even the questions.

As these existential curiosities gained momentum throughout the 60s, the conventional religious community also struggled with providing intellectually satisfying responses to the deepest questions of our being. This led the American youth to look elsewhere for answers and often to the "Eastern" teachings of philosophy, mysticism, and spirituality.

Throughout college campuses across America, student ideology began to change, and many young students were now more interested in the meaning of life than learning about the conventional post-secondary subject matter to further a career in the future. They were looking for enlightenment. It was something they felt was far more important than studies in capitalism.

In addition, with the draft sending young men to fight and die in the Vietnam War, those left behind were left to ponder what was *really* important in life. After all, they were witnesses to many of their friends and neighbors being snatched in the prime of their life and placed in the living hell of Vietnam.

Fashion also continued to evolve into more colorful clothing mimicking the bizarre new psychedelic music and the artists who performed it. Men's hairstyles de-evolved into no hairstyle at all as they began to grow their hair beyond their shoulders and sported unshaven bearded faces as well.

The hippie subculture may have roots in the early sixties, but it boomed by 1967 and became a prominent fixture in American culture through the remainder of the decade and beyond. This subculture embraced several major political themes during this period. They strongly supported the civil rights movement and were highly engaged in anti-war protests. In addition, they supported the use of recreational drugs as a method of "mind expansion" and the concept of "free love," which promoted increased sexual promiscuity. Peace and love were the nomenclatures the hippie subculture built their belief system primarily upon during this period. Hippie phrases such as "make love not war," "turn on, tune in, and drop out," and "let your freak flag fly" were common phrases that defined and separated this group from conventional ideology and were often in conflict with the far more conservation older generation.

The Hippie Generation

From my perspective, the hippies were indeed an odd group. My parents made it clear they were to be avoided as they were "freeloaders" and "drug users." However, what I observed of the hippie culture, coupled with my limited contact with them, told a different story than my parents' judgmental observations. They seemed to be gentle, open-minded people that accepted almost everything but the war in Vietnam and "squares."

My two uncles, who were seven and fourteen years older than me, respectively, had become pseudo-hippies themselves, and I maintained a very good relationship with both of them. Therefore hippies were "ok" in my book, though I know my parents kept a concerning eye on my admiration for their lifestyle and views on life. In the end, I liked hippies and thought they were "cool," but I also kept my distance as they were still a good ten years older than I, and they behaved in ways I didn't fully understand or even believe I should understand at my age.

The penultimate moment of the hippie era came in August of 1969 with the music festival "Woodstock" in Bethel, New York. Estimates of over four hundred thousand people attended the three-day festival, which included some of the biggest rock acts of the time. Some of the notable musical acts that played at the festival were: Joan Baez, Santana, The Grateful Dead, Creedence Clearwater Revival, Janis Joplin, Sly and the Family Stone, The Who, Jefferson Airplane, The Band, (Crosby, Stills, Nash & Young), and Jimi Hendrix. It was three days of communion, drug use, freedom, peace, promiscuity, and, of course, singing and dancing. Not that there weren't issues at Woodstock. There was plenty, from the inclement weather, lack of facilities and food to the "bad acid" that had been distributed. There were two confirmed deaths and two confirmed births at the event, which ended on the third day with a depleted, worn-out crowd witnessing a historic performance by Jimi Hendrix.

Woodstock

Things had already begun to change by the time of Woodstock, but for one last moment, late in the summer of 1969, the hippie generation did let their "freak flag" fly proud and high before it began to crash down around them in the months to follow.

Drug use, which had initially begun with the idea of mind expansion and the promotion of greater existential understanding, was now beginning to morph into the world of heavy narcotics. The era of peace, love and understanding was about to change into an era of darkness, addiction and death.

Heroin which had been introduced into the drug culture, would wreak havoc on the rock music collective, destroying the lives of such icons as Janis Joplin, Jim Morrison, and Jimi Hendrix, leading to their untimely deaths by mid-1971, just less than two years after Woodstock. For every high, there is a low, and even the existential-minded hippie generation could not avoid the duality of our existence.

Lone Star President

Lyndon Baines Johnson was sworn in as the 36th President of the United States on November 22, 1963, just two hours after the assassination of John F. Kennedy. Johnson, often referred to as "LBJ," was a well-established politician, including senate majority leader, before John Kennedy selected him as his running mate in the 1960 presidential campaign. The Kennedy/Johnson ticket would go on to beat incumbent Vice President Richard Nixon in one of the closest presidential races in history. Sadly, to the horror of everyone in America, Kennedy's tenure as President was cut short by an assassin's bullet.

Lyndon Johnson

Johnson, known as a "wheel'n deal'n Texan," had sought the democratic nomination for the presidency in 1960 but had failed in his attempt, losing to the more charming and charismatic Kennedy. Kennedy, realizing the importance of garnering the southern democratic vote in the general election, eventually asked Johnson to be his running mate. As fate would have it, LBJ would soon find himself as the United States commander-in-chief after the shocking murder of the President.

Fortunately for Johnson, at the time of the Kennedy assignation, the American economy had been showing signs of significant growth, and unemployment across the country was low. In addition, although the cold war was becoming a serious issue and Vietnam was soon to blow up in his face, at the time Johnson assumed the Presidency, world affairs were relatively calm. This allowed LBJ to focus his efforts on the domestic policies Kennedy had built positive momentum towards delivering prior to his untimely death.

Johnson was determined to utilize the legacy of the fallen President and the emotion behind his death to forward many initiatives Kennedy had promoted during his time as President. These initiatives included tax cuts and a push towards passing a Civil Rights bill which Kennedy had submitted to congress in June of 1963. Johnson, promoting a societal reform ideology, pronounced his "War on Poverty" in his "State of the Union Address" in January of 1964.

Riding the wave of support after he assumed office, Johnson easily defeated his counterpart, Barry Gold Water, in the 1964 presidential election by over 15 million votes. It was a clear sign that the American public supported the completion of Kennedy's vision for the future. It would be up to Johnson, who had promised to finish what Kennedy had started, to sell his domestic agenda to congress and the American public.

As Johnson began his first term as the "elected President," he continued to introduce social welfare legislation, creating many social welfare programs that still exist in some form today. Programs created during his administration included: Jobs Corps, Head Start, Food Stamp, Medicare, and Medicaid. He argued that these new social reforms would lead to a "Great Society," eventually, this phrase was used to reference his domestic agenda.

Lyndon Johnson

Perhaps the two most significant pieces of legislation Johnson promoted and signed into law were the Civil Rights Act of 1964 and the Voting Rights Act of 1965. These two pieces of legislation are historic in their impact on millions of Americans, and it once and for all made it clear, from a federal perspective, that racism and bigotry would no longer be tolerated in America. The legislation certainly did not solve all of the issues America faced regarding equality. However, it was the moment when the country would officially condemn behavior and attitudes built upon the past. A future had now been established, free of public policy or whim designed to discriminate against others, thanks to the efforts of people such as John F. Kennedy, Lyndon Johnson, Martin Luther King Jr., and others.

The Signing of the Civil Rights Act

The Civil Rights Act was the premier piece of legislation ending racial segregation in America and banned employment discrimination on the basis of race, sex, religion, or national origin. This was a huge moment in American history when the issues of discrimination were officially dealt with through the formation of public policy and implementation of federal legislation designed to protect the individual and their rights as human beings. Martin Luther King Jr., an observer of the signing of the bill, was given one of the pens used by Johnson in the signing of the legislation. King Jr. would proclaim that the signing of the bill was nothing less "than a second emancipation."

The Voting Rights Act, signed in 1965, eliminated all state and local efforts to prevent African Americans from voting. The act banned literacy tests as a method to turn black voters away from the voting polls, and it also provided federal oversight of voter registration. Intense efforts had been made, particularly in the southern states, to derive ways to prevent blacks from voting creatively. The Voting Rights Act eliminated all those practices and enabled federal oversight of state and local voting methodology.

It is true that many localities, in particular in the south, chose to ignore the new federal law and still imposed unfair voting practices. However, it did give blacks legal recourse to challenge these illegal practices. The Voting Rights Act would turn out to have a major impact on the participation of blacks in the voting process. For example, in Mississippi alone, black voting participation increased from 6 percent in 1964 to 59 percent by 1969.

Although Johnson was able to build on the momentum established by Kennedy before his death and was successful in passing several important social reform legislative bills, it would be the Vietnam war that eventually would cause his undoing. The success of his domestic agenda could not overcome several major foreign policy blunders he made, which only worsened the war effort and public support for it.

On March 31, 1968, Johnson announced he would not seek the nomination for President. This was stunning news, as almost always is the case in American politics the incumbent seeks re-election. Johnson had grown weary and uncertain of his leadership regarding the Vietnam war. As much as he had shown success in his domestic policies, the war had drug him down into a quagmire of controversy and dissent among the American people. At the time of his announcement that he would not seek re-election, Johnson's approval rating had dropped to 36 percent. The support he had enjoyed in the immediate years after the assassination of Kennedy had evaporated in the fog of war.

Johnson had dramatically escalated American military involvement in Vietnam during his years as President, expanding U.S. presence from 16,000 in 1964 to more than 550,000 by 1969. This massive increase of troops and support units in the area was designed to tip the scales of the war in favor of the Vietnamese. However, it only created more public outcry and dissent against American involvement in Vietnam. Johnson, time and again, claimed the war was being won due to the influx of American presence in the region.

After the "Tet Offensive" in 1968, where the North Vietnamese army initiated coordinated attacks against over a hundred South Vietnamese cities and outposts, it was clear Johnson had been misleading the American people on the state of the war. Johnson had lied when he insisted the war was being won, and the media coverage of the massive offensive conducted by the Vietcong spread like wild fire. This was a major turning point in the war, and public support for sending young Americans into the jungles a Vietnam began to wane. Johnson had lost the trust of the American people over his deceitful statements regarding Vietnam and could not win it back.

He would leave office in 1968 somewhat of a broken man because of the atrocities of a war he had only made worse during his tenure. Later Johnson would speak of the weight and guilt he felt sending so many young Americans to their death for a failed cause. His decisions during that time and his misrepresentation of the truth to the American people would haunt the former President until his death in 1973.

The Long Shadow of War

I can't even speak of how I got there and didn't know how to get out. Somehow some way, I found myself in the depths of hell, or in other words, the depths of a southeast Asian jungle. Our platoon slowly walked through the thick undergrowth. A light rain fell, only adding to the misery of the oppressive humidity that sucked the breath right out of you.

As I looked around at the soldier's faces surrounding me, they all looked the same. There was a sterile indifference about them, as if they had seen too much and didn't really care about anything anymore. A half-dead yet selfish look in their dull eyes told me the only thing that continued to push them forward was the cold instinct of self-preservation and nothing more.

My pack was heavy, and my arms were tired as I carried my rifle near my chest. My legs felt like rubber, but somehow, they kept moving through the mud as my boots made a sucking sound with each step pulling away from the slosh beneath them. It seemed like we had been walking for years, but that just couldn't be correct. The night was turning into the morning, and as the sun peeked above the horizon, steam began to rise from the rain-soaked jungle undergrowth like ghosts escaping mortality. It was miserable and inescapable, and it went on for eternity, or at least until we came upon a small clearing.

With one fluid motion, the lieutenant stopped in his tracks and raised his fist into the air signaling a "full stop." It was eerily silent, and the stench of death was in the air. We all smelled and felt it. The tension was palatable.

In the distance, voices could now be heard emanating from further into the jungle. Up ahead, the Vietcong were scurrying around like rats entering into their tunnels and displacing into the depths of the thick vegetation. Much like a lethal plague, the Vietcong could arrive unannounced and just as quickly dissipate into thin air leaving only carnage and death in their wake. They were deadly as hell and conniving little fucks who knew the jungle like the back of their hands. To say we were at a disadvantage fighting the Viet Cong on their home turf would be an understatement.

After holding our position for nearly fifteen minutes, the lieutenant eventually waved us forward into the clearing. As we slowly entered the open space, it looked as if we had walked into a haunted graveyard. The sun, now shining brightly, created an ocean of steam rising from the moist grassy floor and wafting into the air. As we moved into the heart of the clearing, a huge tree appeared like a mighty beast towering over the steam, and its sprawling limbs groped outward toward us in a menacing fashion. On its lower limbs, dangling in the swirling mist like Christmas tree ornaments, lifeless silhouettes hung, twisting in the breeze.

Vietnam

As the leading edge of our platoon arrived near the base of the tree, I could hear phrases like "Jesus Christ," "What the Fuck," and "Oh my God" being uttered by the soldiers who had come face to face with the harsh reality in front of them. Some soldiers vomited, some ran back to the core of the platoon, while others just wondered about aimlessly. For a moment, I froze, my feet glued to the muddy grass.

The lieutenant began to yell loudly, directing soldiers to surround the tree in a defensive position. They scurried about encircling the immediate area with rifles poised, pointing aimlessly into the surrounding jungle. It was at that moment when something began to pull me near the tree. I was certain my legs were not moving, but nonetheless, as if a rope was tied to my waste, I was drawn forward like a skater gliding on a sheet of ice. My mind said stop! However, the force of this unscripted undeterred nightmare would have its way. Suddenly I was at the base of the tree in the midst of this unspeakable carnage that had no moral boundaries and showed no mercy to the living or the dead. It was epic.

As I looked above my head, soldiers were hanging from their bare feet by ropes tied to the tree's monstrous limbs. It looked as if those limbs were pridefully brandishing their prey for the world to see, and what a site it was. I counted at least a dozen American soldiers all disemboweled and their throats cut.

Directly above me was the hapless body of a soldier who's throat was cut from ear to ear, flies eagerly laying their eggs in the open wound. His face was streaked with the blood from his sliced neck, and gravity had done the rest, blood still slowly dripping onto his dog tags that dangled below his head.

My brain began to spin, at first slowly, then increasing with rapidity like a carnival ride. Faster and faster until the world around me was nothing but a confused, disoriented blur. I tried to grab onto something but only found the stale air. Faster and faster, the world spun about me. Then strange voices, distant but growing closer and closer, could be heard swirling around me. They were speaking Vietnamese, and it was the Vietcong. Gunfire erupted around me like fire crackers crackling in stereo as I spun into the abyss. I screamed with all my might awaiting for death to take me. However, there are two different realities; the physical and the dream state.

Death did not take me. Instead, physical reality yanked me free from my dream state, and I found myself sitting straight up in my bed screaming into the darkness. The jungles of Vietnam had vanished and had been replaced by the softness of my own bed, but regardless of that, for a moment, I *was there*.

The truth is that Vietnam has been a part of my conscious reality and buried deep in my unconscious fears for 55 years. This relationship began in the mid-sixties at a time when the war was heating up in the jungles of South East Asia, and debates began to rage in the American political arena.

As mentioned previously, America's involvement in Vietnam was, in essence, a prevention strategy against the spread of communism. The Domino theory doctrine, born from the fear bred by the cold war between the Soviet Union and the United States, was the main political impetus for increased engagement in Vietnam.

American involvement in the region actually began under the Truman administration in the early 1950s. The first group of military advisors was sent to Vietnam to assist the French, who at the time still claimed Vietnam as a colony. Eventually, the French were forced to back out when it became clear by 1954 that the imperialistic hold they had once held in the Indochina region had fallen apart.

By 1961 Kennedy had approved sending additional military advisors, including special forces to help support the South Vietnamese democratic government, which only furthered America's engagement in the region. In 1964 The Gulf of Tonkin Resolution enacted by congress authorized President Lyndon Johnson to "take all necessary measures to repel any armed attack against the forces of the United States and to prevent further aggression."

As they say in sports, with the enactment of the Gulf of Tonkin Resolution by congress, "game on." America would find itself entangled in a war that would scar a generation, blacken its soul and, in the end, find itself leaving the region with its tail securely placed between its legs. A result that would repeat again 45 years later in Afghanistan due to the incompetence of the Biden administration.

I suppose I likely became engaged in the war initially through my strange curiosity about "world news" at such a young age. I clearly remember watching Walter Cronkite, the "CBS Evening News" anchor, open his daily broadcast with the number of American soldiers dead, wounded, or missing in action... a sad routine that would go on for years.

The visions, images, and stories of the Vietnam War broadcasted into our family living room will live with me until my death. I have never been shot at or have been directly subjected to the horrors of war (at least not in this life). However, I certainly have been impacted indirectly by images that have been ingrained in my psyche, like a photograph image imposed upon a negative.

Two of the major circumstances that propagated my lifelong trauma of Vietnam can be attributed to my mother's ignorance of what damage the images and stories I was absorbing from the news were causing me and, of course, the reporting of the war itself by the media. No war in our history had been brought into our living rooms in "living color" like Vietnam. Television was still in its infancy during the Korean War, and the technology was not readily available to provide live and in-depth coverage of life on the front lines. By the time Vietnam had blossomed into a full-blown war, the technology and the availability of affordable color tv sets brought the war into almost every American family's living room.

The Violence of War

As I have mentioned, my mother had a complete lack of understanding of what these images of war were doing to her child's mind. Perhaps because to her, it may have seemed mild compared to what she witnessed as a child. My mother had been a direct observer of the horrors of war herself as a child living in Berlin during WW II. She witnessed bombings, the thundering sound of planes flying directly above her head, and loud, violent explosions which resulted in destroyed homes and buildings.

Near the end of the war, with the Russians closing in for the kill in east Berlin, her family was forced to flee the city with only the belongings they could carry with them. There is little doubt that these experiences my mother endured have stayed with her for her entire life. The shadow of war is indeed long and unending.

The American press, far less naive than my mother, had little oversight or guidance regarding what should and should not be allowed as "appropriate" family viewing of the war in Vietnam. This lack of guidance created an open pallet, for the most part, to present images with little censorship and to portray the war with whatever political bent served the media's best interest.

The problem this created was two fold. First and most importantly, depending on their political view point, journalists were able to paint a picture of just exactly what young American men were facing in the jungles of Vietnam. This enabled journalists to present the terrible images of war directly into the living rooms of American families, which in turn made many Americans question, "Just what in the hell are we doing over there in the first place?"

Eventually, these images, coupled with detailed stories of what was occurring in "real-time" or what had recently occurred, turned the majority of Americans against our involvement in Vietnam. It can be argued that the consistent daily coverage of "the goings on" in

Vietnam led to the demise of morale in the public psyche, and eventually, support for the war greatly waned throughout America.

The second issue, which I do not believe has ever been given proper consideration or historical scrutiny, is the impact the first "television war" had on an entire generation of children. These children witnessed the carnage of a war that may have been thousands of miles away, but its brutal images were just five feet from them on the family tv set.

There are several distinct moments during my viewing of the war on tv that I have never forgotten. Most of the images and stories I observed throughout the war years have all melded into one massive collage of violence, chaos, despair, and fear, often visiting me in the hours of my dream state. However, two distinct incidents will pop into my consciousness at times, always followed by feelings of overwhelming sadness and latent fear.

The first incident was told by a soldier lying in bed at some hospital, and I can't remember where but my guess is it was likely a VA hospital… location is unknown. He told a tale of war that horrified me and gave me nightmares for decades to follow. He told a story that made me want to run to my mother and bury my head in the safety of her bosom. He told a story that no living being should ever have to tell. He told a story of the hell of war.

The details of his experience have long since blurred in my mind, such as how many individuals were involved and where this occurred in Vietnam, but the general theme is still crystal clear. I do remember him lying in bed, his arms completely bandaged and his face scarred by burns. He slowly and painfully recalled the events leading to his hospitalization to a reporter who held a microphone near his face.

He and a handful of buddies, perhaps 7 or 8, were returning to base from a Christmas gathering held by a neighboring unit in some village in some God-forsaken jungle in Vietnam. On their way back, they were ambushed by the Vietcong, all of them gunned down by the automatic rifle fire. However, the bandaged soldier lying in his hospital bed described how he had only been slightly wounded. He decided he would feign death and lie motionless on the jungle floor, hoping the enemy would move along satisfied with the "kills" they had just made. They were not satisfied.

As he continued to "play dead," the Vietcong dragged him and the other fallen soldiers into a nearby clearing, and to his horror, they stacked his dead comrades on top of him. After pouring gasoline over the bodies, they lit the pile of dead soldiers on fire and scurried off, quickly disappearing into the dense jungle.

I recall how he described the smell of burning flesh, waiting as long as possible to be certain the Vietcong were gone before extricating himself from the pile of burning bodies. Wounded and burned, he eventually made it back to the safety of his unit and lived to tell his holiday story, Merry Christmas.

I have half-heartedly tried to research this event in recent years, but with very little detail left in my memory to refine my search, I have been unable to find such an incident occurring. Could it perhaps be a story conjured up in my mind, a sort of amalgamation of the images and stories I endured as a child? I suppose so. However, I have no reason to believe it did not actually occur. In any case, my belief is that it did occur, and therefore the accuracy of the story is irrelevant. Belief becomes a reality for the true believer, the power of the mind.

My Lai Massacre

The second significant incident that occurred drew wide spread media coverage and would become a major scar on the soul of America. Coverage of the "My Lai massacre" could not be avoided once it became public fodder. It was big news in America, casting a shadow upon our own morality and spurring global condemnation due to its level of brutality. The incident, once again, forced Americans to ask the question, "Just what in the hell are our boys doing over there in the first place?" It greatly fueled an already burgeoning anti-war sentiment in America that was beginning to rage by 1969.

In March 1968, roughly 350 to 500 unarmed South Vietnamese civilians were murdered by American troops from "Charlie Company." Men, women, children, and infants were all victims of this atrocity. Some women were gang raped, and their bodies were badly mutilated.

The incident was initially "covered up," and the truth was withheld for nearly a year and a half until finally, in late 1969, it was revealed to the public. Suffice it to say public condemnation was swift and harsh as the massacre was a clear representation that America's supposedly pious efforts to free the South Vietnamese from the "evils of communism" had morphed into a perverse and heinous endeavor for all involved.

My memory of this event is centered around one particular aspect of the massacre. I distinctly recall the reporting involving a group of defenseless villagers, around 80, who were rounded up and then pushed into an irrigation ditch. American soldiers then stood above on the edges of the trench with their automatic M16 rifles firing round after round into the ditch.

When the smoke cleared, innocent men, women, children, and babies were all dead. It was evil to run amuck. Young men, who not long ago had been drinking sodas at their local malt shop in "any town USA," had lost their moral compass and spiritual conscience. Both of these necessary aspects of humanity had been lost somewhere in the heat and deprivation of a South East Asian jungle. These young men, mostly just kids, really had seen too much absorbing the darkness and evil that had enveloped them. They had learned to fear nothing and everything at the same time, both feelings converging upon one another, leaving nothing behind but chaos and confusion in their wake.

As for me, it was the first time in my life that the "good guys" had become "bad guys." How could this be true? We had sent our young treasure to Vietnam spilling their precious blood in an effort to save and help people not to kill them. I didn't understand any of this as my mind was too young to grasp the concept of how people's hearts can be changed through high levels of stress and pain. I recall being very confused by this incident, and it was like finding out Santa Claus was a mass murderer—my first hard lesson on how things aren't always as they appear to be.

Both of these incidents had a devastating impact on my young psyche. They had turned my content and the safe world on its head. As much as the Beatles had made me happy, filling my mind with wonder, Vietnam had injected darkness, death, and fear into my world. For every positive, there is a negative, and for every dark night, there is the brightness of a new day. It is the nature of our existence and is, indeed, the design of everything. As harsh and jarring as the contradiction of "opposites" is, at times, one must be confident that, in the end, all is as it should be.

American Soldiers at War

When I was young, there were certain things I understood as absolutes. I had no prior experience, wisdom, or contradicting information to have me believe otherwise. These were things I knew to be true because they had always been true since my conscious world began. The things I knew as a fact were: that my dad was the strongest and smartest man alive. If I were good, Santa would be sure to reward me at Christmas time. If I left my tooth under my pillow, the tooth fairy would replace it with money, and when I grew up, I would have to fight in the war in Vietnam.

This was an inescapable truth that haunted me. I saw what war was like on tv, and it was simply a matter of time before I found myself in the jungles of Vietnam with a rifle in my hand. It was kind of a death sentence or, at the very least, the death of a peaceful way of life. From what I knew, young men were being plucked away from their homes and the safety of their neighborhoods, dragged half way across the world to some strange land near China. I knew this to be true because it happened to young men we knew in our neighborhood. Even within our own family, we feared it would be the fate of my Uncle until he was finally admitted into the University of Texas. That was my way out; go to college! Is it any surprise that I ended up getting my degree?

In any case, I was fully aware of the draft, and to be drafted meant the end of everything I had known. I would lay at night thinking how horrible it would be forced to leave my mother and be shipped halfway across the world. What if I got scared in Vietnam? My mom would not be there to comfort me. I would be totally alone, far from the people and surroundings I had grown to know, thrown into the midst of people who were complete strangers.

The entire proposition of being drafted, even after the draft and the war had long ended, haunted me for decades. Not until I turned 30 did I finally draw a sigh of relief with the belief that I had finally reached the age where the military would no longer want me. Getting older is not always a bad thing.

Meanwhile, back in the neighborhoods across America, families were not only dealing with the real possibility that their sons could be taken from their grasp and sent off to Vietnam. Others faced the far worse fate of meeting their son at the airport, flying back home in a box with an American flag draped over it. I'm not sure how anyone during the decade of the sixties avoided witnessing the calamity that was Vietnam. Pain, confusion, and anger were dished out like tarot cards to the American public during this time while unfortunate mothers were being paid visits by Army chaplains.

The Return of Our Dead

Our family's closet friends at the time lost their brother to the war, and just down the road from our house, another family lost their son. I recall my dad driving by their house slowly and speaking to my mother about the sadness the grieving parents must be enduring. My parents knew the family at a cursory "hi neighbor" level, but in the end, they put more effort into avoiding them than attempting to engage with them. I'm sure many other neighbors had done the same as well, but I am not quite sure what could be said to comfort the bereaved family or if anything should be said at all.

The war seeped into the schoolyards as well. I recall seeing children wearing "Missing in Action" bracelets in memory of their older brothers who had been lost somewhere in an unforgiving jungle far away. The bracelet was a representation of hope that their sibling may still be alive and would come home one day. On the other hand, it was also the symbol of the shadow of death, dogging them consistently until they went to sleep at night and found peace.

Then again, all of us children were reminded of the "evils of war" and the long shadow of death every time we had a bomb drill at our school. These drills were common practice throughout the 1960s. The purpose of this drill was simple and direct; the Russians were capable and willing to drop nuclear weapons upon our heads, and we all needed to be prepared for that possibility. However, looking back, I doubt our actions would have done much to save our lives. Hiding crouched beneath our desks, last time I checked, does not prevent radiation from seeping into our bodies or protect us from a nuclear explosion. I suppose it made the adults feel better that we were doing "something," regardless of how ridiculous it might have been.

War Protests

Of course, at the post-secondary educational level, there was much debate, including massive protests against our involvement in Vietnam. This had become a common place activity on college campuses throughout the country. For the first time in American history, the "younger generation" had a real voice in politics, and they indeed had a very legitimate reason for voicing their opinions. After all, it was their generation being sent to Vietnam against their will. It was only logical that they would have a voice in the political arena, and they indeed let their voices be heard, even to the point of fermenting violence and chaos in the process.

The anti-war protests were not just centered around the draft issue but also around the moral implications of the war. There were serious questions regarding America's involvement in a war where many felt the Vietnamese people were fighting for their independence from an oppressive regime. These protests received considerable media coverage that only grew over time due to increased awareness of what was occurring in Vietnam and because of the violence propagated at such highly charged events.

It was not uncommon to see images of police wielding night sticks, dressed in riot gear, aggressively pushing back on a raucous crowd of protestors. Invariably violent clashes between protestors and police occurred, and the dark shadow of Vietnam had found a new home on our college campuses and city streets.

One of the more heartbreaking things I remember about these protests is how some protestors had turned on the soldiers, painting signs that read "Baby Killers," accusing them of murdering innocent civilians.

The "My Lai Massacre" did nothing to help the image of the American soldier. However, to blame and generalize all of these young men sent to Vietnam (many against their will) as "baby killers" was unforgivable. I remember reflecting at the time, "Oh great, I'm going to be forced to fight in Vietnam and will probably die there, and if I do survive, I won't come home a hero as my grandfather did... no, I will be chastised and called a " baby killer." Not one damn good thing ever came out of that war.

Of course, all wars end, and though Vietnam would go beyond the decade of the sixties, it would finally come to an end for America in March of 1973 when the final military unit was pulled out of Vietnam.

On April 30th, 1975, the South Vietnamese government surrendered Saigon to the North Vietnamese Army, thus ending the war entirely. All of the pain, blood, and American treasure lost in the jungles of South East Asia turned out to be for nothing. The South Vietnamese government, for which the USA sought to support and defend, had ultimately surrendered. A generation of young men had been subjected to the hells of war for a political ideology that, in the end, would hold no merit with the fall of the Soviet Union in 1989.

As for me, I will bear the scars of Vietnam for the rest of my life. Decades later, I had the opportunity to visit the Vietnam Memorial in Washington D.C., and I am not ashamed to say I found myself with tears rolling down my cheeks as I pressed my hand against the black marble wall bearing the names of the fallen. It was a healing moment for me, but I will never be completely healed. There are my dreams, of course (though subsiding in recent years), that will continue to haunt me, and the pain that lies deep in my heart cannot be assuaged. Vietnam will always be an unwanted companion in my life, and no matter how hard I try, it is a trauma I cannot run from. Such is the long shadow of war.

Fantasy and Adventure

There is nothing quite like play time as a kid. The free use of a vivid imagination coupled with youthful exuberance is a recipe for unabated fun. The opportunities for fun are almost as unlimited as our imaginations. We have all seen the solitary kid in a neighbor's yard with only a stick in hand and yet appearing to be having the time of his life. Hell, I've held a stick in my hand pretending I was the great Zorro defending my family from evil doers.

The wonders of an imagination not grounded by logic can produce inspiring results. Sadly over time, almost all of us lose the ability to combine naivety with boundless imagination. We feel silly and embarrassed at the thought of playing like a child. I wish this weren't so, but I see no way around it. The magic of believing in Santa Claus and playing only with a stick in hand seems to be in the purview of the very young.

Often we attempt to relive these moments of wonder and fun vicariously through our children and then grandchildren. We can attach ourselves to their wonderment of being engaged in new experiences and, in a sense, relive them again. Much like observing a person watching one of your favorite movies for the first time, you can almost relive the excitement you felt the first time you viewed the film. Our children and grandchildren, in effect, become our surrogates to the world of the young, and through them, we can feel anew again. It is one of the blessings of having children, and it keeps us young at heart.

That being said, I still remember my days of youth and often find myself drifting back to relive moments so unique they are unlike any other experiences in my life. I could swear that on one Christmas Eve night, I even caught a glimpse of Rudolph's red nose flying across the starry sky above.

Now logic tells me that reign deer cannot fly and certainly do not have glowing red noses. In addition, Santa Claus himself appears to be immortal, which from my observations of physical reality, seems to be highly unlikely. However, at that moment, at age seven, I *knew* what I saw, and I would have sworn in a court of law as to my observations that evening. Was Santa really flying across the sky with Rudolph leading the way? The answer is an unequivocal "yes."

My seven-year-old imagination created this undeniable reality for which I was certain, but could I prove it? Nope, however, I know what I saw that evening, and the imagination of a young mind is not bound to the laws of physics or logic. The fact is, all that we see and experience is really nothing more than an illusion in the first place. So let's just call my observation on Christmas Eve in 1968 an illusion within an illusion, which, when you think about it, is not so different from experiences we incur during our dream state.

But let's not get too far away from discussing the world of play. While living in Salem, I was fortunate to live near a park. It was just on the other side of the homes that lined the street across from us and around three acres in size. It included all the amenities a park should have, i.e., basketball courts, swings, slides, and a merry-go-round. In addition, on the park grounds was an outdoor public pool for use during the summer months. It was an ideal place for a young kid to play, and the fact that it was so close to our home made it absolutely perfect.

I may be sounding like my parents when I say this, but back in those days, there was far less concern regarding "safety issues" for the children that played there. Sure, we all were taught not to talk to adult strangers and to avoid them if approached in the park, but in the 1960s, the concern for child safety was certainly not at the level it is today.

My best friend, Brett Crawford, lived directly across the street from us, and his backyard backed up against the park. We would meet in the park along with the other cadre of friends our age and play football or tag or any number of games that kids play. One of our favorite endeavors was playing pirates on the playground equipment. We would spend hours at the park enjoying all the things kids enjoy doing.

One of my friends, Tracy Tuss, had a brother named Mark who was two years older than us and led his own little gang of friends. When Mark and his posse came around, there was certain to be trouble. Just like a biker gang riding in on their Harleys, Mark and his group of friends would peddle in on their stingray bikes, looking for trouble at the park. One of their favorite past times was commandeering the slides and swings and chasing off the other children.

Those who knew of this gang of unruly kids would scatter the moment they were spotted. However, there always seemed to be a few hapless children who either didn't see Mark's gang coming or were unaware of their exploits. For those unfortunate few, who did not extricate themselves from this perilous situation, well, they would be caught in the world of bullying and harassment. No one dared help them as all of us made sure to keep a safe distance from the mayhem. Just like in the jungle, when push came to shove, self-preservation was the fundamental rule of the park.

One day we were playing football when Mark and his gang paid us a visit. They started out with the obligatory insults "You throw like a girl," "What a bunch of wusses," etc. Tracy, who would be the only kid to talk back to Mark, challenged him and his group of thugs to a football game. Of course, the rest of us thought this was a terrible idea, but it was too late Mark and his boys agreed to a game.

I don't remember many of the details of the game, but I do remember my friends and I opening up a can of "whoop ass" on the older boys. As it went on, the more physical and aggressive Mark's gang became. On this day, though, it didn't matter. We may have been younger, but we didn't play like it. We were not intimidated, and for every elbow they threw, we threw one back at them.

It wasn't long before the game turned into a brawl, as Mark and his gang were tired of being embarrassed on the football field. It was then that the rule of self-preservation kicked in. My friends and I began to scatter after seeing Tracy take a fist in the face from his older brother. Whatever "machoism" we had possessed in our beat down of Mark's gang on the football field evaporated when Tracy took that shot to the face.

Running in multiple directions, we scattered like a herd of gazelle being chased by hungry lions, all of us hoping to reach our homes before being run down by the beasts. Some of us made it, while others did not. Some were chased down and beaten, but fortunately, I was not one of them. I followed Brett to safety as we both climbed over his backyard fence before we could be taken down.

The next day I saw Tracy sporting a black eye and a swollen cheek, as well as several of my other friends who failed to escape with assorted bumps and bruises. It was a watershed moment in the neighborhood. However, as Tracy told me, his brother had been grounded, and several of his friends' parents had also been informed of the incident and their children's participation in the beatdown.

Things were different after that incident in the park and in the neighborhood. Mark and his gang never physically attacked us again, though they would still skirt around the fringes of where we were playing and lob insults at us. It appeared Tracy's parents had set Mark straight after punching his brother in the face. That would be the end of his gang activities, at least as far as I knew, and the park became a much more relaxed place to play without the fear of the "bad boys" making trouble.

Those days playing in the park and neighborhood with my childhood friends are some of my best memories of the early years of my life. We had such fun, and the summers seemed endless and fraught with unimaginable possibilities. A ride around the neighborhood on our bikes could yield an adventure we had no idea awaited us. My friend Brett and I had many such adventures, even in his garage, where we would pretend to play astronaut in his mom's dryer. There was no limit to our explorations or what we could manifest out of thin air to initiate our next big adventure.

Of all the great fun I had as a child, nothing matched the fun of playing Hot Wheels with my friend Brett. Hot Wheels were miniature dye-cast cars that Mattel had developed in the late sixties. Initially created as an alternative choice to the "Matchbox" car collection that had ruled the miniature toy car industry for years, Hot Wheels were more stylish and had wider wheels that allowed for racing. Matchbox cars were designed to be pushed around by the kids who played with them, and Hot Wheels were designed for racing on a track utilizing gravity and their design of balance to maximize speed. I absolutely loved Hot Wheel cars, and I still do.

My first car was a yellow/green Camaro with a black roof. It was my reward for enduring a visit to the dentist. Subsequently, after every visit to the dentist, my mom would take me Hot Wheel shopping; more on that later. The track, which you could purchase separately, was bright orange and narrow enough to keep the cars guided within its boundaries without flying off. I never played with my cars in the dirt our concrete as they were far more valuable as race cars careening down the orange track. I took very good care of my cars as they were the "crown jewel" of all my toys, and racing was their purpose.

Our house sat at the top of a big hill on the street we called "Big 18th". And though the main part of our back yard had been leveled off, on the south end, it sloped significantly. This was perfect for Hot Wheel racing. Brett would bring his case of cars, and between the two of us, we had enough orange race track to run two parallel tracks for racing cars. We enjoyed hours and hours of fun racing our cars, and nothing was more exciting than getting a phone call from a friend informing us of a new Hot Wheel purchase. Showing off your new Hot Wheel was the pinnacle of pride. Some engaged in trading cars, but I only did that one time. I developed a strong attachment to all my cars and could not part with them. My one trade was a big one, however. I traded four of my cars for the special edition "Boss Hoss" it was a mean-looking Chrome Ford Mustang with black stripes. It was a special release at the time and, to this day, is my favorite car.

Cars From Personal Collection

I still have around thirty of my original cars, which now hold considerable value as collectors will pay significant money for the original "red line" Hot Wheels, which simply means cars that have red lines around their tires. The value of my collection was around $3,000 the last time I priced it out.

Sadly I once had double the amount of original red-line cars. However, in the act of sheer meanness, my first wife sold at least 30 of them, unbeknownst to me, for pennies on the dollar in the 1990s at a garage sale. During one of her many manic episodes, others suffered the fate of having their tires popped off or purposefully bent as I helplessly watched. Much more about her exploits later, but the good news is I still have the best of my original collection still in my possession. The truth is I could NEVER sell them and have already instructed my daughter that they will be left in her hands upon my passing.

My childhood was an amazing experience that I often reflect on with great reverence. Between my friends, my neighborhood, and the time I grew up, I could not have asked for a better experience as a child. The only thing I would change about it is that I wish it would have lasted longer, but by the summer of 1970, that magical time of my life would sadly come to an end.

Up Up, and Away…

Speaking of adventure… one of the greatest adventures in the history of humankind would occur during the summer of 1969. It was an endless summer that year, and it carries some of the fondest memories of my youth. I had plenty of adventures going on myself that summer, including building my first tree house and first underground fort. However, as great as those adventures were, they paled in comparison to what was going on in the sky above me.

As promised by President Kennedy in the summer of 1962, the United States was about to fulfill the dream of landing a man on the moon. The space race had been won by the United States, and landing on the moon was the defining moment in a decade-long competition with the Soviet Union. Anyone who is old enough to remember *anything* likely remembers July 20, 1969. It was a moment like none other.

America Watches Apollo 11 Mission

I was out in the backyard that evening playing with my sisters when my mother yelled through the screen door, "They're getting ready to walk on the moon!" We immediately dropped what we were doing and scampered into the house. Like so many families across the United States, that evening, we all sat near the tv set gazing with amazement at what we were seeing, Neil Armstrong slowly walking down the steps of the lunar module. I remember being a little disappointed that the image coming from the moon was in black and white and a bit fuzzy, but my overwhelming sense was a feeling of pride for my country… for America.

"That's one small step for man... one giant leap for mankind", Neil Armstrong pronounced through his space suit as he stepped onto the lunar surface. We had landed a man on the moon, and with the planting of the American flag on its surface, the United States had boldly proclaimed itself as the greatest nation ever created under God. Whether that was true or not was irrelevant, for in that moment, we were.

Neil Armstrong Steps Onto Lunar Surface

I recall later that evening, after the sun had gone down, walking into the backyard with my father, both of us gazing up at the moon. I pointed to the moon and said, "Our astronauts are up there, Dad... way up there on the moon." I realized, at that moment, staring at the moon, just how amazing it all was! My father smiled, put his arm around my shoulders, and said, "I bet they miss their families don't you think?" That thought had never crossed my mind, but my dad wanted me to understand that these were *real people,* not just some "spacemen figures" as seen on tv.

It was a moment I have never forgotten as I felt a strong sense of sadness standing so close to my father and thinking just how lonely those men must be so far away from home. That night I prayed for their safe return to earth, as I'm sure millions of others did that evening. I prayed they would be reunited with their families again, just as I was so united with mine.

The astronauts, however, were not alone. For every night, morning is born, and everything must ultimately exist beneath the spectrum of light created by God, a light that immerses all of us, whether here on Earth or on the moon above. No matter how far away from home or alone we may feel, we are never without the light of God shining upon us.

The First Time We Fall in Love

When I was young, I believed you fell in love only once. Sure, I loved my mom and dad, sisters and grandparents, but that was already "built-in" love. I had never fallen in love. I believed that one day, in the distant future, I would run into a girl, look into her eyes, and know that she was my one and only true love. Why did I believe that? Reflecting back, I suppose some of it was based on my conscious awareness of how love was being presented to me on tv and in children's fairytale stories. Cognitively limited and lacking experience, I had formulated my belief system on a fundamental naive assumption which then became fact as far as I was concerned. After all, perception invariably becomes a reality.

I remember the first time I fell in love. It was an evening not unlike many others in 1968. I was sitting on the carpeted floor in our living room in front of the family tv set. I don't recall anyone else being around that evening, but likely because I was so immersed in the movie I was watching.

There was absolutely nothing real contained in the creation of images and sound I found myself absorbed in that evening. It was simply a video signal sent to our tv from the airways above. The signal had been converted into dancing electrons and focused into thousands of pixels through a picture tube and projected onto our tv screen. Not very romantic when you think about it. It was all an illusion created by human technology and the art of theater, but nonetheless, I was taken to a realm of new emotional discovery, a realm where the longing for something transcendental clashed with the laws of reality.

In the movie, a teenage girl runs away from home by the method of jumping from freight train to freight train in an effort to get as far away from her parents as possible. I don't remember the reasons why she felt compelled to leave everything she had known behind, but I do recall her bravery in doing so. I remember her face being soft and gentle, but it was her eyes I fell in love with as they were deep, expressive eyes exposing her strengths and fears. She was free now from her parents, but she was also alone and facing a big unforgiving world. I suppose it was her bravery coupled with her sadness that drew me to her, and it would be the first time, but certainly not the last, I felt the helpless pain of love.

The movie, of course, eventually ended, and I do not recall the final disposition of her circumstance, but I have a sense she never went back home. As for me, I was left with these new powerful emotions but absolutely nowhere to place my feelings. They just hung in the air with no recourse or resolution. I knew what I felt, but I had no idea what to do with my feelings. I longed for her with an emptiness in my heart as I knew our paths would never cross again. It was a sweet pain that was filled with contradictions being wonderful and terrible at the same time. I felt invigorated and energized by this new feeling, but I also felt broken and beaten by the inevitable outcome. Dare I say it was "the best and worst of times."

As with most bouts of lost love, the pain eventually subsided, and I was left with only the sweet memory, which I carry with me to this day. A love that cannot be sustained eventually finds its resting place, perhaps not in your heart but can reside in your mind forever.

As fate would have it, less than a year later, I saw the movie "The Graduate" and realized Catherine Ross was *really* my true love and not the young girl who had run away from her parents. Sure, I still thought of that brave young teenager, but she no longer resided in my heart. She resided in my memories now.

Catherine Ross

Catherine Ross was a beautiful brunette with a charming smile and a touch of innocence about her. I thought of her often, and there was no doubt that the familiar ache in my heart had returned again. I would listen to my transistor radio all day, hoping to hear the song "Scarborough Affair" by Simon and Garfunkel, who had written and performed the music for the movie. I would drift into a hazy mist of longing and desire, imagining her stroll across the Berkley campus to meet me near a large fountain.

Of course, I was only eight and had no means of traveling down to Berkley, and certainly, there may have been some inherent issues, primarily the difference in our ages. However, anything is possible with a little imagination, and my young mind had plenty of imagination to power this fantasy of mine.

Fortunately, Catherine Ross had become a star (unlike the unknown freight train hoping girl). Therefore I was not left with the staggering thought that our paths would never cross again. For this reason alone, I didn't feel so abandoned, with no place to deposit my emotions. If nothing else, I could hear "Scarborough Affair" on the radio, and somehow she felt near to me.

It wasn't long after "The Graduate" that I would see Catherine Ross again in the movie "Butch Cassidy and the Sundance Kid." In this movie, however, I was stunned to discover she was a much different person than the one I had fallen in love with. She was still somewhat soft-spoken but far from naive or innocent. She was more likened to a clever thief with a penchant for hanging around the "bad guys" than a young, pretty college student. Worst of all, she was far too interested in Robert Redford for my liking and not unlike many men of that era, I felt a little 'out of my league" when trying to compete against Redford for the hand of a beautiful woman.

I felt an odd sense of rejection and disappointment that she had fooled me in "The Graduate" as she was clearly not the person she had portrayed herself as being. She wasn't an angel, and she wasn't a princess. She was something much darker than that and nothing like the young woman in my childish fantasies.

Sadly this would be an experience that would be repeated throughout my life. There is, of course, the superficial individual that we are allowed to see, and then there is the *real person* that is hidden behind a curtain. As time goes by, we begin to learn the truth about people the more the curtain is slowly and carefully pulled back. The darkness of secrets that had been cleverly hidden behind the veil of socially acceptable behavior slowly began to appear.

These are the warning signs that many of us do not recognize or refuse to see. We rationalize and make excuses for behavior that we know is not copasetic to our lifestyle or beliefs. We want to believe the best in a person because we have *seen* the best in them and are too often more than willing to ignore their dark side that peeks through the veil from time to time.

I have learned it is best to trust your instinct or "gut feeling" when this occurs because, like a dripping faucet, the issue will not go away by ignoring it. On the contrary, over time, it is certain only to get worse. However, because of the time we have spent and the emotional investment we have made, the decision to "part ways" becomes far more difficult. Some never make it out, and others who do are left with emotional scars.

Love, it can be argued, is the most powerful force in the universe; hence this power has the potential to uplift or destroy. How love is perceived and how it is applied will ultimately determine what type of outcome will be derived from its presence. This brings us to the most basic question. What is love? How can it be defined with absolute certainty? This invisible force can be translated through our physical actions and reactions. However, our physical manifestations and mental observations of love are simply tools to express this experience that we all hold within our being.

Love is ubiquitous, yet it is also intensely individualistic and unique to each person or living being. Our world is filled with love. It cannot be avoided or ignored. It is a transcendental experience encompassing "the all" and being, so it is hard for us to comprehend the vastness and power that it wields. We observe and feel its impacts. However, to describe love as interpreted by our senses is an exercise in futility. As they say, love is "something in the heart," but that is pure symbolism

assigning a transcendental experience to an organ in the body.

Love goes beyond the senses and reaches deep into our emotional being. It can certainly impact our physical well-being, but anything of the mind is capable of doing so. It exists deep within ourselves and operates independently and powerfully over most any other emotion.

There is something about love that is simply a natural part of our world, and yet also it is also something beyond our world. If there is evidence that God exists, love is likely the best evidence we have to support his existence. We have all been impacted by its power, and we have all learned how it can save or destroy lives. As I discovered at a young age, love is a flame that, when ignited, can bring out a part of us so profound that the memory lingers on long after the flame has been extinguished.

"Eddie"

I remember lazy care free summer days when I would awake with nothing but adventure in front of me, and by the time night fell and the adventure was complete, I was exhausted and ready for sleep. However, the other part of our existence, our sleep state, could also be quite an adventure. I recall having one reoccurring dream, which included my nemesis, "Eddie," whose sole goal was to raise hell upon my young psyche. The dreams with Eddie were always in black and white, and he looked to be a child of around eight. However, this was no "average" kid of eight. Eddie appeared to be the son of Satan, complete with horns and a tail with a spear-shaped tip.

He always wore a mischievous smile on his face as if to remind me he could kill me anytime he wanted but preferred to terrorize me instead. The worst thing you could do was run from Eddie. Much like that vicious neighborhood dog, if you chose to run, Eddie would be certain to chase. In my dreams, Eddie invariably would force me to run down the long hallway of our house, and it appeared that the more I ran, the longer the hallway stretched. Faster and faster, I would run, the hallway stretching out like an accordion, I was just out of reach of Eddie, but so close I could feel his breath on my neck.

By the grace of God, somehow, I would make it to the kitchen where my parents would be washing dishes. I looked back at Eddie as he stood in the dining room with a mischievous smile on his face, appearing very content that he had me cornered.

At my parents' feet, I had found safety from Eddie, knowing he couldn't catch or harm me with my parents so near. What I didn't realize was that Eddie, being a dream of my own making, had unlimited powers, including transmutation. He always won in my dreams. There was just no escaping that fact, though time and time again, I fell into the trap of believing there was a way out of his evil clutches.

I would grab my father's pant leg imploring both him and my mother to save me from this black-and-white devil child. It was then that I would notice something out of the corner of my eye. I caught my mother's reflection in the kitchen window, and to my horror, it was in black and white! "Oh dear lord, it can't be true," but indeed it was. My parents would then gaze down upon me with black eyes and "Eddie" faces grinning from ear to ear. As I mentioned, in the end, there was no escaping the reach of Eddie.

Eventually, as I grew older, he chose to leave me alone and terrorize other children, I'm sure. However, to say I don't still fear him, well, that would be a lie. To this day, when I lie in the darkness of my bedroom, I will occasionally think of that black-and-white devil child and wonder if one day he will return.

The Race of 68

With the stunning news in March of 1968 that Lyndon Johnson would not seek re-election, the democrat nomination for president became a wide-open race. Who would come out of the fray after Johnson's surprising announcement was anyone's guess? Robert Kennedy, a late entry into the race, had hit the ground running, quickly building momentum for his campaign with several major primary victories. It appeared to many that Kennedy, the former Attorney General and current United States senator, could actually be the one to rise above the fray and garner the nomination. That belief came to a crashing end with his assassination that June.

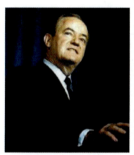
Hubert Humphrey

Vice President Hubert H. Humphrey joined the primary race soon after Johnson had announced he would not seek re-election. Humphrey tried to tow a fine line between not being critical of the President's Vietnam policies while also trying not to alienate the many voters who supported the anti-war movement. This was a difficult balance for Humphrey to achieve as the other two primary candidates, Eugene McCarthy and Robert Kennedy, openly campaigned against America's involvement in the war.

The death of Kennedy, however, would give Humphrey the advantage he needed. Many of the delegates who were obligated to cast their vote for Kennedy would swing their support to Humphrey, giving him the advantage going into the convention. In the end, Humphrey would be selected as the nominee during the democratic national convention, though for many, it felt as if he was a "default" choice.

I am convinced that had Kennedy not been assassinated, he would have most certainly been the democratic nominee. He had garnered immense momentum in just a short period of time. The night Kennedy was killed he had just earned a huge victory in the California primary, and it became obvious momentum was clearly on his side. However, as fate would have it, his nomination was not to be. Humphrey was put forward to challenge the republican candidate and former Vice President, Richard Nixon.

Nixon, who had served two terms as Vice President to Dwight Eisenhower, had lost a close election to John Kennedy in 1960. Undeterred by his defeat to Kennedy and then his subsequent loss for the Governorship of California, Nixon resurfaced in 1968 to once again challenge for the office of President.

Nixon campaigned as an advocate for the "silent majority," meaning the middle and working class. During the Johnson administration, much of the focus had been on the less fortunate, people who were argued to need the "helping hand" of government. Nixon took the stance that throughout the implementation of Johnson's progressive domestic agenda, the middle class had been ignored and their needs not met.

Richard Nixon

He promised the "silent majority" would be heard if he was elected. Nixon also campaigned on the idea of uniting Americans and healing the divisions between them. These divisions had only been exacerbated by Vietnam and civil rights protests that, at times, became quite violent. He campaigned using the phrase "Peace with honor" as his promise to extricate America from the entanglement of the Vietnam war.

In the end, Americans looking for a way out of the war and tired of the eight years of failure by democrat administrations to do so chose Nixon over Humphrey. The fact was, between Kennedy and

Johnson, the democrats had only drug the United States further into the quagmire of Vietnam. Although Nixon had yet to clearly outline his plan on how to exit Vietnam with honor, Americans were willing to give him a chance to get the job done after the failure of the democrats.

The 1968 election was the first Presidential election I was engaged in. Although only seven years old, I followed the news coverage leading up to the first Tuesday in November when I sat with my parents and watched the election results on tv. Nixon won the election by one of the closet margins in American history. However, he failed to garner over 50 percent of the popular vote due to a third candidate, George Wallace, who garnered 14 percent of the national vote and drew votes away from both Nixon and Humphrey in the process. I was very much on the side of Richard Nixon throughout the campaign season, and I think for no other reason, he had promised to get Americans out of Vietnam. I had developed, as unfair as it might have been, a negative opinion of Johnson because of his escalation of the war effort. I saw him as someone who didn't care how many young Americans died and was certainly a hindrance to peace.

Nixon would run into his own issues when it came to Vietnam. Eventually, he did spearhead successful efforts, which led to the end of America's involvement in the war, but it was only after he suffered extreme criticism for the bombings in Cambodia that he had ordered. He did have a watershed moment in his presidency with his visit to China and the opening of relations with the communist country. He also made inroads in the Cold War with the Soviet Union in reaching an agreement on the limitation of nuclear weaponry between the two super powers. In the end, Nixon would be forced to resign in disgrace in August of 1974 due to his involvement in the cover-up of the Watergate scandal.

The Birth of a Phobia

"Phobia" can be defined as: "An extreme or irrational fear of something." There are many types of phobias. Some of the more well-known may involve a fear of heights, closed-in spaces, or needles. Often these phobias have no rational basis, while others may be a result of childhood trauma that lingers well into adulthood.

My mother, for example, had a traumatic experience with water as a child where she feared she would be drowned. That experience, and the subsequent trauma it created, impacted her view of water for her entire life. I have never seen her step into a pool or any body of water for that matter. In fact, her phobia also impacted my life long perception as well. Though I don't have a great fear of water, I'm certainly not the first one in the pool or one to ever swim in the ocean.

The birth of my own personal phobia occurred in 1968 in the most unassuming fashion. My mother had told me she was going to take me, Johnny Vierra and his mother out for an ice cream treat. What a great way to spend a summer afternoon, going with family and friends and getting two scoops of my favorite flavor! I wasn't sure *why* out of nowhere, she decided to take all of us out for ice cream, but that was of no concern to me until, of course, it was.

While romping around in the back of the station wagon with Johnny, he casually mentioned something that made absolutely no sense. He intimated that my mother was taking me to the dentist, and they were simply along for the ride. I first ignored his assertion as nonsense and continued to horse around in the back of the station wagon. However, when he mentioned the dentist again and asked me if I was scared to have my teeth pulled, well, that certainly got my attention!

I immediately yelled up to the front of the station wagon and asked my mom where we were going. There was dead silence. A chill ran down my spine as I yelled even louder, asking her again about our destination. She turned and looked at me with guilty eyes, and it was at that moment that I knew I was in trouble. She sheepishly confirmed that what Johnny had told me was accurate, and a rush of heat flushed my face. My fate that sunny afternoon was indeed not a tasty ice cream treat but an appointment with Dr. PAIN in a dental chair! Johnny just looked at me and nodded his head in an "I told you so" fashion.

The next few minutes were filled with a blurred, chaotic, and confused sense of panic. With every green light, with every turn, I was drawn closer to the dental holocaust, and there wasn't a damn thing I could do about it. For a moment, I foolishly thought of opening the back gate of the station wagon and jumping out to escape at the next light, but I didn't even know where I was! I was trapped in a station wagon to hell.

I went into the dentist's office that day in tears and left in tears. I had two teeth pulled, and many more would be removed at the hands of a dentist. My mouth was sadly too small for the number of teeth I had coming in, and the remedy apparently was to pull out my permanent teeth to avoid braces. I would indeed avoid braces, but would have so many teeth pulled throughout my lifetime that I have lost track of the number pulled. Initially, it was simply an effort to remove teeth that did not fit in my mouth. However, later, it was my own desire to avoid the dentist at all costs, which would create even more issues for me in the long run.

All of my dental woes can be traced back to that fateful day when my mother deceived me and took me to the dentist for teeth extractions instead of the ice cream shop. There is no doubt that is when my fear began and the phobia was born. Through the decades, I have had an irrational fear of the dentist, which has caused me to avoid oral health care. This irrational fear, of course, has caused even more unnecessary dental grief. It has become a self-fulfilling prophecy that, even with all of my advances in mentalism and mental discipline, I have yet to overcome.

I talked to my mother about her decision to deceive me on that fateful day, and she has long since apologized, but the damage had been done. I firmly believe that had I been told the truth from the beginning, I would have been able to prepare for the dental visit, and the trauma would not have occurred. However, I also know that being a parent is a tough job, and my mother did what she thought best at the time. Who hasn't made multiple mistakes as a parent? I hold no malice towards my mom for her decision, but I also cannot deny that she made a big mistake that has negatively impacted me throughout my life. It's just one of those things, I suppose, but I sure wish it hadn't occurred.

Your Ballroom Days are Over

The 1960s, without a doubt, had been filled with some incredible socio-political events, from a Presidential assassination to major civil rights advancements and what seemed like everything else in between. The final year of the decade would be no different, and it would send the 60's off into history with more incredible stories and events that would be remembered more than half a century later.

In 1969 we went to the moon, and we saw the end of the Beatles. Woodstock would also be remembered as the swan song for the "hippie" generation, as opioids would forever change the culture of "free love" and peace. Vietnam would still rage into the 70s, and the struggle to solve civil rights issues would continue for decades beyond the 60s. However, the "dark side" of the decade would rear its ugly head one last time in 1969 with an absolutely heinous and terrifying act of evil. The "Tate-LaBianca Murders" occurred in August of 1969, and it rocked the country, in particular the west coast, with its brutality and bizarre circumstances.

This event scared me significantly as it was the first time I clearly understood the level of evil that could be propagated by our species. These murders were not a result of the "fog of war" when lines of morality are confused with the will to survive. These were crimes of the soul that had manifested into the form of evil.

The "Tate-LaBianca Murders" occurred in Los Angeles, California, and were perpetrated by cult members of the "Manson Family" led by Charles Manson. The murders occurred over a two-day period and were ordered to be carried out by Manson. The sheer brutality of these murders stunned the country and severely damaged the reputation of the hippie counter-culture, as Manson, an aspiring musician and self-proclaimed user of LSD, identified himself as part of this counter-culture.

In total, seven people were murdered by means of beatings, stabbings, and gunshot wounds. Sharon Tate, an actress and model, who was 8 1/2 months pregnant, was stabbed sixteen times while begging for her life and that of her unborn child. She was then hung. The crime scenes of both sets of murders were unspeakable scenes of gore and blood. Using Sharon Tate's blood, the Manson family members wrote phrases such as "Pig" on the front door of her residence and "Helter Skelter" (title of a Beatles song) on the refrigerator door of LiBianca's residence.

Charles Manson

Manson believed the Beatles' "White Album" was a call to arms in an imminent race war between whites and blacks. In particular, he believed and also convinced his followers that the song "Helter Skelter" was filled with subliminal messages calling for violence.

Manson did not personally kill any of the victims. However, he did orchestrate the killings. He possessed a powerful hold over his followers, and they indeed carried out his direction to commit mayhem and murder on subsequent evenings. He claimed it was the Beatles who had inspired him and his followers to kill. In his own words, Manson said, "It's the Beatles, the music they're putting out. These kids listen to this music and pick up the message. It's subliminal. It is not my music. I hear what it relates to. It says rise. It says kill. Why blame it on me? I didn't write the music."

The subsequent arraignment and trial of Charles Manson and the "Manson Family" members was big news, and the media coverage only fueled the disgust and shock of the American public. The bizarre images of Manson and his "cult family" as they were brought into court were surreal and filled with representations of latent incoherent violence. I recall seeing young women involved in the killings (one with an "X" carved into her forehead) smiling with vacant eyes as they were escorted into their court hearings. To me, it looked as if they were in a trance, and they looked possessed. In the end, all of those involved in the killings were either sentenced to death or life in prison, including Manson. In 1972 the California Supreme Court abolished the death penalty, and Manson and his followers' death sentences were reduced to life in prison.

When these murders occurred, the common question uttered from the lips of most Americans was, "What could have possibly driven these young people to the point of madness and level of barbarism?" Some blamed it on the hippie culture, some blamed it on LSD, while others blamed it on society.

The cold hard truth is that in every decade since the "Tate and LaBianca Murders," heinous events such as this have and will no doubt continue to occur. Is it really our society that generates these events that too often now manifest themselves in the form of public mass killing scenarios such as school shootings? This is, of course, a difficult question to answer as many variables are in play at the same time coalescing into a perfect storm of latent evil which rises to the surface. However, I believe there are some fundamental reasons for the occurrence of such unthinkable events, and they are indeed a result of corrupted belief systems that have infected all of us at some level.

It begins with personal ego but ultimately expands into societal "group think." You don't have to look very far or hard to see it in everyone and in almost every man-made nomenclature created.

It is the quest to satisfy personal desires through materialistic acquisition as well as the craving for power and control over others, that drives far too many in our society in the wrong direction. If continued unchecked, this "unholy trinity" of lust, power, and greed creates an imbalance in the human equation.

Ultimately this "imbalance" promotes societal dysfunction where large masses of individuals lose their connection with the higher purpose of serving humanity. They become lost in a finite existence that is tied to materialism instead of an infinite existence with God. More about this later, but in summation, until we as a species rid ourselves of selfish desires and focus on the "whole" of humanity instead of ourselves, evil shall continue to manifest itself. Violence will continue in many forms, from mass shootings and terrorist attacks to all-out wars between nations.

Something has to change, and we as a species are capable of making these changes though we are still far from engaging in this endeavor. It begins with the *individual,* meaning all of us can do our part by modeling unselfish behavior. We must begin living a life dedicated to humanity instead of a narrow focus on ourselves, our family, and our friends.

It requires a new thought process that demands we see all people as part of our immediate family, worth our love and respect, as in the end, all of us are from the same seed of God.

Ask any astronaut who has gazed upon the earth from space, and they will tell you there are no "borders" on the planet Earth, only the borders we have mentally created and then manifested into physical form. We are responsible for these self-made divisions of thought; therefore, it is logical to assume our thinking can also change a destiny currently filled with violence and division.

Is this likely to happen? Absolutely not. The "unholy trinity" has grown far too powerful and has no plans to relinquish its power... the politicians and corporate CEOs will make certain of that. However, as individuals, we can commit to not submitting to the trappings of lust, power, and greed by curtailing our own personal desires and replacing them with an unselfish and open heart to all of humanity and, of course, also to God.

George and "The Duke"

Duke was the meanest son of a bitch I have ever known. He was cold-hearted, and he was vicious, showing no mercy to those he preyed upon. It was as if he had no conscience whatsoever or certainly none that I was aware of. He would attack just about anyone who came within his purview without remorse or regret. I hated him with a passion, and I feared him even more. I avoided him at all costs and would have nightmares regarding his brutality. He was "The Duke of Terror" as far as I was concerned.

George, on the other hand, was one of the most gentle souls I had come across in my youth. He was a boy my age who had a fragility about him, and yet he did not let that deter him from being part of our group of friends. I'm not sure what medical issues George had, but it was clear he was different than the rest of us. He walked with a slight drag of his right foot, and his right arm appeared to be stuck at a 45-degree angle, his limp hand dangled, ineffective in its use for the most part.

George, however, did not let this handicap stop him from being part of our neighborhood group of boys. He acted as if he had no defect whatsoever and would play football or any other activity we indulged in without a second thought. All of us treated him as an equal, as he expected that of us and of himself. There was no "victim" role played by George, and because of that, we treated him not as inferior but as an equal. We never made fun of him, and we all had an internal respect for his courage though we never spoke of it between ourselves. George was a good kid that found a way to fit in at an age that isn't always easy to be accepted.

Duke had no interest in fitting in. He hated all of us kids and made it clear every time we passed by him. His eyes were filled with hate and madness. Given the opportunity, I'm sure he would have maimed us all. Thankfully his opportunities were limited as he was chained to a tree in the front yard of my best friend's home. He was a full-blooded German Sheppard sired by "King," his father, and "Queen," his mother, who lived down the street with the Vierra's. He was sold to Brett's family and instantly became the worst dog on the block. He was nothing like his parents, who, by all accounts, including my own personal experience, were good dogs and family pets. Duke was a bad seed born from Satan, and if "Eddie" had ridden a beast, I'm certain it would have been Duke.

As I mentioned, Duke was chained to a tree in the front yard, which just happened to be near the walkway to Brett's front door. Every time I would go to Brett's house, I would have to walk right by Duke as he lurched forward at me, snapping his chain taught until it choked him. He would literally get within two feet of me as he bared his teeth, snarling and barking wildly, his eyes afire with hatred. I was terrified of this beast, and many a time, I pondered what would become of me if his chain ever snapped.

I would ring the doorbell and stand there petrified as Duke yanked and leaped at me, growling and showing his fangs. Seconds seemed like hours as I waited for that door to open. When it was finally answered, it would be Brett or his mother at the door, and they would engage in the obligatory scolding of this monster, telling him "to shut up and go lay down," which he never did. They then would tell me, "Don't mind him... he's all bark and no bite." I didn't believe their words for a second, and my belief would be validated in the summer of 1969 when Duke would have his way with George.

It all started innocuously enough. We were playing basketball in Brett's driveway when George said it was time for him to head home. We all said goodbye to George, but frankly, we weren't really paying attention as he left because we were focused on playing ball. Upon our arrival, as per usual, Brett had put Duke in the house. No one wanted a threatening barking dog (who was a broken chain away from wreaking havoc) anywhere near them while playing basketball. What none of us knew was that Brett's little sister had let Duke out into the backyard. What we also didn't know was that George had decided to take a shortcut through Brett's backyard and across the park back to his house.

It wasn't long after we had said our goodbyes to George that we heard shrieking coming from Brett's backyard. Instantly we all ran towards the shrieking to see what the commotion was. As we entered the backyard, it was clear what had occurred. Duke was circling around George snapping and biting at him as he lay crouched in the corner. Brett immediately yelled at Duke, grabbed him by the collar, and yanked him away from George, but the damage had been done.

In my over sixties years of living, I have never seen so much blood on a human being. George crying uncontrollably, had blood all over him. It was matted in his blonde hair, on his neck, hands, arm, and legs. He was understandably terrified and almost in shock, as far as I could tell. Duke had bitten him multiple times and had scratched him in the neck and face. George was a bloody mess.

After putting Duke in the house, Brett returned with a damp washcloth and several bandaids. We patched poor George up the best we could, and after a period of time, we got him to calm down and stop crying. Eventually, all of us walked him home and delivered him to his understandably very upset mother. I didn't see much of George after that. I suppose his mother kept him closer to home after the incident. By the end of the summer, the news had circulated that he and his family had moved. I will never forget what I witnessed that afternoon and the blood bath that Duke had propagated on our disabled friend.

As for Duke, he continued to terrorize people chained to the tree by Brett's front door. I'm not sure what came from the incident in the "adult world." I never heard or perhaps forgotten what Brett told me regarding the final disposition of the incident. It was George who had chosen to go into the backyard without notifying Brett or getting his approval. Whether there was any legal action available to George's parents, I'm not sure. I do know the dog continued to be "The Duke of Terror" long after the bloody assault upon George.

I have never trusted the German Sheppard breed since and always feel on guard and uneasy around them. I certainly never approach them and do my best to avoid contact anytime one is near. As for George, I wouldn't blame him a bit if he felt the same way about the breed, but then again, he was a special kid with unusually strong fortitude. Hell, that being said, he may just own a couple of those beasts. He was just that kind of a guy.

All They Wanted Was to Be Free

I would be remiss in not mentioning the movie "Easy Rider" before closing the era of the 1960s. "Easy Rider" was a biker film written by Peter Fonda, Dennis Hopper, and Terry Southern. It was an independent low-budget film that exceeded all expectations at the box office as well as critical acclaim.

Easy Rider

The film, made on a budget of just four hundred thousand dollars, grossed over sixty million worldwide. It became a cultural centerpiece for its representation of, in particular, the youth counter-culture, which had blossomed during this period of time. The film was nominated for two Academy Awards and was selected for preservation by the Library of Congress for being "culturally, historically, or aesthetically significant."

I became aware of the movie through my two uncles, who were enamored by the film upon seeing it. I recall both of them telling me, "It was the best movie they had ever seen." If my uncles, who I believed were extremely "cool," had thought that highly of the movie, I knew it must be something amazing.

The story and theme behind the movie is really quite simple. Two young men acquire wealth through a big cocaine sale trade for a meager living for a free, unfettered lifestyle. They are no longer slaves to a capitalistic society. They are their own men now, owing nothing to anyone. The money they acquired through their drug deal had freed them to do whatever they wanted.

The two main characters, "Wyatt" and "Billy," were an interesting pair indeed. Wyatt, the leader, appeared quiet, sincere, and possessed depth in his thinking. In contrast, Billy appeared selfish, lacking in intelligence, and superficial. He was more interested in selfish desires and instant gratification, while Wyatt, although he wasn't sure where to look and what he might ultimately find, was looking for something "deeper." It was as if the pair represented the best of the hippie culture as well as its falsehoods and misgivings.

Riding on two spectacular "chopper style" motorcycles, which they had just purchased with their newfound wealth, the pair set out for adventure in a cross-country ride to Florida. The rest of the movie is a chronicle of the people they meet and the experiences they encounter along the way to their final destination. In a poignant moment, near the beginning of the film, Wyatt removes his watch and takes a good long look at it before he throws it onto the ground. Time no longer has a hold on these two men. They have freed themselves from its constraints.

As the movie unwinds, we are reminded of the many themes that were prevalent during the decade of the sixties. Racism and bigotry are addressed, as well as senseless violence towards those who are not understood or feared due to the blind ignorance of others. The film also takes a deep dive into the hippie culture in a raw but warm-hearted commune scene. Young people are depicted working together to grow their own crops to feed themselves. They are poor and have really nothing of value, but what they do have, they share, including a common love for one another. Wyatt is touched by what he sees, while Billy quickly gets bored with it all and wants to move on.

Near the end of the movie Wyatt, having premonitions of the pair's untimely deaths, thoughtfully says to Billy, "We blew it." Billy looks at Wyatt, confused and disturbed, not understanding the depth of Wyatt's statement. As far as Billy was concerned, they had accomplished exactly what they had set out to do, but for Wyatt, that was not the case.

For decades I also was confused by Wyatt's statement, and I am embarrassed to say it didn't dawn on me until I was in my early fifties what he had meant. Throughout their journey across America, Wyatt had taken stock of how people lived, and he learned, sadly too late, both he and Billy had not earned their freedom or their right to happiness.

Through their adventures, Wyatt observed the admirable qualities of hard work and self-sacrifice. He realized that he and Billy had taken the *easy* way out, and it had left him unsatisfied and empty.

They had not toiled and worked for their wealth, nor had they taken any responsibility for the care of others. They had cheated their way to freedom, only caring about themselves and their own happiness without a thought for anyone or anything else. In the end, it left Wyatt empty inside as their freedom, when scrutinized, had no merit.

When the movie came out, I was not able to see it, as my parents, already leery of the influence the hippie culture might be having on me, would not allow it. I already owned the album soundtrack and several of the "Easy Rider" posters, but that was as far as my parents would let me take it. I was finally allowed to see the movie in my teens, and though I didn't really understand the meaning behind the film, there was no doubt I found it very cool.

Easy Rider

Looking back, of all the movies I have seen in my life, "Easy Rider" had the greatest impact on me. The film has always been neatly tucked away in my immediate memory, and many of my life experiences have gone through the filter of that movie. In fact, upon my retirement, the first thing I made sure to do was frame a photo of Dennis Hopper, "Billy," giving "the finger" directly into the camera while sitting on his chopper.

To this day, that photo is proudly presented on our family room wall. It is what I like to call "my retirement certificate." One last act of simple defiance, giving the finger to "the man." Figuratively my watch has been thrown onto the ground, and time, or no one for that matter, owns me anymore.

Everything Must Pass

By late 1969 my dad had accepted a promotion to become the manager of Commercial Credit's Portland Branch. Portland was forty miles north of Salem, and my father dutifully drove the 80 miles round trip for months until he and my mom broke the news to us children that in late spring of 1970, we were putting our house up for sale and moving to Portland.

I don't believe any of us kids were all too happy to hear the news, but personally, I hated the idea of moving. I spent the first few weeks in denial, thinking my mom and dad would come to their senses and change their minds. However, it became quite clear that would not be the case when "Ted Morrison" reality staked their claim to our property with a for sale sign in our front yard.

I hated Ted Morrison's Reality, and I hated the real estate agent who came to visit us with his phony smile and deceit in his heart. Every time he would drive up in his green Mercury Cougar to visit my parents, I would send evil thoughts his way and hope Eddie would pay him a visit late in the night.

When you are young, I suppose hope springs eternal until reality slaps you in the face. By mid-summer, reality came crashing down on my misguided belief that something would happen to change the course we were on. Our house had been sold, and I was devastated. I cried alone in my bed that night, feeling the same feeling of desperation of a lost love with no hope of getting it back. I was about to lose everything I grew to know and love, with the exception of course of my siblings and my parents. In the end, that would be enough to sustain me as I made the rough transition of relocating.

The last few days I spent in Salem were filled with sadness. I recall scratching on the foundation of our house, my initials, and the date. This gave me some relief in the belief that although I may be leaving, I was leaving my mark for as long as the house would stand. It was a futile childish effort, but I suppose it was the best I could do, having no control over the circumstances I faced.

My lasting memory of our departure was looking through the back window of our Ford Fair Lane family sedan, waving to my best friend Brett as he stood in the middle of the street waving back. I waved until his silhouette grew smaller and smaller, ultimately disappearing into the horizon.

We all have moments like these in our lives, the pivotal moments that shift our fate from one direction to another. I didn't know what lay ahead of me; I only knew what I was leaving behind. I had no idea at the time, even with all my sadness at the moment, that my life would never be the same again.

Looking back at the first decade of my life, I can't tell you if it was my age, where I lived, or perhaps even the decade of the 60s, but whatever the case, it was truly a magical time for me. I fondly recall the decade of the 60s as being my own slice of "Camelot," and I can honestly say I have never been as happy or filled with wonder as I was during that time.

I've chased happiness throughout the decades that followed but never found what I had living in Salem. It wasn't until I was well into my 50's I quit chasing the happiness that once prevailed over me during the first decade of my life. It took me that long to relinquish the belief that I could recapture the magic of those days.

Today I have laid all of that to rest and accept those years for what they were and what they still mean to me. However, as they say, "You are only a kid once," and I suppose I made the most of it. I would change nothing about those days as they were indeed the best days of my life.

This by no means is a negative reflection of the years and the decades that have followed. There has no doubt been some amazing times since those early years in my life, and many I will discuss in the pages to follow. That being said, there is something special about being a child before the world begins to tug you in so many different directions and before the complexity of life steals simplicity from your existence.

There is something special about believing your dad is the strongest man in the world and your mother loves no one as much as she loves you. That sense of security and well-being is the foundation to build a strong life and is an important tonic for ensuring happiness well into the future.

The potential magic and value of youth can never be underestimated, and I thank my parents for providing me with a safe, loving environment to excel in. It reminds me that all of us, parents and grandparents, have a responsibility to provide our children an opportunity to experience the joy and wonderment of youth. Through the years, as they grow older, the magical days of youth will always be a welcomed companion and a great source of joy and will continue to feed their souls throughout the decades to follow.

Part Two
(The 70s)

Change is in the Air

By late summer 1970, I found myself immersed in an entirely different environment. Our family had completed its relocation 40 miles north of Salem to Lake Oswego, a suburb of Portland. It was not the first move I had made in my life, but it was indeed the most profound. I had zero desire to move away from Salem and the familiarity it had provided me. All that I had known had been summarily abandoned and left far behind on Interstate 5.

In Salem, I had lived on top of a hill amongst the wide open spaces and an extended view of the horizon. In Lake Oswego, I found myself buried beneath huge Douglas Fir trees that towered a hundred feet above my head. It was like our family had landed in the middle of some strange dense forest world.

In this new "forest world" I was now immersed in, there would be no viewing of sunsets or observing the distant coastal mountain range. Everything was now "closed in" and darker. At night the giant Douglass Fir trees around me were ominous. Their huge limbs moved independently from one another in the wind like an octopus's arms reaching out to grab unsuspecting children below. To say the transition from Salem to Lake Oswego was easy would be to say the giant fir trees surrounding my new home did not intimidate me. It would take some getting used to this new forest environment.

There was some good news. I still had a month until school started, meaning there was still plenty of time to make new friends before entering a new school environment. The problem was that I didn't. My sisters found immediate friends in the cul-de-sac where we lived. They would run over to the house across the street and play Barbies with their new friends for hours. How did I know this? Well, because I tagged along! I would bring my "GI. Joe" and "Captain Action" dolls (the term "action figure" had not yet been created) and play "house" with my sisters and their friends. This, of course, was not my first choice for a playtime activity. I would have preferred playing Hot Wheels or football with my friends back in Salem, but I was a long way from that neighborhood with no hope of getting back. Life moves on even at times you wish it wouldn't.

My mother, upon discovering my daily routine of playing "house" with my sisters and their Barbies, needless to say, was concerned about my non-conformity in playtime activities. She clearly felt this was not a gender-appropriate activity for me to be engaged in, and I really didn't disagree with her. The fact is, though, some play, whatever its context, is still better than no play at all. Although I could play well alone, I still enjoyed playing with others at times. Having no friends of my own left me with only one available option, and that was to engage in play with my sisters, and so I did.

In any case, my mother instantly went into action and ordered my sisters to take me around the neighborhood and knock on doors to inquire if there was a boy my age that would play with me. Pretty pathetic right? My sisters, as one might imagine, were not happy about having to drag their little brother around and introduce him to people *they* didn't even know. As for me, I was embarrassed as well, but I had no choice in the decision-making process.

So, off we went door to door, with me being exhibited as the ugly puppy who no one wanted. After doing this for several days, my sisters pleaded with my mom to stop the madness. I confirmed that my sisters had dutifully followed her instructions to knock on every door in a two-block radius. The results of their efforts were clear from the beginning. All three of us were humiliated. I felt I received the worst of it as my sisters were only trying to sell "the dog-faced boy" to others. They at least *weren't* the "dog-faced boy."

In the end, it did absolutely nothing to help with my loneliness, as no one wanted to play with the friendless boy. As the saying goes, when you're down and out, nobody loves you. I spent the rest of summer resisting the urge to play with my sisters, knowing what that would bring. Instead, I passed the time throwing the football in the front yard catching my own passes, and playing with my hot wheel cars in my room.

School was coming soon enough, and it would be an opportunity for me to make friends, which I did with ease when the time came. That being said, my first summer of the new decade had been a struggle, to say the least. Looking back, it was one of the worst summers of my life. I had survived the move from Salem but just barely. Once school started, I found new friends and established a routine that eased the loss of my old way of life. However, the first summer in Lake Oswego had no doubt been very difficult for me.

I remember my dad telling us kids why he chose Lake Oswego as our new home. He informed us that the community he chose had a reputation for "really good schools." I don't think his claim had a big impact on any of his three children, as we all thought the school we had previously attended was perfectly fine. However, what none of us kids knew (and I would not discover until entering college) was that we had moved into a very wealthy community. Lake Oswego, at the time, was likely the wealthiest community in the entire state of Oregon and, to this day, is a bastion of affluence. It was the community where all the Portland Trailblazers (Portland's only professional sports team at the time) lived, as well as the coaches for the team. In fact, the head coach of the Trailblazers, Jack Ramsay, daughter, attended my high school. If you had money and lived in Portland, you likely lived in the suburb of Lake Oswego.

Looking back, it's odd that I never made the connection to the wealth attached to my community. Only after I left the protected world of Lake Oswego as a young adult did I realize there was a vast difference in the distribution of wealth in our society. I thought most people lived like we did and had what we had. I would come to understand the impact wealth (or lack thereof) had on the thought processes of communities and the individuals who resided within them. It was a sobering realization of which I only became aware when I left the friendly confines of my parent's home and went to college.

The More Things Change…

Kent State Massacre

Although I was facing many changes in my life by the summer of 1970, some of the same issues that dogged America in the 1960s continued into the new decade. The war in Vietnam showed no signs of slowing down and, if anything, accelerated with President Nixon's bombing of Cambodia. There was mounting public pressure to begin the removal of American troops from Vietnam as Nixon had promised "peace with honor" during his campaign. The bombing of Cambodia, followed by a ground invasion in April of 1970, created more outcry to end the war as soon as possible. At the time, Nixon believed these measures were necessary to disrupt the supply lines and destroy the weapons depots the Vietcong had established in the region.

Whether this was, a strategically sound military decision became irrelevant to many Americans. The anti-war sentiment and protests only accelerated with news of the bombings and subsequent invasion of Cambodia. Many people believed this was an attack on innocent human beings who were stuck in the middle of the conflict between North and South Vietnam. With news of this increased American aggression in South East Asia, protests once again irrupted throughout the country. College campuses, in particular, began to coordinate anti-war protests nationally, with their anger focused on Nixon and his attacks on Cambodia.

College students became more aggressive towards the police at these anti-war rallies, and in turn, the police reciprocated this aggressiveness back at the unruly crowds. Protests on college campuses hit their peak in violent behavior on May 4th, 1970, on the campus of Kent State University. Four students were killed, and nine others wounded when the Ohio National Guard opened fire during a peace rally protesting America's expanding war efforts.

Organized protests of the war had continued to be more contentious between its participants and those attempting to maintain order. The mass shooting at Kent State, however, was the moment when the country realized the war had metastasized into the heartland of America. The public response to the shooting of unarmed students at Kent State was swift in its condemnation. Media coverage painted an accurate picture of the carnage that had unfolded at Kent State. Ultimately it was concluded that there was no legitimate reason for the National Guardsman to have opened fire on the defenseless students.

As in most cases, confusion and fear were the primary contributors to the shootings that left four dead. A chain of events compounded upon one another, eventually leading to the guardsman firing into the crowd of unarmed protest participants.

Vietnam Protests

There was little compassion for the guardsmen who were involved in the killings. They were seen as part of the authoritarian structure that supported the war in Vietnam. The shootings at Kent State magnified the belief that those in authority not only supported the violence in Vietnam but had now brought it onto the college campuses of America.

Public outcry against the war increased even more after Kent State, and mistrust and anger towards those who supported or defended our involvement in the war became intense. It was clear that public sentiment had strongly swung to the side of the anti-war faction. President Nixon found himself in the untenable situation of trying to win a war that most of America wanted no part of anymore.

As for me, the Kent State killings only caused greater concern for my future. It seemed to me that there was no "right side" to the war, and those who had been dragged into the war and forced to fight were hated as much as those who had forced them to go. The police had become the "bad guys" often in these anti-war rallies, and the protestors appeared unruly and overly aggressive towards authority.

The fog of war had crept deep into America's soul, poisoning its societal structure of right and wrong. Up appeared down to me and, of course, down up. Our own National Guardsmen had shot and killed unarmed college students protesting the war, while on the other side of the equation, students attacked soldiers and police at these so-called "peace rallies."

Meanwhile, the young men returning from the war in Vietnam were treated with venomous hatred by those opposed to America's involvement. Protestors focused their anger on these young men whose only crime had been being drafted and sent to fight against their will. These young men were now literally spitting on upon their return home and called "baby killers." They did not return home as heroes like those who had returned 25 years earlier after World War II. Instead, they were ridiculed and despised for something which had been completely out of their control. In my mind, it was an absolutely untenable situation for our country as there were no winners, only losers. I kept hoping for an end to the madness, but there was no end in sight. It just went on and on and continued to escalate.

Let it Be

In 1970 the world was also beginning to adjust to life without the artistic power and influence of the Beatles. The "Fab Four," having endured an incredible and torturous six years of unprecedented fame, had finally folded under the pressure of their own immense popularity.

Their business venture, Apple Corps. founded in 1968, failed to live up to its expectations primarily due to the Beatles' lack of business acumen and desire to focus on the details of "running a business." Great composers and Imagineers, certainly. Astute and disciplined business executives, not so much.

The Beatles 1969

In the end, the conflict of attempting to run a corporation and the stress of their own deteriorating relationships proved to be too much to overcome. Bitterness and resentment simmered just beneath the surface of the band, along with a burgeoning mistrust of one another's motives. Ultimately these factors, along with the unrelenting stress of their extreme fame, fractured the band beyond repair.

In April of 1970, Paul McCartney issued a press release announcing he would no longer be "working with the band." This surprised the other members of the Beatles and, in particular, enraged John Lennon, who seven months earlier had privately informed the group he was leaving. It was McCartney who had convinced Lennon not to publicly announce his departure until after the release of their last album, "Let It Be," only to turn around then and make the announcement himself that he would be leaving the group.

Needless to say, the band broke up with plenty of hurt feelings and anger, which led to legal entanglements against one another that would continue long after their relationship had ended. The band who promoted peace and love in the 1960s, now in the decade of the 70s, were practicing the art of anger and retribution.

However, as they say in show business, "the show must go on," and all four Beatles continued to move forward with successful solo careers of their own. The radio airways were still permeated with the original music from the "Fab Four," but it was also now filled with the solo efforts of John, Paul, George, and Ringo. To no one's surprise, all of them found success apart from the band and continued to produce music for the world to enjoy.

Like so many others, I was saddened to see the end of the Beatles, but within each of their solo works, I could still hear and feel "the sound" of the band. Sure, the new stuff was different and frankly not as good, but the shadow of the Beatles could still be felt in each of their solo efforts. It would be a large shadow all of the band members would try to run from for decades after their breakup. A shadow that still follows the surviving members to this very day. Such is the price of unprecedented greatness, it's never forgotten or allowed to rest. Strawberry fields forever.

It All Goes Down on the Playground

We all remember days at the playground, the fun and the excitement of playing with others in a world filled with swings, slides, and merry-go-rounds. There were two types of playgrounds, of course, the park playground and the school playground. I was fortunate to have access to both when I lived in Salem, as the park was across the street from our home, but that would all change in 1970.

When we moved to Lake Oswego, I no longer had access to a park, so the playground world was now strictly located at my elementary school. I was, of course, already familiar with playgrounds located at schools and the games played there. However, in Lake Oswego, it was a significantly different experience than in Salem. I'm not sure if it was my advancing age or the new location, but the playground world I now found myself a part of was filled with far more issues than just good old fashion "play."

It began innocent enough, but before long, the school playground I was now immersed in became a battle for power and control. The result of this conflict left me pondering the character of the kids I went to school with and, for that matter, even the integrity of the adults who supervised all of us.

It all started with a kid named Jack refusing to allow a girl to drink out of the outdoor water fountain. His logic seemed sound to me at the time. He did not want "girls' germs" around his drinking water. What Jack did not realize was that this girl, Angela, had an older brother named Donny in the 5th grade. The very next day at recess, Donny confronted Jack regarding the drinking fountain issue.

Now what I came to find out about Jack, through my own observation and stories told about him, was that he was a natural leader. As the "new kid," I did not share any history with him, but many kids in my class had grown up with Jack, and it was clear through the years that he had earned their respect. He led an entire classroom of 4th graders out into recess every day, just as he had likely done the three previous years. He was the master of all he surveyed on the playground, and no 4th grader questioned his stature.

As for me, I was in no position to question his authority and fell in line with the rest of my classmates as a subordinate to him. Besides, Jack, for the most part, appeared to be a benevolent leader. Sure, he established rules that, in retrospect, were unfair to some, but they were often simply an extension of rules already established by the adults in our lives. Was there any question in the adult world women did not hold the same stature as men?

Most women during this era were considered best served as housewives and not part of the workforce in American society. If they did work, their value was considered far less than their male counterparts, and they were compensated at a much lower rate. I saw nothing wrong with any of this, and so when Jack said he did not want "girls' germs" contaminating his drinking water, who was I to argue with him? The fact was, like most boys in my class, I agreed with him.

Of course, our fathers would have been appalled learning we would not allow girls to drink out of the water fountain. They would have scolded us for this level of bigotry, and no doubt would have lectured us regarding the unfairness of our rules. Yes, these were the same fathers who would be upset that dinner was not on the table when they came home from work or that their dress shirts had not been ironed properly by their wives. Life is filled with contradictions and unseen hypocrisy supported by tradition and ignorance.

In any case, Jack had established the rules regarding the drinking fountain, and now Donny came to challenge this rule not because of a higher purpose such as "equity" but most likely out of the chivalrous tradition of defending his sister's honor.

I was not there when this confrontation occurred, but the playground legend has it that Jack was in no way intimidated by Donny's 5th-grade stature. He flatly told him he would not be changing any rules, and to the surprise of many who witnessed this confrontation, Donny simply just walked away.

Of course, Donny held the ultimate recourse to Jack's actions and went straight to one of the teachers who were in charge of playground supervision. He informed her of Jack's unfair rule regarding the drinking fountain, and subsequently, Jack was taken to task and sent back to the classroom to spend the rest of recess reflecting on his actions. As I said, it began innocent enough, but this incident would cause a cascade of events to follow that would bring war into our playground world.

Jack was our leader, not just by "dumb luck." He was our leader because of his smarts and charisma. Immediately after he was scolded by the adult authority at the scene, he began the process of recruiting his own posse aimed at retribution for Donny's cowardly actions. He chose those boys in our classroom who possessed aggressive personalities and were strong enough to fight but also dumb enough not to question why. They would fight simply on the basis of a thinly veiled allegiance to Jack, but mostly they would fight because it was part of their aggressive nature.

In the meantime, Donny made a point to brag about how he had drug Jack's name through the mud by informing a teacher of his misdeeds. He shared with his fellow 5th graders how Jack had cried and pleaded with the teacher not to ban him from the classroom during recess. Of course, he did not plead or cry as Donny had described. It was not in Jack's nature to do so, but Donny had created a new reality with his lies, and his fellow classmates believed him. In addition, his little sister, who had been the focal point of this entire brewing conflict, spread the same lies within our class of fourth grade students.

I have always been loyal to my friends and those I consider quality leaders until, at such a time, I conclude my loyalty has been misplaced or abused. Jack was not a friend of mine, but he was the leader of our class, and therefore, I dutifully stood by his side and did not believe the lies that were being told about him.

There was tension on the playground now, with fierce glances and occasional threats bantered about between the two opposing factions. There had been no physical attacks or direct confrontations, at least not yet. Primarily it had been just "mud-slinging" and increasing rhetoric filled with more outrageous lies about the other side.

It didn't take long for these lies and accusations to spill over from direct attacks on Jack's and Donny's character to others who supported one side or the other. I was surprised one day to hear the opposing side was accusing me of playing "dolls" with my sisters. Whether they knew the truth regarding this accusation or not made me immediately question my sisters' loyalty and who might have "gotten to them" and at what price? The playground conflict had now hit home.

Then one day during math class, our teacher, Mrs. Meyers, abruptly stood up from her desk and asked all of us children to line up against the chalkboard wall. Confused and alarmed by this demand, we all followed her direction and stood with our backs against the wall. She walked towards us with her hands folded behind her back. She slowly walked down the long line of students, much like a Marine drill sergeant reviewing his platoon. With a stern look and an even sterner voice, she informed us that someone had taken the most recent math test answer sheet from her desk. She told us she had placed the sheet in her top desk drawer just prior to recess, and now it was gone.

Her aide then came into the room and whispered something into her ear. Mrs. Meyers rolled her eyes and nodded to her and then informed us they would be searching all of our desks for the test answer sheet. She told us it would be wise for the student who had taken the answer sheet to come forward now before it was found by her or her aid. The classroom was silent as no one came forward with an admission.

To our surprise, Mrs. Meyers and her aide did not start from row to row or from left to right. Instead, they went directly to Jack's desk, lifted the lid, and found the answer sheet lying right on top! Mrs. Meyers looked at Jack with disgust and anger. She raised her voice and said, "You are to go immediately to the Principle's office." Jack stood there for a moment, stunned at what had just occurred. He looked at the test answer sheet Mrs. Meyers now held in her hand and just shook his head in disbelief and stepped out of line towards the door. Mrs. Meyers directed her aid to accompany Jack to the Principle's office, and I wondered if I would ever see him again.

Since it was a Friday afternoon, he never returned to the classroom that day, and I was left to ponder over the weekend if he had actually stolen the answer sheet or had been framed. What did the teacher's aid tell Mrs. Meyers when she entered the room? What information was leaked to her that made her believe they would find the stolen paper on Jack's desk? And, of course, I wondered if he had been sent away for good. I hoped that would not be the case as I wanted to know his side of the story, and yes, I was still loyal to him until I could verify a reason not to be.

Well, Monday morning arrived soon enough, and with it, Jack was back in the classroom. I did not know him well enough to ask him for his side of the story, but I did notice his demeanor had changed. His charisma was gone, and his behavior was somber at best.

Through the classroom grapevine, I learned he still denied taking the test score sheet but would not elaborate on the subject, stating his mother had directed him not to discuss it any further other than to deny his guilt in the matter.

Jack, however, had chosen his loyal posse well. The aggressive group he had initially assembled to defend his playground rules, and exact revenge upon Donny, were now more than eager to engage the opposition in defense of his honor. What could have easily been predicted, their focus quickly turned to Donny's sister, Angela, as the likely suspect in the "frame job" of Jack. After all, she was indeed the classmate who had initially been scorned by him in the "drinking fountain incident." Who else in the class had a better motive to place the test answer sheet on his desk?

It initially began with the subtle harassment of Angela on the playground. Jack's posse, led by his "right-hand man," Sam, would call her names and threaten to spit on her. Mind you that Jack was nowhere to be found during these unruly activities. He quietly played alone or with a small group of kids far away from the action.

Sam was now in charge of the group, and it was clear he had less than honorable intentions. Unlike Jack, Sam had little charisma and certainly fewer smarts, but he did have size and strength and was more than willing to impose his physical stature to coerce and intimidate other kids. I stayed clear of Sam at all costs as my instincts told me he was no one to be messed with or even innocently get in his way. Trouble would soon, no doubt, follow.

Meanwhile, Donny, satisfied with the degradation of Jack's character, went about his life without much involvement with his fourth-grade subordinates. I was certain he was aware and likely involved in the planning of the "test answer sheet scandal." However, it did not appear any of Jack's posse was interested in going after a fifth grader who was bigger and stronger than they were. They were satisfied going after the low-hanging fruit of a fourth-grade girl instead.

As is often the case, harassment eventually leads to violence on the playground. The rhetoric from both sides, and the increased threats, had ultimately manifested from so-called "harmless" words into physical aggression. I myself witnessed the fateful event of Angela falling onto the asphalt from the top step of the playground slide. It was about a six-foot fall, and it instantly snapped her arm as she landed awkwardly on the hard surface.

What happened next, I suppose, was all a matter of perspective and whose side you were on in the conflict. Angela began to scream, whaling in pain, and her friends went running towards her to help. Other kids, including Sam and the rest of Jack's posse, simply just scattered throughout the playground area.

In a matter of seconds, one of the teachers who were supervising recess ran over to assess Angela's injuries. A crowd gathered around Angela, and I was unable to see much of what was going on, but I caught a glimpse of her crying and wailing in pain. Moments later, she scurried off to the nurses' office with her cries of pain still heard as she entered the administrative building.

Of course, there was a thorough investigation into the matter, and I was brought into the principal's office and questioned about what I had observed. The truth was I had not seen what caused Angela to fall. I had just witnessed the fall itself. The classroom grapevine, though, was running rampant with speculation of who was to blame for the accident.

In the end, under the strain of intense questioning and unconfirmed accusations, Sam admitted to pulling Angela's leg as she tried to step on the top wrung of the ladder. This caused her to lose her balance and fall onto the asphalt below. In addition, as the common colloquialism states, Sam "folded like a cheap tent," also accusing Jack of blackmailing him into committing the nefarious deed. He claimed that during a sleepover at Jack's house over the summer, he had admitted, or rather bragged to him, about stealing chewing tobacco from the local "Mom and Pop" store. Also, unbeknownst to Sam, Jack had recorded the entire conversation on his tape recorder, which he had hidden in a shoe box near his bed.

Sam, through his tears, told a story of how Jack, after being framed by Angela, met with him and played the tape of Sam admitting to stealing from the local store. He spoke of how Jack instructed him to make Angela pay for her misdeeds through physical trauma. Sam claimed Jack was incredibly angry about the "test answer sheet scandal" but realized he in no way could be directly involved in his plans for revenge as he would be considered the primary suspect.

Sam's testimony made perfect sense and aligned with the fact that after the "test answer sheet scandal," Jack had publicly become reserved and stayed clear of any activities during recess that could be perceived as aggressive. As I previously mentioned, he had begun to play by himself or with a small group of kids away from the action.

Sam claimed Jack had made it clear to him that if he did not follow his direction to hurt Angela, the tape recording of his admission to stealing chewing tobacco would find its way into the hands of the school and his parents. In Sam's mind, he had no choice but to carry out his wishes, and ultimately, that's exactly what he did.

The fallout from this event was widespread and sent shock waves throughout our classroom and the playground. Sam was suspended for a week as well as Jack, and both never really recovered from the scandal. As for me, my loyalty to Jack was gone, as was it for all of my classmates as well. He had cleverly used all of us and fooled us into believing he was something he wasn't. Behind his strength and charisma was a dark soul seeking personal gain and power over others.

As far as Angela and Donny, well, things ultimately did not go well for them either. Angela discovered the value of playing the "innocent victim" and firmly placed it in her playbook to get her way and avoid trouble. Anytime something went awry for her, she would immediately point fingers at others and claim she was being "picked on." In the end, this left her with very few friends, as she was perceived as being weak and selfish. She grew to expect handouts and unearned favors for no other reason than her crying wolf and claiming she was a victim. Eventually, she began to believe her own lies and became uselessly dependent on others to take care of her needs and lost her ambition to better herself, instead focusing her time on her own victimhood.

Donny fell into a scandal of his own doing when several "Playboy" magazines were found on his desk. He claimed he had been framed and someone had placed them there, but the classroom grapevine showed no mercy to a kid who had skillfully avoided all the trouble that Jack and Sam had encountered. He was incessantly mocked by his peers, and even the teachers laughed at him behind his back. He quickly found himself ostracized as some sort of a pervert and later was labeled as the "The Little Perv" by his classmates.

As far as the final disposition of Jack and Sam, both would be gone by the next school year. Why they left, no one was certain. Some said their families were "run out of town," and others said they had simply moved to another town as families often do. After a few years had passed, one thing, however, was quite clear. All the drama, all the self-serving behavior, all the hurt feelings, and all pain inflicted on one another no longer meant a damn thing.

All of us had moved on, and the major players of the playground drama that year, their aspirations, motives, and desires were now just dust in the wind. No one cared anymore, life had moved on without them, and with it all, the pettiness and poor behavior of those involved went as well. They were now nothing more than useful jackasses for the butt of bad jokes designed to mock them and their unethical behavior.

Looking back, what had occurred should have been used as a cautionary tale, but for most, it was simply a story of some poor fools whose only use now was for a good laugh. Besides, the students were far too busy creating their own personal dramas filled with lies and deceit to spend time pondering what might have been learned. They had no time to be concerned with those who had already burned in the trash heap of the playground world. They were building their own bonfires now, and the cycle would just feed on itself over and over without end.

This is an appalling story that makes one wonder how children could behave this way and who is ultimately responsible for their actions. Their behavior was dominated by self-serving motives lacking integrity and compassion for their fellow classmates. How could children behave in such a reprehensible manner lacking the ethical and moral standards required in a well-functioning, equitable society?

The truth is that this story is a simple allegory about our own politicians. Does it make you feel any better that this story is *not* about children; instead, it is about our *adult* leaders whom we have entrusted to lead our county. Are you sighing with relief that children would not behave this way and that it is the adults who behave in such a disgusting manner?

This is what we have grown to accept as tolerable behavior from our politicians. We just shrug our shoulders and say, "It's politics," and give it little thought beyond the recognition of "business as usual." We accept the fact that our leaders are liars, backstabbers, cheaters, and manipulators who are ego-centric and feign compassion for the people they claim to serve. They amass wealth and power on the backs of their constituents, making empty promises to them over and over again with little repercussions.

Did all of these politicians start out this way when they first joined the "playground" of politics? My personal belief is that they did not. Many, I believe, came into the arena with the desire to make a difference and to serve the people who elected them. However, the playground is filled with a culture that is dark and corrupt, and eventually, one joins the club of the deviants or is run out.

The temptations that lure these once-honest people into the world of darkness are immense and attack the source of humankind's greatest weaknesses. The "unholy trinity" of power, lust, and greed will eventually take control over most politicians.

Through money, sex, and self-ideation of their own perceived power, these individuals become infected with corruption and selfishness, willing to crush anyone who gets in their way. Their sickness is so deep that they actually believe they hold the right to do what they please and to hurt whoever they want. They have become pathetic examples of human beings and will reap the karmic correction which is waiting for them at the end of their journey.

How can this disgusting example of human behavior ever be changed? The outlook, frankly, is not promising. It takes all of us as individuals to stop looking the other way and accept the culture of politics as "it is what it is." Things will never change until the individual, you and I, put our foot down and say "no more." The victory towards true righteousness and justice begins with one heart, with one soul at a time. It begins with you and I saying "no more" and then living the type of life we expect our public figures to live.. free from lies, deceit, and greed.

Do I expect this to occur? Certainly not. I have little faith that we are capable of changing our attitudes and our tolerance of the unworthy people we choose to lead our society. We have become far too brainwashed and controlled even to begin to realize the potential of the individual to inspire the necessary changes. It would take a cataclysmic event of such magnitude that I find it unimaginable even to perceive it. However, you and I can decide to make the necessary changes in our lives and know that others may follow and choose to respond as we have. Eventually, over the decades and centuries, the playground of politics may one day be filled with peace and justice instead of pain and deceit.

The Same as it Ever Was

In November 1972, President Nixon was re-elected by an astounding margin that set an electoral record at the time. Nixon carried 49 states earning 520 electoral votes, while his opponent, George McGovern, received 17. There was no doubt America had put its faith in the Republican candidate who promised to end the Vietnam War, improve the economy and provide tax cuts to millions of Americans.

In addition, Nixon, during his previous four years as President, had leveled inflation, established relations with China (an American President first), and negotiated a level of stability with the Soviet Union and the ongoing cold war between the two superpowers. There was certainly reason to be optimistic about the next four years under the Nixon administration. However, that optimism quickly morphed into disbelief and mistrust due to the Watergate scandal and the subsequent cover-up.

Prior to the election of 1972, the "Watergate coverup" initiated by Nixon was already brewing in the bowels of his administration. It all began nearly five months earlier, on June 17th, when five individuals were apprehended and charged with burglary and attempted interception of telephones and other communications at the Watergate office building (the home of the Democratic National Committee). This criminal activity initiated by members of Nixon's own republican party started a cascade of events that would end in his resignation.

Nixon, who initially was not even aware of or involved in the planning of the Watergate break-in, attempted to cover up the criminal activity to avoid public scrutiny. Ironically his efforts to cover up the event would lead to one of the biggest scandals in American history and would be the basis for his undoing and not the break-in itself. Had Nixon acknowledged the break-in from the beginning, he would likely have never been forced to resign as President.

Richard Nixon

However, as is the case with most politicians, Nixon chose to lie and cover up the nefarious activities at the Democratic National Committee's headquarters. This effort to deny and refute the claims of the break-in and the planting of "bugging devices" in the DNC offices led to a series of lies built upon one another until it all unraveled in the Senate hearings investigating the matter.

The hearings, broadcasted live to the American public during late spring and summer of 1974, revealed the Nixon administration's constant efforts to obstruct the investigation and hide the truth. I vividly remember the senate hearing coverage being relentlessly viewed by my uncle, who was recovering from an appendectomy at our home. He watched day after day and week after week. He viewed the senate hearings with great interest while I lamented the fact I was missing my favorite tv shows.

I was aware of the trouble Nixon had created for himself but was not aware of just how serious it was becoming. We only had one tv in our house at the time, and I was more upset with my uncle monopolizing my only viewing source than I was at the prospect of the constitutional crisis.

By early August, facing three articles of impeachment which included: obstruction of justice, abuse of power, and contempt of Congress, Nixon found himself in an untenable and unsustainable situation. The country, and even some of his most ardent supporters all had to face that Nixon, with his series of lies and intimidation of others, was now finished as President of the United States.

Clearly facing certain impeachment and ultimately removal from office, Nixon, on the evening of August 8th, announced he would be resigning as President of the United States. I remember this event with great clarity and was saddened by the news. I liked President Nixon and had not followed the tale of Watergate enough to understand just how badly he had behaved while occupying the highest office in our country.

It was a devastating blow to many Americans to see a once honorable man be reduced to a pathetic lair and subjugator of the truth. The recently appointed Vice President, Gerald Ford, immediately became America's new president. Nixon would be the only President to resign in American history, and in a moment that will live in infamy, the American people found themselves, literally overnight, with a new leader.

What initially could have been easily avoided through a simple recognition by Nixon of the Watergate break-in had ballooned into a heinous act of corruption by the President himself. Nixon's own demented belief he could control this incident through the power he wielded from the presidential office had led him down the path of self-destruction. Politics had corrupted the man and his thinking. He believed he was above the law, just as so many politicians before and after have fallen for the same illusion.

This sickness, often brought about in high-level politics, deceives those in power into believing their importance and need for self-preservation is greater than the constitutional laws they were elected to protect. In the end, the stench of their corruption cannot be contained with the lies and deceit they create to deceive. Ultimately they become nothing more than immoral fools justly ridiculed and mocked in the public town square for their self-righteous, arrogant, and corrupt behavior. They have earned the seed they have sowed, and personally, I hold no pity for them or their kind.

As for Watergate itself, the latter "gate" portion of the word is now used as a synonym and attached to practically any scandal in any arena in American society. It has become a fixture in the popular American vernacular. We have all heard it used at one time or another throughout the decades since the original crime and will continue to hear it to define scandalous human folly well into the future.

The Teacher and the Student

My father was born in 1931 in a farmhouse that had no indoor plumbing or electricity. It was located near a small town named Reydon, Oklahoma, with a population of maybe several hundred people. His family lived off the main road on a modest parcel of farmland growing cotton and raising a very small herd of cattle. When he was around five years old, "dust bowl" conditions forced his family to move out west to California in search of work.

Decades of "over farming" coupled with drought conditions had made the panhandle area of Oklahoma a veritable wasteland. Massive dust storms blew through the area, and life on the farm had not only become unprofitable but damn near unlivable.

The Great Depression of the 1930s gripped the entire country, and this only exacerbated an already untenable situation for families living in the "dust bowl region." The migration west to California was a common landing place for many lifelong Midwestern farmers and ranchers.

My father's family was just one of the thousands who would abandon their life on the farm in search of a more profitable existence elsewhere. Such was the life and times of the 1930s, and as a boy growing up during this period, my father was profoundly impacted by this experience, and it would influence his decision-making process for the rest of his life.

Financially speaking, my father always played things "close to the vest." His conservative approach, born from his experience during the depression, was frustrating to me. I observed many of my friends' fathers buying new cars and pouring money into big fancy homes, but not my dad. I would ask him why he would never buy a new car or why we didn't move into a bigger home. His response was always the same, "Those folks are up to necks in debt, and we are not." He never wanted to be compromised financially by over-extending himself, and thus he never did.

Living in wealthy Lake Oswego, his conservative approach often left us kids on the outside looking in with our friends as they bragged about vacation getaways to Hawaii or ski trips to Sun Valley. One time I recall a friend bragging about how his family had taken a flight to Hawaii for dinner and then flew back that evening. Was it true? Well, I knew for a fact their father worked for the airlines, and they lived on the hill in a big house that looked down upon us. The cars they drove were always new and exciting models. Our cars were never new and were almost always standard Ford family sedans: no color, no flash, no imagination, and no clout.

By the time I had reached high school, my dad, a banker by trade, had risen to become president of several credit unions. However, nothing changed as he continued to maintain his conservative approach. The memories of his youth and his family barely scratching out a living haunted him. He still waited until every last possible drop of oil was emptied from the can and into the car engine, never wanting to waste a single drop. He always looked for a penny to save here...and way over there. He even tried to buy powdered milk as a substitute for the real thing, but Mom put her foot down on that effort.

As far as exciting getaways? Well, we never did fly to any exciting vacation destinations. In fact, we never flew at all. Instead, we drove for hours upon hours or took the train to Amarillo, Texas to visit family. We may have resided in the wealthiest community in Oregon, but we certainly did not live like them.

Now don't get me wrong, our lives were far from impoverished. However, as with all aspects of life, it was just another exercise in relativity. "To the poor, we are swaddled in riches... to the rich, we ain't nothing but poor" is a quote from Micheal Been that speaks of such relativity. In most aspects of life, we could run with the pack along with the rest of our peers, except when it came to the big ticket items such as homes, cars, and extravagant vacations. We *could have* run with them, but as previously stated, my father had no interest in doing so as it was just too risky for his taste.

One day while I working on a high school paper about "careers", I asked my father if he felt he had accomplished what he had dreamed of doing as a young man. His response was, "All I ever wanted to be was a family man. Raising a family has always been the most important thing to me." At the time, I wasn't sure if I really believed him because those certainly were not my aspirations at the time, but as I reflect (now many years later), I'm certain he was telling me the truth. I'm certain of it because that is how he lived his life...always for his family.

Early in my life, he became involved in many of my extracurricular activities, including coaching basketball and football, beginning in the fourth grade. I know he enjoyed coaching, and he was damn good at it, as we always had competitive winning teams. He treated me no differently than any of the kids he coached, and he integrated basic psychology into his coaching methodology. He taught us the mental aspects of competing, which always gave us a decided advantage.

My dad was a busy man but not so busy that he could not find the time to spend with his wife and children. I had great respect for my father, as did all of us within his inner circle. When he spoke, I listened, and what he told me I believed. It was a great responsibility that he bore, and he bore it well. He was careful regarding the subject matter he would teach me and the timing of when to deliver the message. He would always present new ideas to me in a way that would make sense.

At the age of nine, he opened a door for me that would ultimately change my perception of my own personal reality permanently. As I mentioned, he was the coach of our 4th grade YMCA basketball team and had prepared us well for our first "real game" experience. However, he took it a step further with me one night in a discussion after dinner. He asked me if I was nervous about playing in front of an audience and with referees calling the game. I told him I was excited but nervous that I might screw things up for the team.

He told me he wanted me to do something that night before I went to bed. He wanted me to imagine myself playing in the game that Saturday, feeling comfortable and confident. He wanted me to imagine I was not nervous, but rather I was calm and playing under control. I, of course, agreed to honor his request, and that night while lying in bed, I did exactly what he had asked me to do. The next day he asked me if I had imagined myself playing the game and doing well. I told him I had done as he had asked. He smiled and said, "Good... now I want you to do that every night until the game." I agreed I would.

The night before the game, he took me aside and shared something he had read. He told me about two groups of kids who played basketball on a regular basis. In the first group, the coach asked them to shoot ten free throws after every practice in an effort to improve their free throw percentage. The second group was told to imagine themselves shooting free throws and making all of them before they went to sleep at night. He paused and looked at me and said, "Would it surprise you, the kids who did not have a basketball in their hands but just imagined making free throws had a better percentage at the end of the season?" I was surprised, of course, and answered, "Yes." He said, "That's the power of the mind, and don't ever forget that is where your power lies. It will never fail you if you believe in its power to create the reality you desire."

That night I once again imagined playing the basketball game with poise and confidence. I actually dreamt later that evening of the game I was to play. In the dream, I played well and was not intimidated by the environment... it all felt comfortable and familiar.

The next morning as we entered a gym I had never seen before, I was surprised to find it was eerily similar to what I had dreamt the evening before. There were huge windows in the gym that started about twelve feet from the ground and went almost to the height of a very tall ceiling. The large maroon curtains had been pulled back, allowing the morning sun to stream into the gym. The sunlight reflecting off the wooden basketball court was so bright you almost needed sunglasses to diffuse the reflection. Echoes of basketballs bouncing on the court filled the gym air, and there was a comfortable familiarity to everything I observed.

I don't remember much about the game, but I do remember that on the first possession of the game, I stole the ball from my opponent and drove to the basket, made the layup, and was fouled in the process, making a free throw that followed. I began my organized basketball career with a steal and a three-point play with our team winning the basketball game.

The results of that day convinced me that what my dad had instructed me to do to be mentally prepared had worked, and what he had told me about "the power of the mind" was also, without a doubt, true. I would spend the rest of my life forgetting and then remembering this lesson. Sometimes I would forget for months upon months amongst the strain of living. However, I never let go of the string and would always find my way back to the belief that I could create my own reality through my own thinking and faith in the power of the mind.

That was the first lesson I received from my dad regarding the mental aspects of life. He didn't just talk to me about the potential of the mind. He had provided me with a practical method to unleash its power. Of course, at the time, I didn't realize just how important this lesson would be to me, but I did realize there was definitely something to what he was teaching. My belief in its power has never really wavered throughout the many decades of my life since my father's teaching of that lesson. As I have mentioned, to my own detriment, I have forgotten, ignored, or put this belief "on the shelf" at times, but my faith in the power of the mind has never wavered.

Sadly I never thought of inquiring at the time or even in the years that followed as an adult what led my father down the path of "mentalism." I suppose I was far too caught up in my own life experiences to question him on how he found his own path to enlightenment. My mother has since told me that when she met my father, he already held these beliefs. That would have put him in his early twenties but still did not answer the question of what led him down the path of this belief system.

I was always keenly aware that my dad was a veracious reader who often meditated in the late hours of the evening, but I never asked why. I would listen and implement much of the instructive lessons he would teach me but never questioned the origin of his beliefs. I knew he was a man of God, but he appeared to have no affiliation to any organized religion or attachment to any particular religious dogma. He never shared how he came to find his place in the spiritual world, and as I mentioned, I never thought to ask.

Several decades after my father had passed, I finally asked my mom if I could look through the library of books my father had in his possession. I quickly recognized several books I often saw him reading or that were always placed near his "reading chair." Those books would lead me to several unanswered questions about the origins of my father's belief system.

Books written by Paul Brunton, Godfre and Jane Roberts held many of the answers to the questions I had about my father's view on spirituality. On the inside cover of the 1945 hardback printing of "The Wisdom of the Overself" by Paul Brunton, there is a handwritten date of May 1950 with my father's initials next to it. Apparently, that was the month and year he purchased the book. He was just eighteen.

This really is the only clue I have as to when my father may have begun his spiritual journey. I will never know for sure but suffice it to say his journey began at a relatively young age, and he would continue to pursue enlightenment up until his death in 1999.

There is much more to be explored later in this book regarding the subject matter of his studies and those writers who guided and provided him insight into the world of "mentalism" and spirituality. However, for now, it's enough to state that my awareness of a world that expands beyond our known physical reality began for me at the age of nine, and the teacher/student relationship between my father and me would last until his passing.

The Heart of a Champion

Only three times in my life have I witnessed greatness at a level above and beyond what would be considered possible. The fact is, throughout the centuries, there have been moments in time in which humans have observed superior artists, athletes, and "thinkers." These observations validate the premise that there is something greater than ourselves at work here on Earth. The Beatles were the first time I witnessed this occurrence, and the second time would occur nine years later.

As one might justifiably assume, this occurrence, however, was not at the hands of man. In fact, one could argue, as some have, that the hand of man was the one hindrance that stood between this being and the actual realization of "perfection." In any case, Secretariat is considered by many to be the greatest racehorse ever, reaching nothing short of "Superstar" status in the eyes of the American public in 1973.

You may very well be thinking, "A racehorse! That's just ridiculous." Ninety-nine times out of a hundred, I would likely agree with you. However, this was one of those one-in-a-hundred scenarios that are rarely witnessed but statistically do exist. In addition, and let's be clear about this, by no means was Secretariat just "another horse"... not even close.

Secretariat would capture the hearts and admiration of the American public at a level unheard of for an animal primarily due to the large expansion of television sets into American family homes by the early 70s. He ascended to a level of stardom only experienced by a handful of America's greatest human stars of the time. He was a celebrity without any of the typical human flaws attached to him. There were to be no scandals or dubious behavior to drag him down into infamy. His persona would remain unscathed and his deeds unmatched.

Secretariat was the perfect combination of personality, skill, and flawless character that America so desperately needed amidst the era of Vietnam and Watergate. He was, and therefore appropriately labeled a "Super Horse." A mantle of greatness which he wore well with dignity, class, and a pinch of arrogance thrown in for good measure. He became the perfect American hero at a time when America needed one so badly. Once again, the intersection of unscripted "timing" in congruence with immense talent created a brew of inspiration and amazement that still exists today within popular culture.

Secretariat

Secretariat, also known as "Big Red," was a magnificent chestnut red thoroughbred who, even as a foal, impressed his observers. Howard Gentry, the manager of "Meadow Stud" where Secretariat was born, would later state, "He was as perfect a foal that I ever delivered." Secretariat would stand at just 45 minutes old and would nurse just 30 minutes later. Both feats were well above the norm.

Even at a young age, he distinguished himself as the clear leader amongst his peers. Secretariat always ate first while the other horses patiently waited for him. He was as charismatic as a horse could possibly be, playful and mischievous on one hand and arrogant on the other. One close observer stated, "If Secretariat had been human, he would have been a Son of a Bitch". Secretariat knew his place in the pecking order of horses...he sat at the top.

By the age of two, Secretariat began to make a name for himself in race horsing circles. As a two-year-old, he ran in nine races and won seven. During his two-year-old season, he made some physically dazzling moves on the track, which highlighted his strength, speed,

Secretariat in Racing Form

and competitiveness. By the end of the season, he had established himself as a potential "Super Horse" and was the first two-year-old ever to win the coveted "Horse of the Year" award... an award which he would win again the following year.

As for me, I was not aware of Secretariat until his three-year-old season when he would run in the three biggest races in American horse racing: The Kentucky Derby, The Preakness, and The Belmont Stakes. These three races, all occurring within a five-week time frame, are considered the "triple crown" of horse racing, and to win all three is considered one of the most difficult feats in all of sports.

When Secretariat began his three-year-old season, no horse had won the "triple crown" in twenty-five years. Not since Citation in 1958 had it happened. This was about to change. The Kentucky Derby is the first leg of the "triple crown," and Secretariat came in as the favorite even though he had finished third in the previous race, The Wood Memorial, most likely due to an abscess inside his mouth. His trainer, Lucien Laurin, would later state that the abscess caused Secretariat serious discomfort during the race, which led to his sub-par performance.

Secretariat would validate Laurin's claim by easily winning the Kentucky Derby by 2 and 1/2 lengths and in record time in front of the largest derby crowd at the time of over 134,000. He smashed the track record and was the first horse to ever run the mile and quarter track in under two minutes.

Perhaps most astonishing was that Secretariat ran each quarter mile of the race faster than the previous quarter mile! He actually became stronger and faster with each passing quarter mile of the race, which by anyone's standard is an astonishing physical feat that is simply unheard of even to this day.

The next leg of the triple crown is the Preakness Stakes, and at one and 3/16th miles, it is the shortest of the three races with much tighter turns to navigate through. This was of particular concern in the Secretariat camp as he was such a powerful and fast horse that they worried about centripetal force taking him far too wide in the turns.

As he did in the Kentucky Derby, Secretariat broke dead last out of the gate. He was still last going into the first turn. It was then he made one of the most astonishing moves in horse racing history. Ronny Turcott, the jockey of Secretariat, guided him to the outside rail, where he burst to the front with incredible speed in a distance of around one hundred and eighty yards. His acceleration was so astonishing that it appeared as if the other horses were moving in slow motion as he blew past them. He would win the race with ease by 2 and 1/2 lengths, and it became clear that America might just have its first triple crown winner in a quarter century. Secretariat's popularity surged to incredible levels after the race, and he became a bonafide star in America.

The three weeks preceding the final race of the triple crown, The Belmont Stakes, Secretariat's popularity rose to new heights. He made the covers of Time, Newsweek, and Sports Illustrated, a feat never accomplished before or since. Pete Axhelm's article in Newsweek perhaps defined Secretariat best when he wrote:" Secretariat's muscular build identifies him immediately; his glowing reddish coat is a banner of health and rippling power. Magnificent enough at rest,

Super Horse

when he accelerates, he produces a breathtaking explosion that leaves novices and hardened horsemen alike convinced that, for one of those moments that seldom occur in any sport, they have witnessed genuine greatness."

By the time the day of the Belmont Stakes had arrived, the national consciousness had completely focused on this "Super Horse." The public was enamored by his perfection and, of course, his sterling reputation. He was the antithesis of the flailing stars of Hollywood or the ingenuous nature of D.C. politicians. Everyone loved Secretariat as they saw something in him that was pure and genuine and could not be polluted by man's intervention.

Of course, all of the hype and all of the attention thrown upon Secretariat made him an easy target to fail and not live up to the unrealistic expectations placed upon him. He came off prior to the race as a 1-10 favorite which meant if one bet a dollar on Secretariat to win, the payout would be a measly ten cents.

It seemed everyone wanted him to succeed, but secretly all were concerned he would fail as the recent disappointment of Watergate and the failure of the Vietnam War still hung over the heads of the American public. It was a scenario set up for failure for all those who had hoped Secretariat could bring a brief reprieve from the bad news that had filled the airways for far too long. Too much was being asked of this horse, and too many hopes were pinned on his winning. On race day, the tension between a potentially disappointing outcome v.s. a potential victory was palatable across America.

The weather was clear, and the track was labeled "fast" at post time 5:38 PM EDT. An estimated crowd of 70,000 in attendance let out a loud cheer as the horses left the gate. Unlike the prior two races, where Secretariat had broke slow and trailed early, this time, he charged into first place on the rail, taking early command of the race. The problem was, and this was obvious to any seasoned horse race enthusiast, he was going far too fast, far too early. He broke out so quickly and maintained such a fast pace that some felt the jockey had lost control over the horse.

After completing the first turn at a record pace, many believed that Secretariat would fold going down the stretch of this very long race, simply "running out of gas" before the finish line. As the race continued, this scenario became more likely as it was clear Secretariat had no plans of slowing down and began to separate himself from the rest of the horses.

Secretariat Winning The Belmont Stakes

As he approached the final turn of the race, his lead began to grow exponentially, to the astonishment of the stunned crowd. Even Chick Hern, who called the race over the public address system, could not control his amazement when he pronounced, "Secretariat is moving like a tremendous machine!" By the time Secretariat hit the finish line, he had crushed his competition at a level never witnessed before in such a high-stakes race. He won by an astounding 31 lengths with a winning time of 2:24 on the 1 1/2 mile track.

The outpouring of emotion from what the crowd of 70,000 had just witnessed filled the air. People were seen sobbing after the race as they were so absorbed in the moment and what had just occurred. It was as if all who had watched the race knew something miraculous had just occurred and that it would never be repeated.

As for me, I was in Amarillo, Texas, when Secretariat made his run into history. It was our yearly road trip to visit relatives, and it just so happened we arrived at our hotel just prior to the post-time of the race. I desperately pleaded with my dad to sign in at the hotel register as quickly as possible so we could access the tv in our room to watch the race.

By the time we turned the tv on, Secretariat was heading down the home stretch of the race, and for a moment, I was confused at what was happening. None of it made sense to me. Why were there no other horses running in the race with him? That feeling of confusion was quickly replaced by astonishment when I realized the other horses were so far behind that they could not be captured in the same camera shot!

Like so many others who watched the race, I sat there stunned, trying to comprehend what my eyes were telling me. It truly was a surreal event that I will never forget, and for that moment, I witnessed "greatness" personified encased within a racehorse.

For the sake of posterity, it is worth noting that a half-century later Secretariat still holds the track records in all three of the "Triple Crown" races. No horse has beaten his time in any of the storied races and few have even come close. In addition, racehorse experts and casual fans alike believe Secretariat's track time at the Belmont on that fateful day in June will never be beaten as he did what few beings have ever done...making the impossible "possible."

Sixteen years after his amazing run at Belmont Secretariat was euthanized due to a severe case of laminitis. The hoof disease is incredibly painful to a horse. Therefore, the decision was made to end his life and stop the suffering he had been enduring. However, the autopsy of the Secretariat revealed something quite amazing, and its results answered many questions regarding his incredible prowess on the race track.

The average thoroughbred horse has a heart weighing around eight pounds. Secretariat's heart weighed close to twenty-two pounds, nearly three times more than his competitors on the race track. This allowed him to pump oxygen at a much faster rate into his lungs which provided him with superior endurance and power. As it turned out, Secretariat was a "freak of nature," but anyone who had ever watched him race already knew that. God had given him a heart that was so perfectly designed that it appeared from the very beginning of his life that he was destined to be a champion of the grandest kind. A champion of the likes we will never see again.

The Middle School Blues

I don't believe it's a stretch to say that for many, the "middle school years" are considered the most difficult school years to navigate through. It's an awkward time indeed for many reasons. There are those who reach puberty early, and then there are those that never reach it all during this time. You have boys that have already attained a man's baritone tenor, and then you have boys who still sound like girls. You have girls that have begun to look like young women and girls who...well, still look like boys.

The variance in maturity, not only on a physical level but at a mental level, can also be vast in the middle school years. Typically girls begin to demonstrate some level of mental maturity during this time, while boys can still behave like total idiots without caring about maintaining any level of dignity.

In addition, for the first time, social "clicks" become a real phenomenon for middle school kids. It's a phenomenon that will surround them throughout their remaining years in school. For most kids, they have no idea how they ended up in the hierarchy they have been relegated to. It just happens as if it occurred through osmosis. One day you look around and notice the "popular kids" always hang out in the same spot during lunch breaks, and it just so happens it's not where *you* hang out. For some kids, this matters a lot, while others hardly notice, but in either case, all kids abide by the rules of peer social structure.

Unlike elementary school, where there are still some nurturing and inherent protective protocols in place with adult oversight, middle school often feels like the survival of the fittest. What happens in the dark distant hallways away from adult supervision is left to the rule of the strongest and often the meanest. The meek had best avoid the less traveled areas of the middle school jungle as there is no guarantee they will pass through unscathed.

I recall one time in the early morning, just before classes started, I was at my locker gathering my notebooks for class when an 8th grader named Dan Tamasso approached me with two of his friends on either side of him. He was known as a bully in our school and one that showed no mercy to the younger 7th graders. It appeared I was to be his next victim. However, to my surprise, he walked up to me with a gentle smile and, in an inquisitive tone, asked me if I owned a sleeping bag.

Was I scared? Well, yes, initially, but it appeared that maybe he just needed a sleeping bag for camping and was asking me if he could borrow mine. I responded with a smile and said, "Yeah, I've got a sleeping bag." It was then he punched me right in the groin and said, "Well, you better wake it up!" Dan and his buddies burst out in laughter and then casually walked away as I crumpled to the floor in pain. Such was life in middle school.

It wasn't all bad, middle school was also where I began to notice girls, and they noticed me. It would be the first time I would feel romance in the air and the heat of passion, albeit at a junior high sock-hop dance level. The dances in middle school were ritualistic expressions of the feelings and emotions which were slowly beginning to surface within our young psyche. With neither gender fully understanding how to behave or what might be accomplished, rudimentary efforts were all that could be mustered via simple physical expressions and basic non-verbal communication. It was not too far removed from the dance between the zebra and lion on the great Savanahs of Africa, fundamental in its simplicity and yet provocative in its results.

It began with the girls circling the dance floor, placing themselves on display for the boys, who would move in small packs behind them on the outer edges of the circle. This ritual lent itself to some confusion, however, as when the girls turned to look at what pack of boys was directly behind them, it became unclear, from the boy's perspective, who the girl may be looking at. Of course, depending on the confidence level within the pack, some boys would always assume the girls were looking at them, while others, who were less confident, assumed no one was looking at them.

The result of this primitive form of communication of "I want you. Do you want me?" invariably led to some embarrassing moments for both sides. It was middle school drama at its highest level, where hopes died, and miracles happened. Where rejection was tied to brutal humiliation and acceptance was met with sweet affirmation. The stakes were indeed high during this two-hour drama which could make or break a student's school year depending on how it played out under the lights.

There were no guarantees, there were no givens, and the results could be as capricious as the emotions that flowed through our teenage bodies. The sock-hop wasn't for everyone. It took a certain mental fortitude to survive the danger that lurked behind every song the DJ would spin.

I had my share of successes and embarrassments asking girls to dance, but mostly, I let the opportunity pass me due to the fear of rejection and the public humiliation that would follow. There was no compassion from your peers; if the girl said "no," it was incessant mocking and ridicule. Mind you, it was nothing personal. It was just part of the male code and one that I would partake in as well upon the failure of a friend to coax a girl to dance.

There were times, of course when a true romance would sprout in the aftermath of the sock-hop. This would entail the boy and girl holding hands and walking up and down the school hallways prior to school and during breaks. Of course, in the end, the boy preferred to be with his immature male friends, and the girl would be offended and disgusted by his inattentive behavior. The shelf life of a middle school romance was short indeed, but it was practice for high school, where romance became a far more serious endeavor.

Looking back at those middle school years, I have to smile and wince at the same time. It was clearly a transition from childhood into adolescence. The world became a much bigger place, with variables and scenarios expanding into my consciousness. The juggling act of life became a reality during those years in trying to find a balance between what was real and important and what could be ignored. There was a strong pull toward advancing maturity while childhood was reluctantly giving way to things just months before that were of no concern.

The fact is, we all eventually make the transition into the teenage years, some of us going into it smoothly while others go kicking and screaming. The middle school years are a right of passage, if you will, a portal to new discoveries along with bigger problems. However, it is a necessary journey designed to close the door of childhood while opening a new door into adolescence. There are bumps and bruises along the way, but in the end, it prepares you for the next big step in life, the high school years.

The Art of Sneaking

I was a good kid…for the most part. I had my moments of getting into minor trouble but never anything of consequence. By my own admission, I was clever and a bit of a sneak, but when you are clever and a sneak…well, you rarely ever get caught. There were several rules that had to be followed *to the letter* if one was to have success at being a sneak. Ignoring any one of these rules could mean getting exposed, and that was simply not an option for me.

Rule number one: *Attention to detail*

This is where many kids fell short. Details are where a sneak earns his stripes. There are several facets to this rule. A well-laid plan outlining the specifics of the implementation and operational actions required to meet the objective is a must. Close attention to detail is critically important. One must painstakingly go over all aspects of the plan to identify those little details, if not handled correctly, can bring down the whole house of cards.

This leads to the next facet of the *attention to detail rule*…contingency planning. A sneak always has in mind what could go wrong and has a plan in place to address unexpected issues. Nothing ever truly goes as planned, so developing options that can be utilized on the fly is critically important to the overall mission. Contingency planning takes into account all aspects of the mission that could possibly go awry and create chaos.

Rule number two: *Know when to abort*

For many kids, after many hours and perhaps days of planning, the desire to go forward with the *"sneak plan"* can be overwhelming. Usually, the plan entails other kids, so there is additional pressure to go forward with the mission regardless of the current conditions. One must put their emotions aside and weigh the circumstances at hand to determine if logic dictates to proceed or abort. I've witnessed many kids fall short regarding this rule. Their desire to proceed, coupled with their ambitious nature, would lead them to "lie to themselves" and quell the obvious issues that should have stopped them from proceeding.

Rule number three: *Have the courage to take risks*

There is a very fine line to walk when it comes to rule number three. Where that line ultimately will be drawn often depends on circumstance. Differentiating between calculated risks and foolishness is a required attribute of a successful sneak. I have seen both sides of this play out. I have seen kids foolishly take risks that were unnecessary and later find themselves watching the police drive up their parents' driveway. I had also seen kids fail because when the moment came and risk-taking was necessary, they folded under pressure and got caught. As I said, it's a fine line, but if one is to be a successful sneak risk-taking is required.

Rule number four: *Learn from other's failures*

I was fortunate that I had two older sisters to learn from their mistakes and failures. I watched my older sister, in particular, get into trouble time and time again because of stupid decisions and mistakes. Her efforts to keep the devious activities she engaged in from my parents often failed because she reacted in the moment without any preparation or contingency planning. I recall one time I saw her and a friend leaving the high school grounds without permission. She never once looked around or behind her to see who might be observing her actions. She just walked across the football field and out into the public street. Of course, I told on her when I got home, and of course, she was stunned that I had seen her leave school, and of course, she was grounded. I watched her attempt to lie and deceive my parents on many occasions and frankly she just wasn't very good at it. I observed her mistakes in the art of deception and made mental notes on what she had done wrong and how she could have avoided being caught through thoughtful planning.

Her failures taught me many lessons on how *not to succeed* in being a sneak. I also observed the pain and mental anguish her behavior caused my parents. If I were to be a sneak, I was determined to be so damn good at it that my parents would never know. It was very important to avoid being caught, not just for my own sake but perhaps more importantly for my parents' sake. They were good parents and deserved better than constantly questioning their parenting skills because of my own incompetence in appropriate sneaking.

Rule number five: *Choose your co-conspirators well*

The fact is that you are only as strong as your weakest link. Those you choose to be your "partners in crime" must have the highest integrity and respect for the art of sneaking. They must honor the code of "taking the hit" and never "ratting" out their co-conspirators if caught. In addition, it is critically important that they can keep their mouths shut and not share their exploits with anyone. Ideally, this circle of partners should be very small and closed very tight. Any leaks can create a cascade of events that could lead to your behavior being exposed. The biggest trouble I ever found myself in was due to my closest friend being busted for something *he had done*. Through the pressure of intense questioning, he folded and spilled his guts, implicating me on a totally unrelated issue. The bottom line in the world of sneaking, you can never completely trust anyone. It just comes with the territory.

Rule number six: *Always remain humble*

Perhaps of all the rules, rule number six is the most important. The moment one lets their guard down and begins to think they can outsmart or out-sneak anyone is the moment they have failed. It's just a matter of time before this arrogance builds upon itself and the belief that you are untouchable becomes your worst enemy. Make no mistake; arrogance leads to failure. One needs to look no further than the crooked politicians whose deviance has been exposed time and time again due to their own arrogance.

I always took the approach I was being watched and spied upon when I was engaged in deviant behavior. I told myself I was one second away from being caught, and the moment could happen at any time. I never believed I was "home free." Rather, my mindset was to just survive unscathed until the conclusion of my unscrupulous behavior. I greatly respected the power of bad luck and unexpected variables that could wreak havoc on the best-laid plans. This humble approach always provided me with contingency plans that I was mentally prepared to implement at a moment's notice. I was never caught off guard during my adventures because I always mentally planned for the worst-case scenario. Throughout my youth, it was this humble approach that made me a master-level sneak.

One of my favorite adventures was sneaking out of my room in the middle of the night and meeting several of my friends to exact our juvenile exploits upon our neighborhood. Of course, all of it was well laid out and planned in advance. As I have already stated, getting caught was simply not an option.

The first thing which had to be done was to loosen the screen on my bedroom window. It could not be completely pulled off prior, as that would easily be noticed by my father. I would loosen it as best as I could earlier that day so as to minimize the noise it created upon removal. Typically we would meet around midnight, so around 11:30, I would get up and check to see if my parents were tucked safely asleep in bed. It was about a ten minute walk to where we would meet, so at 11:45, I would initiate the "Juvenile's Gone

Wild" mission. I collected my firecrackers which I had hidden under my bed, and the lighter, which I had already confiscated from my unknowing father earlier in the night.

Once I cleared the compound of my parent's home, it was a solo walk in the dark to the designated gathering point. I was the only one who lived on the west side of the neighborhood, so I always was alone in my journey to meet my co-conspirators and then again on my return back to the compound. There were no smartphones to text or call to confirm that the mission was still on and had not been aborted. We had to go on faith that we were all able to clear the security of our parent's homes to meet at the designated time. There were several occasions I made the walk only to wait half an hour with no one ever showing. That was just part of the risk. We all accepted the fact "mission abort" was always possible.

Upon meeting with my fellow juvenile soldiers, we began to implement our plan for the evening. The mission on this particular evening was simple and direct, 'scare the hell out of people'. We would arbitrarily pick a home that had decent cover to complete our mission. We slowly, carefully worked our way up to a bedroom window, and upon arrival at the target site, we carefully laid out a full complement of firecrackers on its ledge. We then lit the fuse and ran like hell for several blocks as bursting firecrackers echoed throughout the neighborhood.

We would repeat this process in different parts of the neighborhood several times and then wait to see if a police car showed up driving around the neighborhood. Sometimes we would see a cop slowly driving through the neighborhood looking for the perpetrators of this mischievous deed, but we never got caught.

At the completion of our mission, we all headed back to our homes, and this was always the scariest part. As I walked back, I couldn't help but ponder the thought, "What if there is a light on in my bedroom?" A "light on" would obviously mean I had been caught, and the only thing to do then was to walk into a firestorm of parent rage bravely. These were tense moments as I got closer and closer to home until I would make the final approach around the corner and see the light off. There was still the possibility they were waiting in the dark for me with scowls on their faces, but at this point, I liked my odds. All that was left to do was climb back through my window and replace the screen back to its original position.

Upon closing the window, the mission was complete, and I could relax knowing I had beaten the odds again. It just didn't get any better than that! However, on this occasion, as I exhaled and the last of the tension slipped away, my father, who was sitting in the dark in the far corner of my room, said, "Did you have a good time?" Just kidding! I told you I was a master class sneak and never did get caught conducting my late-night missions.

This is the End…. Or is It?

Throughout my life, the shadow of death had followed close behind me, clouding my past with darkness and invading my future with fear. The Vietnam War had been a companion of mine since the very beginning always reminding me that life is filled with both light and dark and one cannot exist without the other.

As much as I was amazed at the world around me and the exuberance of life that filled my soul, there was also the fear of my own mortality coming at the hands of the Vietnam War. I had seen far too much and had personally observed others who had direct contact with the shadow of death at the hands of war not to take its threat seriously. It was something one day I would have to face, and much like my nightmarish friend, Eddie (the devil boy adorned in shades of black and white), the war would eventually find me regardless of how far I ran or where I hid.

However, this "nightmare" which haunted me even in my waking hours finally found its end in 1973. Using the term "end," I am referring to American involvement in the war in utilizing our soldiers as a force of aggression and violence in defense of the South Vietnamese government.

America's involvement would continue for several more years on the political front and in a so-called "peacekeeping" role. However, the cessation of direct hostilities from the perspective of our government, and hence our military meant young men would no longer be sent to Vietnam to fight, kill, or be killed. For the first time in my life, and with my limited awareness of the world that surrounded me...there was peace.

On January 27th, 1973, President Nixon signed the Paris Peace Accords, officially ending America's direct involvement in the war.

In addition, the draft was rescinded and an all-volunteer military was reinstated. It was obvious to anyone who followed the course of the war that the Peace Accords were simply a diplomatic way for the United States to "save face" in a conflict they had so badly managed and ultimately lost. It was Nixon's way of mitigating the catastrophic results of the war by claiming that peace had been struck between the two warring factions. Few believed, including me, that this would end the war between North and South Vietnam. It was simply a way for America to extricate itself from an unwinnable scenario.

By late March 1973, the last American military unit left Vietnam. However, as many expected, hostilities continued between the North and South Vietnamese people, with both sides accusing the other of violating the peace treaty. Over time America's support of the South Vietnamese dwindled, and hostilities between the North and the South escalated, costing hundreds of Vietnamese lives daily.

In the end, the South Vietnamese government, crippled by a crumbling economy and a people tired and beaten from years of war, collapsed with the fall of Saigon in April 1975. With the fall of Saigon, the North Vietnamese quickly instituted a military-based government. In July of 1975, South Vietnam was renamed as the "Socialist Republic of Vietnam," ending thirty years of war.

Over 58,000 Americans lost their lives in the war, and another 1,500 to this day are listed as missing or unaccounted for, whereabouts unknown. Estimates of over a million North Vietnamese and VietCong fighters were killed, as well as a quarter million South Vietnamese soldiers died in the 30-year conflict. In addition, it is estimated that more than two million civilians were killed on both sides of the war.

The emotional toll Vietnam took on the American people throughout the years of our involvement was immense. The loss of a generation of young men to a futile cause in a land so disconnected and far away from us is a burden we must all bear.

Of course, we know that war doesn't just "end" for the returning veterans of combat, and Vietnam was no exception. Although it is unclear just how many veterans of the war have committed suicide, there is no doubt it is well into the thousands. This does not include those that survived but had been so mentally damaged that they have struggled to maintain a healthy and prosperous lifestyle.

The scars of war run deep, and time cannot bring back the dead or heal all of the suffering and anguish. I can only say from my perspective that I have the utmost empathy and gratitude for those that served. I only wish they had served and died for a cause that was worth fighting for. It's with great sadness that I see the Vietnam War as nothing but a destructive part of our history with nothing gained and so much lost.

By the end of the war, I was relieved that my fate would not be decided in the jungles of Vietnam. I had somehow avoided my worst fear, but the sad truth is that many others just like me were not as lucky. They had lost their youth, naivety, and for some, even their lives to a useless endeavor. Many lives were lost and families destroyed, supporting a geo-political theory that later, with the fall of the Soviet Union, would be proven to be in error from the very beginning.

As for me, I am unable to rid myself of this terrible war as it is imprinted deep into the recesses of my mind. I thought that perhaps the nightmares of Vietnam were behind me. However, I was wrong. I recently discovered upon writing this book and recalling my memories of Vietnam the dreams have returned.

War does not just evaporate into the ether for those who have experienced its impact. Rather, it becomes a dark companion that reminds us of the cruelty humankind is capable of bestowing upon one another. My scars certainly do not run as deep as others. However, they are scars nonetheless and ones that can never truly be healed. The end of war is never really "the end." It goes on and on throughout a lifetime. It is a burden that is shared and passed down from one generation to the next until, finally, it becomes just another of many stories contained within textbooks that recount the long history of humankind's aggressive and violent nature.

200 Hundred Years and Counting

1976 marked the bicentennial of the United States. It was a time for our country to reflect on where we had started and how far we had come in two hundred years. It was indeed a unique moment to experience as a series of celebrations occurred during the year culminating with the July 4th celebration.

Bicentennial Celebration

It was a proud time for our country as we celebrated the accomplishments of our past while also holding out hope for an even brighter future. We honored the genius of our forefathers, who had devised a system of government that continued to flourish after two centuries. It was a birthday celebration like none other and, frankly, a much-needed respite from the recent failures of our government that had already clouded the decade of the 70s.

The debacles of Watergate and Vietnam were finally behind us, and although the memories of both were still fresh in our minds, the 200th birthday of our country gave us all a chance to forget our disappointments briefly. The celebration gave the country an opportunity to focus on its accomplishments while also injecting a badly needed sense of nationalistic pride.

Bicentennial quarters were issued that year and became ubiquitous for a short period of time, eventually becoming more and more rare as the years passed. It was a grand celebration that continued throughout 1976, and I was grateful to be a part of it. The sense of pride felt throughout the nation that year has rarely been matched since, and sadly, I don't see it happening again. It would appear our country has become far too cynical, and our forefathers are now often painted as "bad human beings" who should be chastised instead of honored.

I would ask what level of ignorance does it take to judge people who lived over two centuries ago against today's standards? Who has the right to pass judgment upon our founding fathers using contemporary morays to measure their morality? All of this, in my opinion, tears at the fabric of our society and weakens the overall health of the nation. I ask this question to all those who seek the defamation of our founding fathers. Since when is it a good idea to defame our heroes? What value is to be gained by doing so?

Perhaps more importantly, I ask those who find joy in defaming these incredible men, "What have you done with your lives that in any way can match the accomplishments of the men you ridicule?" Let's be honest. You haven't done shit compared to these men…not even close. They were certainly not perfect human beings and may have had some unsavory characteristics, but to those who would criticize them, I wonder if their lives could withstand the same scrutiny they impose on others. A hypocrite is nothing more than one who deceives themselves, as well as others, with a facade of unwarranted self-righteousness, therefore I have no interest in their fallacious opinions.

I suggest people who expend energy judging others perhaps would be better-served spending time taking a critical look at themselves and their own behavior. In my opinion, to attack people who lived over 200 years ago, who cannot defend their motives or actions, is ignorant and cowardly.

The Final Frontier

The idea of developing a reusable spacecraft to send astronauts into space initially gained interest after NASA's Apollo moon program had ended. Interest in developing manned space stations became more prevalent after the joint effort between the United States and the Soviet Union. In 1975 the two "cold war" nations agreed to meet in space to execute a peaceful mission called the Apollo/Soyuz Test Project.

Apollo Soyuz Mission

The Apollo/Soyuz mission would help ease 20 years of tension between the two nations and the subsequent "space race," which had begun two decades earlier. This endeavor would turn out to be a grand success as the Apollo spacecraft successfully docked with the Russian spacecraft. American astronauts and Russian cosmonauts would work together on several "science experiments while orbiting the Earth for nearly two days until the two vessels separated for an eventual return home.

It would be the last mission of the Apollo spacecraft as NASA's focus would now be on developing a craft that could efficiently meet the needs of space station development and maintenance. The Apollo/Soyuz mission would initiate the development of international space stations and the need for an effective and economical way to deliver astronauts to these scientific platforms of exploration. It is a need that continues to this very day as space stations are now part of the world community of orbiting space crafts that circle the planet.

The Viking Lander

Almost as an exclamation point of the progress our nation had made over the past two centuries, the "Viking Mars Lander" landed on the surface of Mars during our nation's bicentennial on July 20, 1976. The Viking Lander would soon send photos of the Mars surface to Earth, astounding the world with their clarity and detail. For the first time in human history, we observed images of another planet within our own solar system at an incredibly intimate level.

I remember being amazed at the photos the Viking Lander beamed back to Earth, clearly detailing the surface of a faraway planet. It was inconceivable to me that we could actually land a spacecraft on Mars and send these amazing images back for the world to view. It was indeed a surreal experience.

Mars Surface

I recall gazing at the "Oregonian" newspaper with a large photo of the Mars surface they placed boldly on the front page. The image was in color and composed of red and pink hues revealing a rocky planet's surface and an actually visible sky! As opposed to the images from the moon's surface we had observed seven years earlier, the photos from Mars showed a horizon not unlike our own. The atmosphere of Mars gave it a "daytime" feel, and the red planet did not appear uninhabitable, cold, and barren as the moon had... rather, it looked as if it could sustain life.

The entire mission was an unparalleled feat of human engineering and mathematical mastery. It demonstrated to the world just how far the United States had advanced since its inception 200 years earlier. America conquered the moon and now had successfully landed on Mars...what would be next?

The Second Time We Fall in Love

In the late sixties, I had my first taste of that transcendental experience of "falling in love." It was the first time I felt the experience of longing for someone in a romantic manner. Sure, I was only eight, but as I have already written about, I had my first hopeless "crush" on an actress named Catherine Ross. In the end, however, I felt she had misled me with her portrayal in "The Graduate" being far different than in "Butch Cassidy and the Sundance Kid." She wasn't as young and innocent as I had thought, but at the time, I was young and innocent enough to believe it.

By the time the mid-seventies rolled around, I was a teenager, and hormones were beginning to surge in my body. I no longer saw women as an unattainable mystery whose presence I enjoyed but not really knowing why. I now saw them as a top priority in meeting my needs to develop manhood. I was a boy with aspirations of becoming a man, and nothing in my mind would fulfill that requirement more than the adoration of a beautiful woman. It was clear, even in my grandest fantasy, that was just not going to happen. Therefore I was left gazing from afar at beautiful women knowing they had no interest in me. Sure, it was a one-sided relationship, but hey, you make do with what you have to work with.

Farrah Fawcett

There was no one, and I mean *no one*, I have ever adored more from a distance than Farah Fawcett. As I have mentioned before, the randomness of "timing" can create momentous results. Being in the right place at the right time historically can produce incredible outcomes. As for Farrah, she came at the exact time of my coming of age. Who better to initiate me into the world of heterosexual desires than one of the most beautiful women I had ever seen?

Farrah was a Texan who moved to Hollywood in 1968, looking for a career in film and television. Initially, she landed jobs in tv commercials ranging from toothpaste to cars. Eventually, she landed small acting roles on tv shows such as "I Dream of Jeannie" and continued further career, landing a re-occurring role in the tv drama "Harry O."

I had noticed Farrah in several of the commercials she had been in and was awestruck by her beauty, but it wasn't until I saw her star in the pilot for the television show "Charlie's Angels" that I fell head over heels for her. The show followed the exploits of three female private detectives who worked for the Charles Townshend detective agency. Although the show had two other beauties in starring roles, Kate Jackson and Jaclyn Smith, they frankly were inconsequential in comparison to Farrah Fawcett. This beautiful blonde, who also possessed a natural "girl next door" charm, had stolen my heart and would keep it under lock and key for several years.

The Poster

Farrah's stardom was launched into the stratosphere with the release of her famous "red bathing suit" poster in 1976. This stunning beauty captured the hearts of many men with this groundbreaking poster. If you were a male and breathing, your heart most certainly skipped a beat the first time your eyes came across Farrah in her bathing suit. She looked sexy as hell, but also, her smile was so disarming that you felt like she took the picture personally for you. I bought it immediately upon seeing it for the first time. The poster would sell six million copies in the first year in print and would become the best-selling poster of all time.

I loved Farrah, and so did all my friends, as did every male in my school. Although the show "Charlie's Angels" came on after my bedtime, I was fortunate enough to have a black and white tv in my room and would, in classic "sneak" fashion, secretly turn it on and watch the show at low volume with my dad nearby in the family room. It was always worth the risk of being caught out of bed to watch. One never knew what Farrah might wear or what should look like that week. If the term "must-see tv" was ever appropriately used, it was in the viewing of "Charlie's Angels." Believe me, you didn't want to be the one kid the next day at school who didn't see Farrah in her bikini or white bell-bottom pants the night before.

Many argue Farrah became the most photographed and most popular beauty since Marilynn Monroe. She was on the cover of so many magazines during this period that I could not even fathom a guess on how many covers she adorned at the peak of her popularity. I would have done anything to have met Farrah and spend one romantic evening with her, but the best I could do was gaze at all of her magazine covers and the poster I cherished in my room.

Eventually, Farrah's star dimmed, and my interest in pursuing obtainable girls my own age won out over my fantasies of Farrah and me getting married. However, that does not mean I still don't hold a special place in my heart for the beautiful Texan. Years later, and long after I was married, my father approached me with a poster canister in hand, and inside it was the same famous Farrah poster I had purchased almost twenty years earlier. He smiled at me and said, "I figured one day you would want this back." He had kept it safe for years until I was older and settled into my own home before he gave it back to me. Today it is framed and hung on our guest room wall, along with other memorabilia from the 70s.

The Girl Next Door

Farrah would sadly passed away from cancer in 2009, but anyone who was around my age in the mid 70's will never forget her. On a cold Winter's night, staring at the burning embers of the fire while warming their aging bones, I'm certain many men have drifted back to recall the girl with that special smile for whom they fell in love so very long ago.

The Long and Short of It

The year of the bicentennial was also the winter and spring of my first year in high school. The high school years as a whole, or better yet, my adolescent development between the ages of 14 and 20, molded much of the attitudes and behaviors I would hold as an adult for decades to follow.

To this day, I cannot explain why this "imprinting" of my personal self was so well established during my teenage years or how it was sustained for so long after… it just "happened." I never took the time even to ponder this phenomenon. Instead, I just let the years roll by without retracing my path back to the origin of my established behavior or thought patterns.

In any case, the establishment of my behavior and thoughts began to assert itself at the age of fourteen while I was a freshman in high school. If middle school had been a passage from childhood into adolescence and, in its most dire moments, a simple matter of survival. High school for me was a passage from adolescence into knowing and accepting who I was while also not yet knowing who I could be.

Most of my freshman year was spent trying to figure out why I was so much shorter than everyone else. Unlike some of the boys whose voices had already changed in junior high and now were brandishing razors for their sparse whiskers as freshmen. I had a voice that was no different than my sisters and a stature that was not much taller than my 7th-grade neighbor.

There was no doubt I was young for my grade. I began elementary school at the age of four, but I did not feel the negative effects of this early entry until much later in my school years. I first realized there was something amiss in high school when I caught some older boys mocking and laughing at some poor soul, telling him, "Hey, little boy, the elementary school is down the street!" I looked down the hall behind me to see who this unfortunate child who was being teased was, but to my surprise, there was no one there but me. I took a few steps more, pondering just who in the heck were these high school boys mocking, and then it hit me. They were mocking me! The funny thing was, up until that moment, I never felt like I was a "short kid."

As it turned out, I was the obligatory little dog who thought he was a "big dog" because he existed in a big dog world. In that moment, the little short kid (which I finally realized I was) became just a little smaller. I recall going home and complaining to my dad about this "height challenge," which I had recently become aware existed. Of course, my dad, at a humble 5' 7", was someone who could certainly relate to the challenges of being short. However, my dad did not take the "I know how you feel, son" approach with me. It would have been easy and quite natural for my father to discuss how a shorter person, especially a male, navigates through life with what I perceived as a major barrier.

How was I to compete in athletic endeavors or, for that matter, the courting of young ladies against other males of much larger stature? How was I to be seen or even recognized in a crowd while hovering below a sea of humanity? I looked at my dad and then my mother, who was even shorter than him, and realized my destiny had already been written in stone. I was going to be a short man.

My father, however, had other ideas for me. Through his studies in metaphysics and parapsychology, he had by now bought into the philosophy and probabilities behind "creating your own reality." He was convinced that *the mind* was responsible for creating the reality that surrounds us. Only through the illusion of this supposed physical reality had we allowed ourselves to be convinced we had little control of our past, present, and future.

Although I never thought to ask my father why he had taught me this philosophical and cognitive approach to the fundamental aspects of reality, it did become clear he was sharing the knowledge he had garnered later in life in an effort to mold my mental approach for the future.

After I had finished my rant regarding my "height disability," my dad looked at me and said, "You're are not going to be short... you are going to be tall, just like your grandpa and uncles." The fact was he had made a good point because on my mother's side, her father was six feet tall, and her two brothers stood at 6 '1" and 6 '4". He said, "You are going to get your height from that side of the family, so don't worry about it anymore."

As was my usual practice, I believed what my father had told me and chose to ignore my "shortness" as an issue because I now held the belief that it was only temporary. By late in my senior year, I had reached 6 'tall, and as my dad had predicted, I had inherited my height from my mother's side of the family. However, at the age of twenty, I was informed of a family secret that would change all of this. Apparently, our grandmother had divorced her first husband, our mother's father, after World War II and married an American soldier stationed in Berlin.

This, of course, was a shock to my sisters and me as we had no idea there was not a direct bloodline with our supposed "grandfather." Our actual grandfather was still alive in Germany, and a recent picture of him, which we were finally shown, clearly showed he was indeed a short man. The connection my dad had made with the male side of my mom's family was totally fallacious. Of course, my dad had known this all along but had led me to believe I would acquire my height through a bloodline that was comprised of tall men.

I am convinced I grew to the height of 6 feet because, in my mind, I had created a new reality for my future physical stature. It was this unbending faith in what my father had told me "as fact" that ultimately reshaped my physical reality. I became six feet tall because I believed I would be…it's as simple as that. My mind had reshaped my future physical composition just as the mind can also cure or manifest illness based on individual belief systems.

Life, Love, and the High School Ecosystem

My high school years were filled with the typical dramas associated with the teenage years. They were filled with obligatory decisive victories and devastating defeats. I learned how to behave with enough maturity to garner the interest of a few girls but never really had any serious relationship to speak of. I certainly never fell in love, and I'm even more certain that no one fell in love with me. There were Home Coming, Christmas, and other assorted dances which required a date to attend. Though it took quite a bit of nerve to ask girls to these dances who were taller than me and, in some cases, deeper voices than mine, I did so with grim determination.

The results were poor. I cannot recall how many times I was turned down, but at the end of my sophomore year, I had only been to one dance, even though my efforts to attend these events with a female partner had no doubt been aggressive. In other words, my failures were not due to a lack of trying. One girl, Debbie Kelson, I asked to almost every dance during my first two years in high school. She was a year older than I and preferred her men to be at least 5 '3" or taller with some visible whisker stubble, and I could not meet either of those standards.

Regardless of literally coming up "short" to her standards, I still ventured out and asked her always with the hope that "this time might be different." In the end, it became a sad routine of me gathering up my courage only to be rejected once again. She never did go out with me, and after two years, I finally gave in to the reality of the situation…it just wasn't going to happen.

Besides the dating scene, which had been an abject failure, the first two years of high school were more or less an exercise in trial and error in decision-making. I spent most of my time avoiding situations that would land me in trouble while still pushing the limits of sound thinking in other areas. Early on, I found my circle of friends who happened to be a healthy mix of the conservative and the daring. I quickly adapted to the new high school theme of increased freedom equating to more personal responsibility and seemed to balance the two concepts fairly well.

The academic part of the high school equation was the least of my concern. I easily navigated through the requirements of high school by always doing enough to maintain a "B" average but never doing anything more to excel. I found the business of earning "reasonable" grades a simple matter of focusing when I needed to but never working any harder than was absolutely necessary. By my own admission, I was far too lazy to strive for anything better.

By the end of my sophomore year in 1977, I had gained confidence and developed a routine that would make the next two years of high school much more enjoyable. I had endured the transition from adolescence into semi-adulthood, leaving behind my childhood in favor of increased responsibility along with increased freedom. Better times were ahead for me.

Late in my high school years, I began to work. I held the typical high schooler-type jobs, from bus boy at a local restaurant to the stock boy at a store in the mall. All of them came with their own certain "adventures," and some were more fun than others, but what was most important was that the money I earned gave me a certain level of independence.

I ended my time in High School feeling like I had found a rhythm to my existence within the teenage ecosystem. I was comfortable with myself and had no bouts of depression or had to endure any "bad situations" that caused me considerable grief. Sure, I lost a girlfriend or two, and I never became homecoming king, but for me, high school was a good experience.

As we coasted to the finish line in the last quarter of high school, I recall my best friend and I skipping many classes. Often, we would leave campus to explore the nearby city of Portland. I think we learned more about life during those adventures into the city than anything we learned in the final months of school. We were no doubt ready for new experiences that did not include adult supervision. We had survived the brutality of middle school and the "semi-adult" world of high school and were eager to finally engage in the concept of "independent living" on a college campus. It was time to move away from home and begin to blaze our own trails forging forward into a bold new future.

This is Captain America Falling…

There were also considerable changes occurring in America with the election of Jimmy Carter as President in the fall of 1976. Jimmy Carter, a former peanut farmer and governor of Georgia, had surprisingly won the Democratic nomination in the summer of 1976. He then went on to defeat Gerald Ford in the general election by a narrow margin.

Ford, who had replaced Nixon after his resignation due to the Watergate scandal, no doubt had the deck stacked against him in his bid to retain the presidency. He was not considered a great orator or a polished politician, nor had he distinguished himself as a great leader in the two years he had been President. To be fair, it was mostly the memory of Watergate that led to his demise in the election. Americans were leery of another Republican president, especially one that had been so closely tied to Nixon.

Jimmy Carter

Throughout the rest of the seventies, under the leadership of Jimmy Carter, the country seemed to fall into a funk. Very little appeared to be going right as the country dipped further into "stagflation." Unemployment rose while the price of goods also increased, and wages stagnated. Carter had promised to curb a recession that had been exacerbated by several of Nixon's failed economic policies. However, Carter did nothing to improve the economic doldrums during his administration. By 1979 the country was in the grips of an energy crisis, gasoline shortage, and increasing inflation which caused a steep decline in consumer confidence.

By the late 70s, the country was dealing with considerable economic pain while still living with the recent memory of the

Watergate and Vietnam debacles. The mood of the country was one of frustration and depression. The exuberance that had been briefly felt during the bi-centennial celebration was a long-lost memory by 1979. Under the Carter administration, the general feeling was that nothing was likely to get better while he was in office.

I was certainly more involved in my personal life and the happenings at my local high school than in the economic despair occurring in our country. However, I recall a distinct feeling of frustration and moodiness in the air that seemed to permeate the entire country.

It all came to a head in November of 1979 when 63 American citizens were taken hostage in Iran. It felt like our country had been spit in the face by a group of militant thugs who had been part of the recent Islamic revolution, which had resulted in the overthrow of the Pahlavi monarchy in Iran.

The Iran Hostage Crisis

Carter's initial attempt to free the hostages failed to produce any results and only validated for many the belief that he was an inept leader. The mood of the country grew worse, and doubt crept in whether we were still the world power we had once been and perhaps our best years were behind us.

Public criticism of Carter only increased after a failed attempt to free the remaining 52 hostages resulted in considerable embarrassment after an aborted secret military operation. President Carter had ordered the ill-fated rescue mission, which resulted in the death of eight servicemen and no hostages rescued. The mission designed as an airborne rescue never materialized as three of the eight helicopters used in the proposed mission failed. The aborted mission turned into a military disaster when one of the retreating helicopters collided with a transport plane that was to be used as part of the rescue.

The whole incident received worldwide attention, and the United States, a once proud and fierce nation, seemed to be failing in almost every possible way. Even its military now appeared to be inept and incapable of executing a military rescue operation. President Carter took full responsibility for the failed mission, and his stock as a competent leader hit an all-time low.

The hostages would eventually be freed 270 days later after Carter had been replaced by Ronald Regan as president. Carter's administration, by anyone's standards, failed to deliver for America, and new leadership was on the minds of most Americans by the time of the 1980 Presidential election. Ronald Regan, the governor of California and former movie star, would win a decisive victory in November of 1980, thus bringing a merciful end to four years of Carter administration failures.

Disco Boys v.s. The Rockers

After the sonic awakening of the 60s led by the "British Invasion," what was to follow in the 70s was a potpourri of musical artistry. The Beatles' demise at the turn of the decade opened the door for other musical acts to lead popular music into the new frontier.

Folk singers, Funk artists, and Motown wonders such as Diana Ross and the Supremes and the Jackson Five all found respectable niches in the music industry. There were still plenty of "Rock Star" personas filling the pop charts. In addition, a few new musical styles were also introduced that found immense popularity in the 70s.

Glam rock was one of these new musical creations that originated in the United Kingdom in the early 70s. Contrary to the rock style of the 60s, glam rock focused on superficiality over substance. It had very little to do with musical dignity in its presentation to the masses, and rather, it held its power within the "show" or the "spectacle" of rock music.

Glam rock had shed the decorum which had driven many artists of the '60s to record songs about spiritual awakening or social justice and replaced it with outrageous attire, hairstyles, and makeup. It was, in many ways, the antithesis of the rock of the '60s, focusing on excess and bizarre showmanship instead of thoughtful integrity. It appeared more often like a circus act than a rock act.

Though there were many Glam Rock acts that experienced moderate success in the UK, none did so with the cache which David Bowie brought to the genre. Bowie not only embraced and pushed the Glam Rock scene to new heights. He actually brought a level of true artistry to the music giving it badly needed credibility. Bowie's intellect, combined with his incredible creative prowess, gave Glam Rock exactly what it needed to pierce into the American fan base.

David Bowie

With evocative lyrics and gritty but sonically adept music Bowie brought Glam Rock into mainstream consciousness. Through the creation of his fictitious alter ego, "Ziggy Stardust," Bowie brought rock music into the realm of fantasy as he portrayed an alien rock star who eventually met his demise due to his own fame and a life of excess.

"Ziggy Stardust" brought Bowie international fame and critical acclaim, but more importantly, it cemented Glam Rock as a viable genre in the rock'n roll repertoire. Many bands would follow Bowie's lead by creating characters to portray in their rock shows which were now becoming more attuned to rock'n roll theatre. The music, in some cases, became secondary to the characters portrayed and the exotic behaviors exhibited by musicians adorned in makeup and outlandish attire.

About the time David Bowie was making a splash in America, I was beginning the transition from the world of AM radio music to the far more sophisticated sounds of FM. I had grown up with the Beatles, who had absolutely dominated the AM radio scene. I had very little familiarity with FM radio as it was at an entirely different level of advanced musical content and a signal that most transistor radios were not equipped to carry, or car radios for that matter.

Up until the time I purchased my first stereo in high school, I had been held captive to AM radio and the superficial yet pleasing sounds of the artists of the top 40. I am not one to criticize the pop music of the 70s, as there were many great artists and songs of that era that are worthy of recognition.

By design, however, the depth and creativity of the AM artist were limited to simple "ear candy" and did little to stir one's intellect or perhaps the rebellion brewing inside them. As I would soon discover, most of the artists I had listened to on AM had their best songs playing on FM.

It was late 1975 when I first heard "Rock'n Roll All Nite" by a little-known band called "Kiss." In truth, I first heard the song on AM radio as I had not yet purchased my first Hi-fi system. It was Kiss that drove me to *want* and eventually *need* a stereo of my own that included the FM signal.

Kiss Alive Album

I had no idea what Kiss looked like as I had just heard their one hit and thought it was a good rock song worth paying attention to. That would change when my older sister came home one night with the album "Kiss Alive." I was enamored by what I saw on the album cover, as I had never seen anything like it before.

It was true that David Bowie had brought Glam Rock to America, but he was little known to the AM radio listeners at the time. He was part of the growing counterculture that had seeped into America but had not yet knocked its doors down. Kiss, on the other hand, was an American band that played standard American rock but with a seductive, lyrical edge consisting of lust and excess. They were the essence of hard rock music in the 70s, symbolically fueled by the obligatory "sex, drugs, and rock 'n roll" theme, and I absolutely fell in love with their image and their music. There was no doubt that I now knew my destiny... I was to be a "rocker," and to this day, that is still who I am.

The music of Kiss, from a talent perspective, was nowhere near the talent of Bowie. It consisted of basic repetitive riffs that were powerful but not overly thoughtful in their construction. The impetus behind Kiss was the makeup they wore and the characters they portrayed. They had found the crucial combination of hard rock riffs combined with a theatrical stage presence that drew American youth in masses to their live shows.

They became a huge phenomenon in America with a massive marketing machine behind them. They labeled their fans the "Kiss Army" and rolled into city after city, pleasing tens of thousands of young fans with their stage show and music.

With their stardom reaching new heights in 1978, they starred in their own movie titled "Kiss Meets the Phantom of the Park." The movie was awful by anyone's standards, and even Kiss fans were turned off by the terrible acting and childish script. Nonetheless, the Kiss machine continued to roll along due mainly to their incredible concert performances and stage shows that were considered "top shelf" by rock'n roll standards.

Around the same time, Glam Rock was gaining a modest foothold in America, and Kiss had exploded onto the scene with their "Kiss Alive" album. A new genre of music was finding a place in the nightclubs of the northeast. New York City became the "hotbed" for these types of nightclubs, which soon would become known as discotheques.

If the "hippie rock" of the sixties, comprised of bands such as Buffalo Springfield and later Crosby, Stills, Nash, and Young, had represented "deep thoughts," disco was the antithesis of that style. It was weak in its musical composition, lacking any serious efforts at originality. In addition, the lyrics lacked any level of depth of thought.

The most important aspect of any successful disco song was a beat that could easily be danced to. It was just that simple, and nothing else really mattered other than the beat of the song. This genre was not concerned about bringing awareness to the issues of political corruption, racial division, or social injustice. Rather, it was only concerned about having a "good time." It personified a culture that had turned away from social awareness and now focused on self-gratification and excess. It was the perfect music for those who wanted to forget about life's trouble and just "party." Drugs and sex were abundant in discotheques, along with a heavy dose of narcissistic behavior.

Cocaine became the drug of choice during the '70s. Combined with the shining lights, mirror balls, and beat of disco music, participants of the disco "nightlife" became lost in the euphoria of indulgence. Add to it attire that could only be described as sensual and seductive on the one hand and ridiculously embarrassing on the other…disco nightlife was a venture into superficial debauchery.

With the release of the film "Saturday Night Fever," disco hit new heights of popularity. The film depicted the nightlife of disco enthusiasts with all the drama, self-absorption, and nonsense that went along with it. The film and the soundtrack were a huge success and would make John Travolta a bonafide movie star. It also catapulted the Bee Gees into pop music stardom as the group performed several songs for the movie soundtrack that became one of the best-selling albums in music history.

For a brief shining moment, disco owned the pop music world.

My perspective of disco was that it was an offense to rock music. As a teenager who was now listening to FM radio, I felt disco music was for losers who had no legitimate sense of self-worth. It was a genre right down to the style of dress that typified a lack of substance and originality, and it was clouded with a "wannabe" mentality. Disco was about "dancing" and looking good doing it but not about the art of music. It only used music as a cheap parlor trick to garner attention for people who had no chance of garnering it any other way.

To be blunt, I hated disco and everything it stood for. I saw the young men of disco as wimps and the young women as brainless

The Bee Gees

sluts. There was nothing good about disco other than its predictable death. The image of those that performed disco music compared to those who played rock were on opposite ends of the spectrum. Disco stars such as the Bee Gees presented images of themselves as all glitter and flash with an absolute absence of any toughness or grit. They could dance all right, but could they fight? Not likely. Many rock stars, on the other hand, presented themselves as thoughtful, gritty musicians with big brains.

Pete Townshend of "The Who" epitomized what was good and profound in rock. He was a brilliant songwriter, musician, and

The Who

rocker who appeared to be tough as nails as well. Townshend was steeped in machoism, as was his band, and was the complete opposite of the glitter and flash of the Bee Gees. He wielded his electric guitar as a weapon of chaos and destruction, while the Bee Gees wielded shiny silk shirts and gold necklaces as their weapon of choice. The Who behaved like a street gang who would be more than happy to fight you in the streets or seedy back alleys.

The Bee Gees...well, they appeared to prefer a "dance-off" at a discotheque to fisticuffs in the streets.

In the end, disco could not survive under the weight of its own superficiality. It was simply a fad...a "flash in the pan" genre that did not and could not carry on as a legitimate form of music. It appealed to the masses. However, the "masses" typically have short attention spans and will drop a fad as quickly as a fickle high school beauty drops her boyfriends.

Townshend may have said it best in his anti-disco song penned in 1978 titled "Sister Disco." "I will choose nightmares and cold stormy seas. I will take over your grief and disease. I'll stay beside you and comfort your soul when you are lonely and broken and old."

By the end of the decade, disco was quickly fading into the trash heap of unwanted music, becoming a source of ridicule and bad jokes. It had died an embarrassing death (as bad art often does), and I, for one, was thrilled to see it relegated to the "has been" discounted music shelves of local music stores. Disco never had any other fate available to it other than eventual extinction, while rock would continue strong until the 90s when Nirvana and Grunge Rock would deal it a lethal blow.

My rock 'n roll experience would reach new heights in the late 70s as I began to attend concerts, with the first concert I attended costing me just eight dollars. AC/DC opened up for Aerosmith in a show where AC/DC blew the doors off Aerosmith's drug-induced pathetic excuse for a live performance.

The concert experience was a whole new world of fun and excitement for me. The atmosphere of a rock concert in those days were a bit different than today, including getting into the arena, which at times was an event all in itself. Festival seating was the predominant method most rock concert tickets were sold at the time or, in terms of these days, "general admission." There was no "pre-sale" of tickets or reserved seating available. It was a simple process of whoever got in line first got the best seats...end of story. This, of course, meant extremely long lines waiting for hours upon hours for the auditorium doors to open if you wanted the best available seats.

Many people would even spend the night before the concert outside in the elements and then wait in line the entire next day until the doors opened that evening. This, of course, would set the tone for aggressive behavior to be amplified by the large crowd of tired, anxious kids wanting to get through the doors (once opened) to garner the best seats.

On more than one occasion, I was caught up in the crush of humanity as it lurched forward toward the doors upon their opening. It would often turn into a claustrophobic event with hundreds of kids "gutting it out" to get inside the building. It was literally a free for all, the survival of the fittest, and many folded under the pressure. Those who had waited for hours panicked and gave up their place in line to escape the aggressive mass of humanity pushing forward.

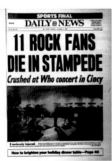

Tragedy In Cincinnati

In December of 1979, this type of scenario reached a new level of intensity ending in catastrophe in Cincinnati, Ohio, before The Who was to perform. Eleven concertgoers lost their lives during a crush of humanity trying to gain entrance into an arena that had opened just two of its doors to accommodate the hundreds trying to gain entrance into the area. Twenty-six people were injured in the incident (due to being trampled), and the eleven who were killed all died of asphyxiation.

After the Cincinnati tragedy, festival seating was eliminated at many rock concert venues and replaced with assigned seating ticket sales. It was a low point for the rock concert industry as many, from a public perspective, deemed the whole idea of "rock shows" being bent on self-destructive behavior by the youth who attended.

As for the rock band "he Who," they were devastated by the tragedy, and the shadow of death from the incident would haunt them for decades. The band would rarely speak of that fateful night and did not return to perform in Cincinnati for 43 years.

By the end of the 70s, I had found my rock 'n roll soul, inspired by a vast catalog of great songs created in an era that is now labeled as "classic rock." It was indeed the heyday of rock 'n roll, comprised of a bounty of talented and creative musicians, many of whom had been inspired by the Beatles a decade earlier.

In the closing years of the 70s, I would expand my album collection immensely and would see many great live acts from Queen to Heart. Just as important, I never participated in a disco-fueled night at the local underage nightclubs, and I never attended a Bee Gees concert...both distinctions I am still very proud of to this day.

Gallons of Trouble

Due to the increasing instability in the Mid-East, primarily the Iranian revolution in 1979, oil markets massively increased the price of crude oil. The increased cost of crude oil, coupled with the decrease in production, created the perfect storm for the second energy crisis of the decade. With a diminished amount of refined crude oil available, a gasoline shortage soon followed. Prices soared, and long lines became commonplace in America. This phenomenon only worsened as consumers panicked in fear of being left without gasoline for their vehicles. It was not uncommon to see long lines at the gas station, along with some very annoyed and impatient people. The increase in gas prices only created more aggravation for the consumer.

Waiting for Gas

Of course, all of this fell on the shoulders of an already beleaguered President Carter, who, under his administration, national confidence and pride continued to wane. The stubborn stagflation issue of the 1970s, which he had promised to solve, but failed in doing so, cost him a great deal of public support. Americans had simply lost faith in his leadership. In addition, the Iranian hostage crisis, which was unceremoniously dropped into his lap, exacerbated the lack of confidence in his administration.

For someone like me, who had little money and drove a gas-guzzling Ford LTD, the gas shortage and increase in prices was difficult to manage. Of course, gas was much cheaper in those days, averaging around 86 cents a gallon, but when you only had three-quarters in your pocket, it just doesn't get you too far down the road. I recall a popular song written and performed by the Kinks, "A

Gallon of Gas," in 1979, in which the lyrics told the story of the gas shortage. "I went to my local dealer to see if he could set me straight. He said there was a little gas going, but I'd have to wait. He offered some red hot speed and some really high-grade hash. But a gallon of gas can't be purchased anywhere for any amount of cash."

The Sweet Success of Failure

By the fall of 1979, at the age of seventeen, I would move more than two hundred miles away from my home to attend a small college in southern Oregon. There is no doubt I had unprecedented fun along with great adventures for a three-month period. The academic aspect was the least of my concern, as I was having far too much fun exploring life as an independent adult. The problem was that I was still far from being an "adult," and my grades validated that truism at the end of the first term of college. With a bag full of D's and F's, I moved back into my parent's house in Lake Oswego with my tail between my legs. I may have been defined as an "adult" by law, but reality told a different story of my level of maturity.

I can't say I regretted the three months I spent away from home. Those months were fantastic in many ways, and I still fondly recall the numerous new experiences I encountered living independently for the first time. Would I do it over again the same way? Hell, yes, I would. However, along with the success I felt at the time "living free," there is no doubt a latent taste of failure from doing it so poorly.

The decade was over, and it had seen me grow from a sad boy forced to leave his home in Salem to a young man returning home after falling flat on his face in his first attempt to live independently. Sure many things had changed during those ten years, but one thing was clear I still had much more "growing up" to accomplish. In the decade to follow, I would definitely complete that task. However, it was not so much out of desire but out of necessity. My life was about to change in ways I could have never imagined, and it would never be the same again.

Part Three
(The 80s)

Into the Breach

By the time the new decade rolled around, I had been eighteen for just over three months. I had experienced life on my own for the first time and lived further from home than ever before.

The times were certainly changing as I was becoming my own man, or so I believed, but the reality was far different from my perception. I was still a snotty-nosed kid who had illusions of independence but had yet to develop the skills necessary to be successful at it.

After my short three-month stint attending Southern Oregon State College, I found myself back in the friendly confines of my father's domain. I had enrolled in winter classes at Portland State University, accompanied by a firm warning from my dad that he had better see improvement in my grades.

Even then, consumed by all of my immaturity, I understood my father's expectations of me. He was, after all, paying for my education, so the least I could do was make a nominal effort to improve my grades. I made a personal commitment to do better in the upcoming winter term, but until then, it would be party time with my friends.

For some reason, I vividly remember spending that New Year's Eve with my closest friends drinking and raising some suburban hell. I recall all of us sitting in front of the tv watching Dick Clark's countdown to the end of 1979. It was great fun, and I could think of no better way to spend the end of the decade than drinking with my buddies.

I remember at the time thinking the 70s were now behind me and, along with it, my youth. I had entered the decade as a boy and left as a young man. Many things had changed in my life during those ten years, and physically speaking, there would never be another decade that would produce such dramatic gains in my stature.

As I watched the ball in time square slowly descend late that evening, I recall pondering my future. In particular, I was concerned about my academic future and whether I could garner the disciple required to be successful. There was no going back to my youth, I had accepted that reality, but the truth was that even if I could have gone back, I would have chosen against it.

That period of my life was over, and a decade of new experiences awaited me. These would be experiences under the guise of an "adult," which meant my choices and decisions would have much more profound consequences. I was entering the deep end of the pool now as an active participant in society and was no longer swimming in the shallow end with adults watching over me.

That night, after we watched Dick Clark celebrate the coming of the new decade, my friends and I drank beers and played tunes well into the early morning hours. I woke up the next morning with a hangover lying in the same bed and in the same room where I had spent my youth. At the beginning of a new decade, it appeared that the more things had changed, the more they had also stayed the same.

Looking back, I suppose I was no different from many people my age…stuck in the transition between a life I wanted and the reality of who I actually was. I was in no way prepared to stake claim to the world before me, and yet my desires bubbled up the simple concepts of independence and freedom. I wanted to be my own man but still liked the idea of my parents being a safety net if I should fail. I had the will but not yet the maturity to transition into adulthood.

Of course, the real danger was that my intellect was far ahead of any wisdom I may have acquired at the age of eighteen. I knew how to engage society and even how to manipulate many of its constructs, but I had no idea how to maintain consistency in my actions. One moment I would be conversing with a college professor about the fundamentals of economics, and the next moment would find myself taking a "bong hit" in my car in the campus parking garage.

The distinction between who I was and the potential of whom I could become had been blurred by latent immaturity. I wanted to be successful, and I wanted to impress my father, but I also didn't want to work at it. When it came to the conundrum of having fun vs. "buckling down," it was clear fun would win every time.

This battle between where I wanted to go in life and what I wanted to do "in the moment" went on for years. There would be months I would find my "inner maturity" and actually behave like a serious student in search of academic enlightenment. However, it would never last. I ultimately found myself right back in party mode, getting absolutely nothing accomplished but having a damn good time doing it.

As a result, my grades fluctuated considerably for a large part of my post-secondary academic career. I don't recall how many D's or F's I accumulated during this period, but there were enough to eventually have my father throw in the towel and say "no more." He was no longer buying my excuses and feigned promises of improvement and eventually pulled the plug on my funding. He was simply tired of throwing good money away. He saw value in a college education but, based on my efforts, saw no potential return on his investment. As far as he was concerned, he had thrown thousands of dollars away for nothing but a report card filled with D's and F's.

I was never angered by his decision to stop paying for college. How could I be? I knew I had let him down, and myself for that matter, but the lure of partying with my friends still took precedence over everything else, including making my father proud of me. I wanted to impress him, and I wanted a college degree, but it seemed I just didn't want either bad enough.

I'm not sure if wisdom ever did come to me regarding my academic woes. It was never the case of an inability to understand the material that was being taught. However, when you don't go to class, and you don't read the text material assigned, it becomes a challenge to excel in examinations.

I recall one time cramming for an accounting mid-term exam. I had been to class maybe once during the entire term and had not read any of the chapters that were to be covered in the exam. That night before the test (around midnight), I decided it would be prudent for me to open the book and study perhaps. I spent the rest of that night and most of the next day attempting to wade through an accounting textbook popping "No Doz" to stay alert and awake.

About an hour before the mid-term, I realized I was too "wound up" due to lack of sleep and all the caffeine pills I had been ingesting over the past 15 hours. I needed to calm my nerves if I was to have any chance of passing the exam. In my infinite wisdom, I concluded alcohol was the answer to settle my nerves. I proceeded to take a bottle of Jack Daniels from my father's liquor cabinet and pour myself "shots" of bourbon.

I don't recall how many "shots" I took that afternoon, and I don't recall how I made it to the classroom, but I do remember sitting staring at an accounting exam, realizing I was on the edge of being drunk. Needless to say, I received an "F" on the exam and in the class. Such was my life in college. I not only danced on the edge of failure, I willingly jumped right into the breach of academic defeat.

Do You Believe in Miracles?

In December of 1979, the Soviet Union invaded Afghanistan, and in defiance of international condemnation, they proceeded to engage in military operations within the country until early 1989. In the end, the entire effort to seize control of Afghanistan would turn into an embarrassing abject failure for the Soviets. Ultimately the invasion would cost them more than a failed geo-political "power grab". The failed invasion would help fuel the demise of the once-powerful Soviet Union.

The incredible economic strain the Soviets endured during the war would have serious consequences for its long-term viability as a ruling government. In addition, the international sanctions implemented in response to the invasion placed even more pressure on a government trying to maintain stability. The Soviet Union would never recover from their ill-fated attempt to occupy Afghanistan, losing to a rag-tag group of resistors. History would later confirm that the invasion of Afghanistan marked the beginning of the end of the Soviet Union's "Super Power" status. The failure of this endeavor helped to decisively tip the scales of power in favor of America in the "Cold War" era.

Two months after the invasion of Afghanistan, the Xlll Winter Olympic Games were played in Lake Placid, New York. Tensions caused by the Soviet Union's invasion were clear from the beginning of the games. President Carter had already stated he was considering boycotting the Summer Olympics to be held in Moscow later that year. The Cold War between the United States and the Soviet Union was now entering the fifth decade and showed no signs of relenting.

Every four years, the Olympics provided each country the opportunity to flex its athletic muscles on a world stage. Both countries saw the games as an opportunity to demonstrate their superiority over the other through the endeavors of their athletes. It was an opportunity to peacefully promote their culture and form of government without the risk of war.

There was indeed fierce competition between the Soviets and the Americans to garner more Olympic gold medals. To ignore the level of importance in accomplishing this task would be to ignore the last four decades of hostility and rhetoric between the two nations. It meant a great deal to both governments and their citizens to win the "medals race" at the Olympics. Pride was on the line, if not also a subtle form of intimidation at stake for the winner. It would symbolically demonstrate superiority over its long-time nemesis.

Nothing provided a higher level of pride for the Russian people than their outstanding hockey team. The Soviet Union's hockey team was a sports dynasty by anyone's standards. Beginning with the 1964 Olympics, the men's hockey team had accumulated a record of 27-1-1 in Olympic competition.

They were unequivocally considered the greatest hockey team in the world and had held that distinction for almost two decades. Just prior to the XIII Olympics, the Russians had beaten the NHL all-stars (which included 20 future hall-of-fame players) in a three-game series, easily outplaying the best professional players the Canadians and Americans had to offer.

The Russians intimidated all who dared to step on the ice with them. Their physicality and skill level were far superior to any of their opponents, and everyone knew it. They were the undisputed champions of the world and heavy favorites to win the gold medal going into the Olympic Games at Lake Placid.

Enter stage left a group of young American hockey players (all amateurs), with an average age of just twenty-one. They were really just boys playing in a man's game. Make no mistake, they had talent and potential, and thanks to their coach Herb Brooks, they also had been molded into a group of tough, hard-nosed kids who had formed a tight bond. The Americans were by no means in the same league as the Soviet team, but they did have belief and trust in one another and faith in what their coach had taught them.

They knew they didn't have to be a better team than the Russians…they just had to be better on the night they played them. Sure, the odds were long, but the boys on that team believed they could play well enough to beat the Russians just once. They might lose nine out of ten games to the Soviet team, but all of them believed that one sole win could occur during the Olympic Games.

As fate would have it, the Americans and Russians would face each other in the medal round of the tournament. No one really expected the young Americans to win the game. However, the team did have a few things going for them. First: They had performed exceptionally well in the games prior to their date with the Soviet Union. They had amassed four wins, including an impressive tie against formidable Sweden in the first round of the tournament. Second: They had the "home ice" advantage as the game would be played in the United States in front of a raucous partisan American crowd. Finally, they had a coach who had trained them physically and mentally to hold up against a fierce imposing Soviet team, who, by reputation alone, could win most games before the first puck was even dropped.

It was a tall order to be sure, and reality demanded everyone expect a sound beating by the Russians. However, hope springs eternal in the hearts of young men, and these particular young men believed in themselves and their coach. They also believed that *they were in charge* of their own destiny and not the pundits who had already handed them the loss.

The game was very competitive from the outset. At the end of the first period of play, the score was tied at 2-2, with the Americans scoring a late goal in the waning moments of the period to tie the game. The Soviet Union controlled the second period and, for the most part, dominated Team USA. They scored the only goal giving them a 3-2 lead going into the final period of play. It began to appear the Russians were about to shut down the feisty American's effort for an upset.

Victory!

The third and final period saw Team USA fight back and take their first lead of the game with ten minutes left. In those final ten minutes, Team USA endured one frantic effort after another from the Soviets to score a goal and tie the game. These young Americans were now in a position to pull off one of the biggest upsets in sports history, but they would have to fend off the greatest hockey team in the world to complete the shocking upset.

In the end, the Soviets, with all of their skill, physicality, and experience, could not succeed in their desperate efforts to tie the game. Through determined play and by matching the Soviets' intensity on ice, the Americans did not fold under the intense pressure of a desperate team facing defeat. As the final seconds wound down and it became clear that Team USA was about to pull off a stunning upset, Al Micheals (calling the game for ABC on network tv) made the historical statement, "Do you believe in miracles? Yes!!"

What has been mostly forgotten over the decades is that the broadcast of the game had been tape delayed and not shown to the American public until the following day. In 1980 this was not an uncommon practice for a network to broadcast Olympic events in a tape-delayed format.

As for me, I was leaving work that evening when a co-worker yelled at me, "Hey, the Americans won!" Of course, I knew exactly what he meant and walked back to see what else he knew. A friend had called and informed him of the victory but provided few other details. However, that was enough for now. We would have to wait until the next day to see the replay on tv, but we were elated by the news, and a sense of nationalistic pride washed over us.

Gold Medal Ceremony

The next day 34.2 million people watched the tape-delayed broadcast of the game, and two days later, another 32.8 million watched Team USA beat Finland in another "come from behind" victory to capture the gold medal. Coach Herb Brooks and his young team of amateur hockey players shocked the world and captured the hearts of all Americans with their stunning performance in the Olympics.

It was one of the finest moments of national pride I have ever witnessed, watching Team USA collecting their gold medals while sharing their joy with the fans in attendance. It was a decisive statement to the Russians, demonstrating that although America had recently been through some rough times, it still had the heart and the will to rise above the obstacles laid in front of it. It would be the precursor to a new era of prosperity and renewed sense of pride brought on by the election of Ronald Regan in November later that year.

A Mountain of Trouble

Mount St. Helens

Mt. St. Helens had been dormant for 130 years until March of 1980 when there became definite signs that the mountain was beginning to awaken from its long slumber. In the months that would follow, St. Helens would show the world exactly how a mountain can turn from a docile sleeping beauty into a destructive force of terror.

Located less than sixty miles northeast of Portland and part of the volcanic cascade range, St. Helens had been a fixture in the city skyline. I was always impressed with the beauty of St. Helens as it reminded me of pictures I had seen of Mt. Fuji in Japan. To me, it appeared in the Portland skyline as the perfect example of a cone-shaped volcano. I never dreamed I would witness it erupt, bellowing smoke and debris far in the atmosphere above.

In late March, the mountain showed signs of coming back to life with an earthquake of 4.0 magnitude shaking the mountain. A week later, steam vents were observed on the mountain, and for the next several months, a series of more quakes and venting continued. In addition, a massive bulge began forming on the mountain's north side.

I recall viewing news reports on the mountain as they shot video of the active steam vents that continued to emerge from the melting snow. There was a great deal of conjecture from geologists and those living near the mountain about what would happen next, but no one really knew. They only knew the mountain had awakened from its long dormancy and was alive with activity. It was all very fascinating and exciting, but no one expected the catastrophic events that were soon to shake the entire region literally to its core.

In early May, my friend and I decided we would drive as close to the volcano as we possibly could. We wanted to be a part of the action hoping to see anything of interest that we could go back and share with our friends. Eventually, we were stopped by a barricade in the road consisting of a number of forest rangers and sheriff deputies who had commandeered the highway and stopped access to the mountain. We certainly felt we should have been allowed closer to the mountain, and we told them so. However, they turned us away, along with many other curious spectators. Three weeks later, the location where we had been stopped by the authorities would absolutely be annihilated…buried in a sea of mud, ash, and splintered timber.

May 18th 1980

On the morning of May 18th, a large earthquake shook Mt. St. Helens. It weakened the entire north side of the mountain in the area where the large bulge had expanded during the previous months. This quake would initiate the largest landslide in recorded history as the north side of the mountain simply slid away at speeds of 110 to 155 mph toward Spirit Lake, destroying everything in its path. The massive landslide allowed the pressurized molten rock, gas, and steam to be released with violent force sending hot ash, gas, and debris 80,000 feet into the atmosphere. The debris would eventually spread across eleven states. It is estimated that the thermal energy released during the eruption was equal to 26 megatons of TNT.

It is presumed 57 people were killed by the eruption and the subsequent mudslides that followed. The eruption destroyed hundreds of square miles of what once was pristine forested land filled with thousands of animals. It was devastation at an unparalleled level leaving behind in its wake a landscape that looked like it had been hit by an atomic bomb.

There were five more major eruptions of St. Helen after the "big one," all of them spewing ash into the atmosphere. Depending on the prevailing winds, the debris would randomly spread in different geographic regions throughout America. I had experienced some strange things in life, but very few were as surreal as driving into Portland and observing a huge mushroom cloud above the city as if a bomb had been dropped.

Portland Skyline

I recall weather forecasts that year would, at times, include the phrase "light dusting of ash." I watched ash drift down from the sky like light snow covering everything in grey. There were towns in the direct path of the ash cloud where the day would nearly turn into night as the ash was so heavy in the air.

Mt. St Helens eventually settled down after the cataclysmic eruption in May of 1980, but those who were there to experience its wrath will never forget the power "mother nature" unleashed with such destructive force in the Pacific Northwest.

The entire Cascade mountain range is a chain of volcanic peaks extending from northern Washington to northern California. Though this range at the moment appears to be mostly dormant, as we learned from Mt. St. Helens, at any time, one of the giant beasts could awaken. I suppose that's why Volcano Insurance is included in my homeowner's policy.

The King is Dead and so is the Walrus

In August of 1977, the undisputed king of rock, Elvis Presley, was found dead in his Graceland home at the age of 42. It would eventually be disclosed that the cause of death was due to heart failure brought on by his abuse of barbiturates. In his later years, Elvis had become severely addicted to prescription drugs, and his health suffered greatly from this abuse.

Elvis Presley

A once lean and handsome man had become grossly obese and lethargic. It was a sad demise of a legend that inspired an entire generation of musicians. In his prime, there may have never been a more charismatic or handsome performer ever to step on stage. Elvis had looks and charm, as well as possessing indisputable talent. Anyone who disputes Elvis as the "King of Rock'n Roll" just doesn't know the history of rock music.

His death sent shock waves across the world, and thousands upon thousands mourned his death. Even President Jimmy Carter took the time to praise Elvis, stating that he had "permanently changed the face of American popular culture." An estimated 80,000 people lined the processional route of his funeral, and tens of thousands mourned his death across the country. He was indeed a legend that, to this very day, still carries considerable cache' in the pop culture world and will continue to do so for decades well into the future.

I clearly recall the moment I was told of his death. My mother (with tears in her eyes) informed my sisters and me of his untimely death. She adored Elvis and still does to this day. It was a sad moment indeed to see our mother so upset. She was not one to show great emotion about anything, but the loss of Elvis hit her hard, and it still pains her even today to discuss his demise and eventual death due to drug abuse.

Fat Elvis

As for me, the death of Elvis had no great impact. Of course, I was well aware of his stature as a star and well versed in his music and movies. Elvis, however, was my mother's idol...he was not mine. He was a bit before my time, and I was never captured by his charisma or charm as so many in the previous generation had been. I will say this about him...I don't think there has ever been a persona in rock 'n roll history like Elvis Presley. In his prime, I believe he was the "coolest" performer of the 20th century and is without a doubt the undisputed "King of Rock'n Roll."

The Assassination of John Lennon

On December 8th, 1980, rock'n roll would suffer another catastrophic loss. John Lennon (the former Beatle) was gunned down in front of his New York City apartment by Mark David Chapman. The death of John Lennon washed over the tv airwaves like a tidal wave. Walter Cronkite, the same man I had watched reporting soldier casualties in Vietnam a decade earlier, presided over the coverage of the death of a legend. The reporting of this tragic event went well into the night, and America watched in disbelief as the story was told of Lennon's life and his untimely death at the age of 40.

Until the release of his album "Double Fantasy" in November of 1980, Lennon had spent the previous five years living a reclusive life in New York City, raising his son with his wife, Yoko. He had retired from the music business for the most part and attempted to live a life of anonymity far away from the spotlight that had dogged him for years.

Ironically the release of "Double Fantasy" and Lennon's return to the industry that had made him wealthy and famous would cost him his life. Unbeknownst to anyone at the time, a mentally ill Mark David Chapman saw the return of John Lennon as an opportunity to gain fame by killing one of the most beloved figures in pop culture. Chapman was also incensed and jealous of Lennon's fame and lifestyle and took particular exception to Lennon's comments mistakenly taken out of context in 1966 when he said, "The Beatles were bigger than Jesus."

The death of John Lennon ended once and for all the hope that one day the Beatles would reunite as a band. There had been rumors and innuendos through the years, and of course, I had hoped they would someday put their differences behind them and produce more music for the world to enjoy. The three surviving members, however, did put their differences aside after Lennon's death to record a song dedicated to him titled "All those years ago," which they released six months after his death.

Lennon and Mark David Chapman

A photo would later surface showing Lennon actually signing an autograph for Chapman in front of his Dakota home. Several hours later, he would return from his recording studio only to be shot four times in the back by the same person he had kindly autographed a copy of his new album.

The man who had once dubbed himself "the walrus" in the famous Beatles song "I Am the Walrus" was slain in a senseless act of violence that resonates to this day.

Is still remember exactly where I was standing and what I was doing when I was told the news. I felt a wave of sadness wash over me at that moment, not only for John and his family but for myself and the loss of part of my childhood. A Beatle was dead, and all those happy and joyous musical moments they had filled my life with seemed to evaporate into thin air with the news of his murder.

I'm not sure rock 'n roll ever fully recovered from the deaths of its two icons just three years apart from one another. Elvis, the heart and soul of rock 'n roll, and Lennon, the "dreamer," both left this world far too early. The artistic loss of Lennon, in particular, is a vacuum still unfilled to this day, and I sometimes ponder what artistry he might have produced in the decades that have followed since he was stolen from all of us.

Lennon's murder had a profound impact on me, and it would turn out to be a musical pivot point, a crossroads if you will, in my journey with the art form. Until Lennon's death, I had followed a course (like most my age) guided by the current rock music scene listening to contemporary artists such as Styx, Van Halen, and Kiss. However, after Lennon's death, I found myself journeying back in time to the sixties when the British Invasion first hit America. I delved deep into all the Beatle albums and discovered they were so much more than just the hits I had heard on the radio in my youth. In addition, I took deep dives into the catalogs of other great bands that had been formed in the sixties, such as the Doors, the Rolling Stones, Pink Floyd, and the Who.

I spent at least a year after Lennon's death retracing the rock music of the sixties and digesting as much as I could find of that era, and when I finally emerged, I was a changed man. The contemporary mainstream rock music I had been following could no longer hold my interest. It suddenly sounded cheap…lacking in artistry and originality.

After Lennon's death, I quit following the current music trends of the time and stayed fixated on the artistry of the music created in the 60s and early 70s. To this day, I have never really left that platform, and I would debate with anyone that the peak of rock music lies within those two decades.

The Sage Recommends Psychedelics

In 1980 I met someone who would end up impacting me greatly in terms of my growth as a person. I met him through a friend of mine who worked with him. His name was Tom, and he was several years older than me or any of my other friends. From the outset, I could tell he was wiser and more mature than anyone I had befriended before. He was a short-order cook at a nearby restaurant with nothing more than a high school education. I saw him, however, as much more than a cook working at the local "greasy spoon." There was an inner calmness and intuitive nature about him that I picked up from the moment I met him.

Even his looks reminded me a little of John Lennon with eyeglasses to match. I knew there was something unique about this person, and though I really didn't see him that often, I always enjoyed the chance to converse with him. Eventually, my friend rented an apartment with Tom, and this gave me the opportunity to visit with him on a consistent basis.

As I grew to know him, I began to understand myself better as well. He was open about his "sensitive side," which I had never observed anyone near my age brave enough to reveal that side of themselves before. Until Tom, discussions with my friends were mostly superficial, comprised of "macho talk" regarding sports, women, and partying. However, Tom talked about writing poetry and his private feelings of inadequacy and insecurity. He was unafraid to share the type of feelings my friends and I felt were taboo and were never to be revealed.

Tom inspired me to write my first poem at the age of 19, and he opened my eyes to an artistic world I had never considered as being part of my purview. All of us looked up to Tom at some level, if for no other reason, he was 3 or 4 years older and was clearly wiser and more worldly than anyone we had been around. Therefore, I felt that if it was okay for *him* to reveal his sensitive side, no one could mock me for doing the same.

One day while over at his apartment, the subject came up about a large tapestry he had on the wall depicting a "nature scene" with all sorts of different animals intermixed cleverly within the trees and undergrowth of a forest. To be sure, there were a lot of things going on in that tapestry, but I was soon to find out there was much more happening than I would have ever conceived.

I commented to Tom that the tapestry had some interesting aspects to it when you *really* looked at it. He nodded and leaned back in his chair, gazing at the tapestry, and casually replied that there was more to it than what met the eye. I'm sure I must have looked at him rather puzzled, and then he said, "You see, I've been inside that world; I've been a part of that tapestry." I recall feeling a little uncomfortable with his nonsensical response, and I chuckled and said something like, "Yeah, right."

He leaned forward with a serious look and said, "Have you ever dropped LSD?" Well, my experience with LSD was limited to what I had observed in the depiction of its effect in the movie "Easy Rider." I shook my head and said, "No." He responded with something like, "You shouldn't laugh at something you no nothing about then." How could I argue with that? He was exactly right; I had no experience in the world of hallucinogens.

Tom went on to describe how he had been in the forest amongst the trees and the animals of the tapestry. He spoke in great detail about what the experience was like and how he had entered into another plane of existence or "dimension" through his mind with the help of LSD.

Well, all of this sounded "far out" to me and very cool. He went on to describe the whole experience of "dropping acid" from what kind to take and what to expect, and who to do it with. He explained a "trip" could last for hours and that it was important to be around people who had a positive "seeking" approach to life. He also offered up the idea I could try it for the first time with him as he could help guide me through the entire experience.

After talking to Tom about LSD, any fears I had about taking the drug were removed. There was no doubt that I wanted to try it, and someday soon, I would. Tom, over time, would share his experiences with the rest of my close friends until all of us felt comfortable with the idea of giving it a try.

Eventually, all of us did try "acid" and even dropped it with Tom on several occasions. The experience, just as Tom had described, was nothing short of incredible. I saw things I had never seen before. They were not hallucinations, but rather I viewed what was already objectively around me, however, with greater detail and awareness. It was as if another sense had been aroused in my brain above and beyond the five senses I already possessed. It also inspired deeper and more creative thinking, which I embraced with great interest.

The experience of taking LSD was the key that opened the last locked door to the inner creativity I had owned but had been unaware of my entire life. From that moment, my depth of thought and interest in creative ventures has never waned. I have no doubt that Tom (the sage), and the magic brew he had introduced, awakened the expressive nature of my existence, and without either of them, I would likely not be writing this book today.

My experience with LSD, however, was short-lived and lasted only several years that included approximately 20 "trips." As time went on, the "trips" became more intense and less about fun and a good time. They became serious ventures with thoughts so deep they scared me at times. My use ended soon after my best friend had a "bad trip" where he had pondered jumping off a freeway overpass, convinced nothing was real because we were on acid and, therefore, he could do whatever he wanted without consequence. It became clear LSD had been enlightening but it also had become clear it could be dangerous.

I have never regretted my time experimenting with LSD, but I know some who do. That being said, I have no interest in participating in that world ever again. I have lived far too much life since those early days, and I am not nearly brave enough (or perhaps naive enough) to ever go down that road again. It came into my life at the right time and exited before I experienced any ill effects. As I have already spoken of in this book, there are moments when timing can be everything, and my timing in the world of psychedelics turned out to be just right.

As far as Tom (the sage)? The last time I saw him, which was several decades ago, he had earned his master's degree in psychology. The sage had become a counselor, which seemed to me the perfect landing place for a man that had at one time provided me with great insight into my own life.

Acting Presidential

In January 1980, Ronald Reagan became the 40th President of the United States. A former actor in film and television, Reagan appeared in 53 films from 1937 to 1965 before entering the world of politics.

In 1967 Reagan became Governor of California and would serve in that position through 1975. He made his first legitimate presidential run for the Republican nomination in 1976 but lost to incumbent Gerald Ford. Undeterred by his defeat in 1976, Regan once again sought the nomination in 1980, and this time, he easily won over his Republican counterparts.

President Carter's administration had left America emotionally fragile due to the failure of his economic policies to arrest the long-standing stagflation issues of the 70s. He also failed to control soaring energy costs which hit Americans hard in the pocketbook and caused extreme frustration at the gas pump due to long lines and a shortage of gasoline. Coupled with his recent disastrous handling of the Iran hostage crisis, Carter had lost the support of most Americans, and few believed he was a strong leader capable of moving America forward.

Ronald Reagan

Reagan easily won the presidential election over Carter and began the process of rebuilding a staggering economy and, perhaps more importantly, rebuilding America's sense of pride that had taken serious blows due to Vietnam, Watergate, and the weak leadership of the Carter administration.

In his inaugural address, Reagan set the tone for his new administration and his vision for the future when he stated, "In this present crisis, the government is not the solution to our problems; government is the problem."

He believed it was the expansion of government that had created many of the issues America was currently facing. In his campaign, he had made it clear to the American public that his intent was to shrink government and allow the private sector to take the lead in economic growth. He believed tax cuts would stimulate economic growth, reversing the economic doldrums of the 70s.

Literally minutes after Reagan was inaugurated as the 40th President of the United States, the American hostages, who had been held captive in Iran since November of 1979, were freed from their captives. The Carter administration had been heavily engaged in exhaustive negotiations for months attempting to secure the release of the hostages. Carter desperately tried to complete this process before his term ended. However, the Iranian government would not allow Carter to have this final victory before he left office. The hostages instead would be freed in the opening moments of the Reagan administration, preventing Carter from claiming an "official" resolution to the crisis before his departure.

Reagan would immediately begin to restore confidence in government by initiating broad-based tax cuts as promised during his campaign. His promise to limit "government overreach" and put money back in the pockets of taxpayers was ultimately fulfilled and would be known as the focal point of his economic approach, which was later titled "Reaganomics." It was based on the "trickle-down" economic theory that argued cutting taxes on corporations and minimizing government regulations on the private sector would result in economic growth and stimulate job creation.

In the end, "Reaganomics" did reduce inflation and lower unemployment rates; however, social programs suffered, the national debt increased, and the gap between the wealthy and the poor became wider. As with any economic policy, there is a delicate balance that must be achieved to serve the many needs of a large society. Overall the economic policies of the Reagan era were a mixed bag. However, what did work well certainly helped the overall psyche of America's view of the future. The inflation and stagflation issues of the 70s had been successfully addressed, and a sense of optimism for the future once again returned to America.

On March 30, 1981, John Hinkley Jr. attempted to assassinate President Reagan in Washington, D.C. Reagan was entering his limousine after a speaking engagement at the Washington Hilton when Hinkley fired six shots into a small group escorting the President. Reagan was seriously injured when one of the bullets ricocheted off the limousine and struck him in the underarm, breaking a rib, puncturing a lung, and causing extensive internal bleeding. He was rushed to George Washington University Hospital, where he was stabilized and convalesced until his release on April 11th.

Hinkley, having obvious mental health issues, believed that through his assassination attempt on the President, he would draw the attention of actress Jodie Foster. Hinkley had been obsessed with Foster for years and was desperate to gain her attention. He was found not guilty of his crime by reason of insanity and was confined to a psychiatric facility.

The attempted assassination of Reagan ironically would boost the President's public approval rating above the 70 percent margin. His brave approach to the incident and strong recovery from the shooting emboldened his persona as the strong leader America had so desperately needed after Carter and Watergate.

America, not unlike its wounded President, appeared to be on the mend as there was growing optimism that better times were just beyond the next horizon. Regan's political prowess, along with the charismatic delivery of his vision for the future, had given the country just what it needed but had lacked for so long…a sense of confidence.

Challenging Times

Space Shuttle Columbia

On April 12th, 1981, the space shuttle orbiter Columbia made its maiden voyage into space and returned to Earth two days later after orbiting the Earth 36 times. The successful launch and landing of the first reusable winged spacecraft initiated a new era of space flight designed to provide an efficient method to send astronauts to manned space stations orbiting the Earth safely.

The successful launch and return of Columbia in 1981 began an era that has produced many scientific discoveries and further exploration into the cosmos. The development of a reusable spacecraft, including reusable rocket boosters, validated the use of space stations as a hub for scientific experimentation and space exploration.

Christa McAuliffe

After twenty-four successful shuttle craft missions, beginning with Columbia in 1981, tragedy would hit the space program on January 28, 1986. The explosion of the space shuttle Challenger just 73 seconds into its flight killed all seven members aboard and devastated the space shuttle program. On that fateful flight was a school teacher named Christa McAuliffe, who had been part of NASA's "School Teacher in Space" program.

Because a female high school teacher was a member of the crew (a NASA first), media attention was much higher for Challenger compared to other recent flights. In some ways, after twenty-four consecutive successful ventures into space, shuttle missions had become a relatively mundane practice. However, this mission was different due to McAuliffes' participation and her plans to teach two lessons to her class from space.

Many school children across the nation viewed the Challenger launch live. Extensive media coverage before the launch had set the table for schools throughout the country to utilize this historic mission to promote the space shuttle program and space exploration in general.

Challenger Explodes

Sadly, just a little over a minute after launch, children watched in confusion and then fear as debris from the explosion splintered across the sapphire sky. Initially, there was a general sense of disbelief as Challenger broke apart, with large pieces of structure flying off in multiple directions. It was one of those moments when anyone who watched the disaster unfold was caught between the reality of what their eyes were telling them and what their minds refused to believe.

As for me, the Challenger tragedy brought back deep-ceded memories of an incident that occurred nearly 20 years earlier. In February of 1967, the Apollo 1 crew was lost due to asphyxiation caused by an onboard fire during a pre-launch test. I recall the sadness around this incident, and those astronauts that would later speak of it in the years that followed almost spoke of it like it was "family business,"… sharing very little of their thoughts regarding the incident because of the horrific circumstances surrounding their deaths.

The fire in the command module was determined to be electrical in nature, and it spread with extreme speed due to the pressurized pure oxygen atmosphere within the cabin. The astronauts could not open the inward opening hatch due to the internal pressure within the cabin. Hence, they were trapped in the command module with no chance of escape.

Apollo 1 Capsule After Fire

In the case of the space shuttle tragedy, the cause was the failure of both the primary and secondary redundant O-ring seals in the shuttle's right solid rocket booster. Hot gases leaked through unsealed joints reaching the external tank resulting in the collapse of the entire external tank structure, causing catastrophic failure of the entire flight system.

The resulting extensive media coverage after the tragedy only exacerbated the pain felt by Americans. If the disaster wasn't bad enough on its own, the media made sure to show the impact it had on the school children who viewed the disaster in real-time. I was in my mid-twenties and felt the trauma from this incident, and it made me wonder how children were impacted by seeing this tragedy unfold right in front of their eyes. It was no doubt a devastating moment for all Americans and one that I clearly remember to this day.

The Challenger tragedy resulted in the suspension of the entire program for nearly three years as an exhaustive investigation took place to ascertain its effectiveness while also making recommendations for its improvement. It would resume in September of 1988 with the launching of Discovery and would continue launching many successful and scientifically important missions. In 2003, however, tragedy would strike the program once again when the space shuttle Columbia disintegrated while re-entering the earth's atmosphere killing all seven astronauts aboard.

NASA discontinued the Space Shuttle program in 2011 with the goal that private enterprise would begin developing reusable spacecraft to continue the practice of space exploration and scientific experimentation well into the 21st century.

Marginal Utility

Marginal Utility is an economic theory that defines (in the strictest of terms) "the satisfaction gained by the consumer from having one more unit of a product or service." This is a theory that is prevalent in basic Economics courses and one that I first became aware of while attending Portland State University during my freshman year. It is a simple concept that ultimately dovetails well with the law of "diminishing returns."

It is a fact that during my early years of college, I spent little attention to what I was being taught. For some reason, however, Marginal Utility struck me as a fascinating concept from the moment I was taught its meaning. Perhaps it was its simplicity wrapped up in the depth of my own thinking on the subject, but whatever the reason, I instantly identified Marginal Utility not only as an economic theory but a potential way of life.

From my perspective, the theory was fundamentally rooted in "decision-making." It was the consumer in this theory that determined when one more purchase of a particular product or service was no longer worth its cost. There comes a point with the purchase of any product when the perceived value can no longer justify its cost. We have all gone shopping and picked up an item we would like to purchase but, upon looking at the price, placed the product back on the shelf. Although we may have a use for the product and hold value in its acquisition, in the end, we deem it not worth the price we have to pay to obtain it.

I never forgot the theory of Marginal Utility, and throughout my college years, which eventually led to a degree in Sociology, I never came across a more useful concept. Most of what I learned in college I have long forgotten, but this simple economic theory based on the perceived value of goods and services has guided my decision-making my entire adult life.

Whether it was making a judicious decision regarding the purchase of a home, or a decision to continue or discontinue a personal relationship, the application of this theory has been an invaluable tool and one of the keys to my success.

Ultimately it comes down to whether the investment in time, emotion, or monetary expenditure is equal to or less than what I receive in return. If I cannot validate my investment from what I will receive in return, then it is a failed proposition and should be discontinued as soon as possible.

By my own admission, college was a struggle for me and, at times, left me wanting to walk out the door, never to return. However, there were a few lessons learned along the way that made the struggle worthwhile. These valuable lessons have benefited me greatly as I have applied them to "real life" scenarios resulting in positive outcomes. Marginal Utility sits at the top of this list of lessons learned. Without the application of this theory, I would not have had the level of success I have enjoyed in my adult life.

One never knows what pearls of wisdom may lie around the next corner, but the key is to recognize and seize upon this wisdom when you become aware of its presence. It is wise always to keep your senses in tune with any learning possibility, no matter what the source or the circumstances around it. Life is filled with these opportunities, and it's simply just a matter of keeping your mind open, recognizing that wisdom can be found at any time and from many different sources.

The Dating Slump Phenomenon

Throughout most of the summer of 1981, my romantic life had taken the obligatory "face dive" into the world of failure. I spent most of my free time hanging with my friends, busy doing nothing worthwhile. We were a gang of about five, and all big talkers full of testosterone. However, we lacked the experience or charisma to be "charmers" with the ladies.

For the most part, we were resigned to blind hope with the simple goal of procuring a one-night stand. The "macho talk" and feigned confidence we exhibited amongst each other would run and hide when confronted with the smiling face of a beautiful young woman.

At the age of twenty, chasing girls was the number one priority in our lives. It was above drinking, getting stoned, and even sports, but sadly none of us were proficient in "the hunt." All of us certainly had the ingredients to be successful in this endeavor, however, we lacked the one key ingredient to pull it all together, and that was experience.

We were uncomfortable and awkward in our efforts to integrate into a woman's world of advanced thinking and behavior. All of us, for the most part, were simple fools behaving more like sixteen-year-old boys than men in our twenties. Asking any of us to behave in a mature fashion for any sustained period of time was like asking a dog to stop wagging his tail. It was an exercise in futility.

I don't know how many young ladies I "turned off" by just opening my mouth. My appearance might have piqued their interest. However, my behavior would quickly have them looking for an escape route. I couldn't nail down exactly what I was doing wrong, but it was clear that things typically went awry soon after I engaged in conversation.

It is a commonly known fact (at least amongst the male gender) when you are in a dating slump, you can't seem to get a break to go your way. It's as if all women can sense you are on a losing streak and will stay clear of you as if there is a stench of "loser" permeating the air surrounding you.

I recall one time, after months of being on a long losing streak, my good friend tried to give me a helping hand. He, of course, understood the strange phenomenon of women sensing men in a slump as he had "been there.. done that" as well. He set up a meeting with two girls he had met at a party several weeks earlier and told me these two were guaranteed to get me out of my slump. When I inquired which of the two I should focus my attention on, he flippantly responded, "Who cares...trust me, it ain't gonna matter with these two."

All of it seemed like a pretty darn good plan to me, and although my pride might have been slightly damaged with this designed "fix-up," I was more than willing to do whatever it took to break my slump. In addition, it appeared these two young ladies were "just what the doctor ordered," as my friend guaranteed a successful night of unbounded affection with this promiscuous pair.

In the end, it was a grand success…for my friend. I spent the last part of the evening playing chauffeur while he sat in the back seat with two girls cuddling and kissing as I drove them around. I once again felt like that boy who, a decade earlier, had walked around the neighborhood with his sisters looking for someone who wanted to play. It was humiliating and appalling at the same time. In the end, my friend, who had made a sincere effort to help me out, realized the stench of my slump was far too potent to overcome. Knowing I was an anchor to his plans, he made a choice to entertain both young women while I watched in the rearview mirror. It was battlefield conditions, and I couldn't blame him for his actions as he did the only thing he could do at that moment…he saved himself.

More profoundly, however, the question still exists of why this phenomenon occurs. There are some obvious reasons, and then there are more subtle causes for "dating slumps." Perhaps the most important issue is one's own state of mind. Perception often becomes a reality, and if the individual perceives themselves as an unwanted commodity, they have unconsciously already created an aura of failure.

This "aura" can manifest in many forms, but often, it is created through nonverbal communication. The slumped shoulders, quick nervous glances, and solemn smiles are all clues to the observer that confidence is waning in the individual. Many women, I have found, possess an uncanny intuition that can often pick up on these subtle nonverbal clues much better than men. In addition, through the individual's own self-doubt, I believe a negative psychic energy may also be released, which is picked up not only by one but by many within a group setting.

In a very true sense, the individual experiencing a "dating slump" has unknowingly exacerbated the situation through their own thoughts. A negative reality is thus created not only for themselves but also projected into the minds of others. Often a person will become what they perceive themselves to be, resulting in others unconsciously abiding by these same projected perceptions.

This phenomenon, of course, can be extrapolated far beyond the "dating scene" and can impact all areas of our lives, from our sense of overall happiness to our physical health. It is, of course, this mental aspect of existence itself that indeed creates our perception of physical reality as well as the perception of ourselves. It ultimately will define everything we know and everything we feel.

Losing control of your positive mental imagery and the perception of your own self-worth can indeed be a dangerous proposition. The loss of a positive mental approach to life and instead embracing the world of negativity can create catastrophic outcomes. It can lead anyone towards an existence filled with unhappiness derived from a false belief of "unworthiness." It is always wise to walk towards the light of optimism and avoid the dark path of negativity.

Eventually, I fought my way through the "dating slump" by not giving into my current circumstance. I continued to take my turn at bat, and whether I struck out or not was nearly as important as having the courage to continue to step up to the plate. Either through random luck or persistence, things began to fall my way, and the small victories I experienced eventually coalesced into newfound confidence. Those around me, including the young ladies I was trying to impress, could sense the growing confidence within me as well as the positive energy I was now projecting. The slump had ended because my mental approach demanded outcomes that would result in success rather than failure.

And Then I Saw Her Face....

It was a crisp fall evening, October 23rd, 1981, to be exact. I had turned twenty the prior month and was beginning my third year of futility at Portland State University. I had started the school year with a new sense of purpose and had struck out to do much better or at least make an attempt to attend my classes.

I had left my teenage years behind and entered the decade of my twenties with a new sense of determination. I was ready to take the next step in my life, finally assuming responsibility for my future and taking the "present" much more seriously. I had done just that during the first month of school, and it appeared I had found some sense of rhythm and balance between the activities of school, work, and play.

About this same time, I began the practice of attending fraternity parties located in the west hills near the campus of Portland State. It had become one of my favorite leisure time activities on weekends. The two main reasons for my interest in "frat parties" was a mystery to no one who attended these social affairs. Underage drinking was condoned, and beer flowed from kegs like wine from the carafes in the fancy restaurants located in the city below. In addition, there was a fresh new stock of young female students who were always invited to attend.

I did not belong to a fraternity, nor did any of my friends, but we were students of the university and therefore had been clued into the "happenings" of these late-night parties. Gaining entrance into these social gatherings was never an issue, and only a nominal fee was required. The investment in time and money seemed almost always to pay dividends.

A good time was guaranteed for all, with plenty of loud rock music to enjoy along with an organized distribution of beer, unlike anything I had ever seen before. It was an advanced course in "partying," to be sure, coupled with unparalleled efficiency and a sense of purpose. There was no question these parties were a grade above your standard after work or "friend of a friend" party, and they included the most important aspect for any twenty-year-old male.. a vast array of female counterparts to pursue.

On the evening of October 23rd, I attended one of these frat parties and met the girl I would eventually marry. She stood alone in the basement of the fraternity house where the kegs of beer had been placed. I poured myself two beers and approached her with one in each hand. I offered her one of the beers, and she flashed a fragile smile and said, "Thank You."

Kim was a blonde with ice-blue eyes and possessed a homespun "natural" look, which I found attractive. She was of Norwegian descent, and her appearance fit that description quite nicely. She was not someone who would necessarily have stood out in a crowd, but if one looked hard enough, her natural beauty was on display.

Although she was not charismatic in the least, she did appear affable and willing to engage in conversation with me. We talked at length, at times almost yelling, in an effort to hear above the loud music. I discovered she was not a student at Portland State, rather, she had been invited by a girlfriend who attended the university, and it had been a last-minute decision for her even to attend the party.

We spent the rest of the evening conversing and laughing and making the usual "small talk" to get through the awkward moments. When it was time to go, I boldly asked if I could drive her home, and to my surprise, she accepted the offer. I drove her across town to her parent's home in a remote but wealthy area of east Portland and left with her phone number in hand.

It was not long after that first encounter that we began our relationship as a couple. She was my first steady girlfriend to speak of, and I enjoyed having a female counterpart to do adult things with. Our endeavors together were far different from my usual "hanging with the boys," chugging beer and throwing up. I quickly fell for Kim and was more than willing to sacrifice my time with my friends and redirect it toward her.

It wasn't long after our first meeting though that I observed some cracks in her mental health. I pushed these observations aside because I was enjoying myself too much, and I was falling in love with the idea of "falling in love." Kim's upbringing had been far different than mine, and her outlook on life and perception of herself was less than positive, in my opinion. Her self-image had been damaged during her upbringing, and she saw life not full of exciting possibilities but filled with potential dread and eventual disappointment. She had no concept of how to "control your own reality," as I had been taught by my father. Instead, Kim believed she was a victim of life and had little or no control over her happiness, and it was in the hands of others to determine her fate.

I learned over time through Kim and my own personal observations that her mother was inflicted with serious mental health issues. Particularly obvious to me was her manic behavior. Kim had told me stories of enduring not only mental abuse from her mother on a regular basis but also physical abuse at times as well. Deep down, Kim may have had a heart of gold, but it had been severely tarnished by a mother whose mental health issues permeated and destroyed any positive aspects Kim tried to develop as a child.

The emotional abuse at the hands of her mother would leave scars that were never to be healed. It is a prime example of just how important it is as parents that we create a loving, positive environment free from dysfunction for our children. The humbling truth is that the dysfunction exposed to our children will most likely be passed down to the next generation. It becomes a perpetuating cycle of pain and sadness, often burdening those we love the most for the rest of their lives.

As for me, my immaturity did not help the situation. I sensed her weakness and took advantage of it to do as I pleased. The novelty of having a girlfriend soon wore off, and I was back to wanting to party with my friends. Instead of nurturing Kim and showing her a way out of her untenable situation with her mother, I piled on at times, offering no relief from the dysfunction that was embedded into her family life.

At twenty, I was completely devoid of any wisdom about how to handle this sensitive situation. I was selfish and steeped in "machoism" and in no way prepared to deal with such deep psychological matters. Kim would have been much better off dating an older, more mature man, but either by choice or by random circumstance, she chose poorly… as did I.

It no longer matters who is to blame or what choices we could have made that might have yielded different results. The randomness of life had thrown us together, and neither of us possessed the wisdom or fortitude to walk away from a relationship destined to fail. It would indeed be a relationship we both would learn to regret in the years that would follow. There was no crystal ball to look into our future, so we simply just followed the path we currently found ourselves on. It didn't matter where it was headed. Even if we had wanted to change course, we lacked the wisdom to do so.

The time would come when we would face the reckoning of our own bad choices and behavior. However, before that would occur, we would drain our very souls to save a relationship that was never worth saving in the first place. It would be a destiny that we should have and could have avoided, but instead, we drug each other into deep waters and drown ourselves in heartbreak and failure.

I Want My MTV

In August of 1981, a new cable program premiered titled "MTV." The establishment of this network, designed to promote popular music utilizing video accompaniment, became a massive success in

MTV

the decade of the 80s. The first video aired on the new cable network, "Video Killed the Radio Star," ironically foretold the future of popular music, where visual presentation became just as important as the music itself. MTV's impact on popular music cannot be understated. It changed the entire industry in the sense that it created a new medium to market music and promoted the artists that performed it.

Michael Nesmith of "The Monkees" fame is widely considered the creator of the first contemporary music video. Unlike all videos before, which simply filmed musicians performing a song, Nesmith's video for his song "Rio" had a "skit-like" feel designed

Michael Nesmith

to support the lyrics of the song. "Rio" was released in 1977 and received critical acclaim for its originality in presenting music in this new video format of "storytelling." Inspired by its success, Nesmith continued to push the idea of the music video and is credited for the creation of the first cable music video show, "Pop Clips," which aired on the Nickelodeon cable network in 1980. The show was subsequently sold to the Time Warner/Amex consortium, which developed "Pop Clips" into MTV.

MTV found a youthful audience almost immediately as it provided around-the-clock music videos to digest at any time of the day. The show was hosted by "VJs" (Video Jockey), who played the role of a typical Disc Jockey who spun records on the radio. The beauty of MTV was that it expanded not only the reach of popular music but also the variety of music available to the viewer. It wasn't long after MTV was introduced that music from groups who received no radio airplay was in demand at record stores due to their music videos being played on the network. Soon after its debut, music industry executives realized the power of MTV in marketing their products. It was indeed a powerful marketing tool that grabbed its audience with a new visual aspect added to the music they were already listening to.

There is no doubt the music video was the impetus for some "ordinary" mainstream artists to gain a strong foothold in popularity due to their release of a video to accompany their music. While other's, in particular newcomers, used the music video to launch their careers, with some gaining immediate notoriety for their creative depiction of their music utilizing the video format.

Perhaps no artist benefited more from the music video than Madonna. It was one thing to listen to Madonna's music which was fresh and innovative, but quite another to see her perform her songs in the video format. Madonna exuded confidence and charisma rarely seen before in a female performer. She was bold, unafraid, and incredibly sexy, all in the same breath. Madonnas' 1984 hit "Like a Virgin" showed her seductively rolling around in a white wedding dress, and it was simply eye-popping. I recall watching the video for the first time and wanting to rewind it and watch it over again immediately.

Madonna

That was the genius of MTV; the videos would grab your attention, leaving you always wanting more. Madonna, with her undeniable sex appeal coupled with obvious talent, quickly became the "Queen of Pop." She claimed this title primarily through the success of her unforgettable music video performances in which she pushed the limits of what was deemed "appropriate" for young viewers at the time.

There are far too many groups and individuals of note that found incredible success through MTV. However, some of the most notable in the decade were: Duran Duran, Hall & Oats, Madonna, Micheal Jackson, and Billy Idol, but there were also many more. Soon after MTV's arrival, the music video took on the role of not only a marketing tool but an actual art form. It could express the complete idea and intent of the performer's musical creation like no other medium. Eventually, it became unclear at times whether the video was made for the song or the song made for the video, but it didn't matter as this new medium had found a permanent place in popular music.

Thriller

Perhaps the pinnacle of the "music video" occurred in 1983 with the release of Micheal Jacksons' "Thriller." Made at a cost of half a million dollars, the video was directed by well-known Hollywood director John Landis and was an unprecedented 14 minutes long. It was more in the vein of a short film than an actual music video, and with pop's biggest icon performing in the starring role, the video was simply a "can't miss" piece of popular art.

I recall watching the premier of the video and was raptured by the entire production of it, from the storyline to the music and the incredible dancing. With "Thriller," the music video reached a new level of music entertainment, and it catapulted Micheal Jackson into even greater stardom, doubling the sales of his album of the same name and helping it to become the best-selling album in history.

There is no doubt that the birth of the MTV network was one the biggest events in popular music since the Beatles, and much like the Beatles, its lasting impact is still felt to this day. Sadly MTV would later become a shadow of its former self, more focused on "reality shows" than the art form it helped to create.

Big City Lights

By the summer of 1983, I was fed up with the climate of the Pacific Northwest, and that summer produced some of the worst weather in Portland I could ever remember. Cloudy skies and cool temperatures had ruined the precious few months of warm weather and sunshine Oregonians counted on.

Kim and I had just returned from a trip to Los Angeles to visit my sister (Kelly) and her boyfriend (Dieter), and I fell in love with the palm trees and sunny skies that permeated the Southern California region. I was also enthralled by the fast pace and flash of a big city, and this was just not another big city by any means. This was home to Hollywood and all the glitter and glamour that came with it. Los Angeles had everything a young man could dream of, and I was determined to move and experience life outside the confines of Portland, Oregon.

The opportunity to move south came soon enough through Dieter, who had procured a job for me where he worked. It was a Customs House brokerage firm located in downtown L.A. and was a professional-level opportunity for me, unlike the retail job I currently held. I had also recently given up on college, as my dad had, in no uncertain terms, stopped funding my academic failures. I had long ago stopped caring about getting a degree, and it was a relief to have all that behind me finally. There was nothing keeping me tied to the city of Portland other than Kim, and I had successfully talked her into joining me on this bold Southern California adventure.

We departed in August of 1983, and for the first time in my life, I had moved far away from home. Sure, I had lived some 200 miles away during my freshman year of college, but this move was in a different state and nearly a thousand miles away from Portland. Kim and I packed up all of our belongings into a U-Haul and left the rain of the Pacific Northwest behind, and headed for the sunshine of southern California.

We shared an apartment located just off Hollywood Boulevard with Kelly and Dieter. It was a major departure for both Kim and me in almost every possible way, and it was all new and exciting to us. Every day seemed like an adventure living in a new environment with different jobs and a far different culture. On the weekends, we went to Santa Monica or Venice and frolicked on the beach. It was great fun to be young and feel free in such a beautiful area. In the evenings, we would make our sojourn into the heart of Hollywood onto Sunset Boulevard, where we would hit our favorite weekend night spot. The Rainbow Bar and Grill.

The Rainbow was a historic rock 'n roll venue as a decade earlier, the likes of Alice Cooper, John Lennon, Harry Nilsen, Keith Moon, Ringo Starr, and others would often frequent it. These rock stars would convene upstairs in an area they had named "The Lair of the Vampires" and would participate in heavy drinking and partying well into the night. There was certainly a mystique about the Rainbow, and it was a fantastic place to drink, listen to music, and dance. Occasionally one would even see a celebrity hanging out at the club, and though the Rainbow was no longer the draw it had once been for rock stars of the 70s, it still carried considerable cache'.

We had great fun participating in the nightlife of Hollywood, and there was a sense that I was now part of the glamour and mystique I had grown up hearing about. This was where the stars of the '50s and '60s had made their home. It was where Marilyn Monroe and James Dean had once walked, and it was where I was now roaming.

What made it even more intriguing was that Dieter had an uncanny resemblance to Rod Stewart, and to some degree, I resembled another rock star named Rick Springfield. It would not be that uncommon to see us strutting down the boulevard with heads turning and people believing they were in the presence of rock stars. Hey, it was LA, and anything was possible!

Several years later, when we walked downtown Portland our rock star images had turned to dust. Instead of looks of awe from those we passed, we were accosted with phrases such as "God damn faggots!" A thousand miles can make a big difference in how people perceive you.

In any case, Los Angeles was great fun…for a while. Sadly Kim did not adjust to life as easily as I had done, and she soon became disenchanted with the entire adventure. Her mood swings became more frequent and, at times, became public spectacles. One time while at Disneyland, Kim, for reasons I cannot remember, physically assaulted me in "Tomorrow Land" in front of a large crowd. Through her shrills and pounding fists, I could see mothers grabbing their children, shielding them from the debacle which was unfolding in front of them. The whole experience was embarrassing and traumatic. It would be a scenario repeated on several occasions in the public domain from Hollywood to Pasadena and often and with little warning.

Her hysterical behavior could now be expected to occur at the most unexpected times, and this variable alone made it difficult to relax and fully enjoy any outing in public. One could never be quite sure if Kim was going to have a "manic event" at the most inopportune time. All of this only added stress to our relationship.

In fairness, I did my part to denigrate the relationship even further through my descent into the world of gambling. Prior to my move to Los Angeles, I had never considered gambling or even how to go about it if I wanted to place a bet. Then one day, a co-worker confided that he was a "bookie," and if I ever wanted to place a bet, he could handle the transaction for me. As a long-time fan of football, I was instantly intrigued by this prospect and foolishly thought that my extensive knowledge of football would make gambling an easy money maker for me. Boy, was I wrong!!

Of course, the worst thing that could have possibly happened occurred right from the beginning…I won. This only instilled the naive assumption that I was in for a windfall of cash. I soon began to daydream about all the furniture I would buy and, with a little luck, possibly even a new car. I figured that eventually, I could quit my 9 to 5 job and just gamble for a living. Who needed a college degree with my acumen in football?

It wasn't long after these fantasies of "easy money" originated in my brain that the wheels came off on my new business venture. I found myself swearing at the tv while watching football and sweating out the results of games. I was baffled and stunned that I was actually losing money on my bets. However, that didn't stop me from gambling.

Every weekend became a cascade of one bad decision compounded by another and then another. I began Sunday morning with two $50 dollar bets and would subsequently lose both. Knowing I couldn't really afford to lose the $100, I would then bet an equal amount on two-afternoon games in an effort to "break even." Of course, as fate would have it, I would lose both of those games as well and found myself in a $200 hole.

Knowing there was no way I could afford to lose $200, I did the only reasonable thing any gambler would have done. I bet $200 on the "Monday Night Football" game to recover my losses. Sadly, by Tuesday morning, I was facing a $400 hole, and I was left staring at my face in the mirror in total disgust. I can honestly say it was the only time I have ever "hated myself" as I was so ashamed of losing so much money.. and for nothing. It got to the point where I would receive my paycheck on Friday, go to the bank, and cash it, only to hand all of it over to my bookie.

It wasn't long after I began throwing money away that Kim began to question me on why we were struggling to pay our bills. She had no idea I was gambling, but she also had little budgeting experience and allowed me to handle the bill paying. Because of this, I was able to bullshit my way out of the corner I had painted us both into. She would say things like, "We are making good money. Why can't we pay our bills on time?" My response would be a simple shrug of my shoulders, saying something like, "Hey, it's LA. It's expensive here."

Things came to a head in early December when Kim decided she had enough of me and of Los Angeles. She packed up her belongings and left sometime around Christmas. I can't say I was devastated, but I also wasn't happy about her departure. Things were not the same after she left, and the excitement of LA had been drained from me due to my betting exploits and a failed relationship.

Fortunately, I had gotten off the gambling merry-go-round and had saved a little money to finance a trip back home a few months later. But once again, I returned with my tail between my legs in another failed effort to live independently from home. Upon arrival back in Portland, I was able to get my old retail job back, and soon after, I found myself back in the old routine of doing a whole lot of nothing with my friends. I then went about pursuing Kim in an effort to get her back, and to the detriment of both of us, she relented, and we became a dysfunctional couple once again. There is nothing quite like repeating the same mistake over and over, and we both got really good at it.

And Now for Act II...

By the fall of 1984, the race for the Presidency was in full throttle. Ronald Reagan, the incumbent, had built an incredibly strong backing due to the success of the prior four years of his administration. Reagan was credited for many things that, at a minimum, had a huge impact on the psyche of Americans.

Known as the "Great Communicator," he effectively gained wide support throughout the country due to not only the policies he had implemented but through his ability to "reach" his fellow Americans. He was charismatic and possessed a good sense of humor, but more importantly, he also presented himself as a strong, confident leader.

Reagan had put the doldrums of the 70s behind us and replaced them with a sense of patriotism and strong family values. Both of these valued characteristics had seen considerable erosion over the previous two decades. He had Americans believing in America once again, and the sense of pride he stirred within its citizens was something I had not witnessed in my lifetime.

The momentum he had created with his successful abatement of the long-standing stagnation and inflation issues was felt throughout the country. His determination to deregulate industry to stimulate the economy had worked, and most Americans felt optimistic about the future.

In addition, Reagan had stood up to the Soviets and demonstrated a certain "mettle" not seen since John F. Kennedy. He boldly spoke about the evils of communism and the Soviet Union and showed no weakness or hesitation when it came to his approach. In fact, he did just the opposite by revolutionizing the United States' national defense through increased technological exploration in an effort to enhance its military prowess.

Under President Carter, the United States military appeared feckless and unprepared, especially after the Iranian hostage debacle. Reagan wiped away all of those misconceptions during his four years as president. Americans once again felt confident the nation could defend itself against "all comers" bold enough to challenge the greatest democracy in the world. With Reagan holding the reign, Americans once again took the attitude of "You want a fight…we'll give you a fight." It felt good to believe in America again.

In 1984 Reagan was pitted against Democrat Walter Mondale in the run for the White House. Mondale had chosen Geraldine Ferraro as his Vice Presidential running mate, which was a first. No major party had ever chosen a female to be part of a presidential ticket prior to this choice. Mondale himself had been Vice President under Jimmy Carter and had just won a difficult primary race, having not been decided until the Democratic National Convention.

Mondale attempted to differentiate himself from Reagan in four major areas. He promised to reduce the federal debt, expand social programs, and implement a nuclear freeze, and he pushed for the passing of the Equal Rights Amendment. In the end, he had no chance against Reagan, who enjoyed an approval rating of 58% on the eve of the election. In what would be one of the largest victories in American history, Reagan ran away with the election. He garnered 525 of the available 538 electoral votes, with Mondale only winning (by the slightest margin) his home state of Minnesota. It was a major testament to Reagan's popularity and the country's overall satisfaction with his policies and leadership over the previous four years.

Big News Heard Around "My World"

It was a cold December morning in 1984, and it started out with great anticipation of fun and good times. Dieter (who was visiting from Los Angeles) and I were embarking on a ski trip to Mount Hood. We had loaded ourselves on the public ski bus, which ran daily to Timberline Lodge, one of the most popular skiing areas in Oregon. Just a mere 50 miles from Portland, it was an easy jaunt for those who resided in the city, and it also offered night skiing which was an experience unto itself.

We arrived in the late morning with light snow falling…it was pristine. The skiing was great, and later in the afternoon, we joined some friends who had driven up later in the day. We skied all day, drinking Southern Comfort from bota bags and enjoying life. In fact, we were having so much fun that Dieter and I decided to stay well into the evening with our friends as we chose to bale on our bus ride home that had left late in the afternoon. Of course, this meant our only way off of the mountain was to hitch a ride with our friends. The problem with that scenario was that they had driven a Ford Courier to the lodge, and it was a very small pickup truck, only having room for two people in the cab. After many draws off of the bota bag Dieter and I had concluded, "Just how bad could it be riding in the back of a pickup truck in sub-freezing temperatures from Oregon's tallest peak at night?"

Well it was a certainly cold ride home, but we bundled up best we could and stared at the blanket of stars above us to pass the time. The "Walkman" cassette player we had brought and had been listening to on the way home eventually froze up due to the cold and slowly came to a grinding halt.

I can't say it was a terrible trip home. On the contrary, it was unique, and unlike any ride I had been on in my life. Would I do it again…well, probably not, but I was young and free and didn't have a care in the world. It was fun, and it would certainly be a story worth telling for years to come. Little did I know, however, that it would be the last time I would feel that way in my life. Things were about to change radically, and it would happen at the end of that magical trip home.

I was dropped off at Kim's apartment at approximately 11:00 that evening, and by 11:30, I was immersed in another storm of her hysterical behavior. This time, however, it wasn't based on the fact that I had arrived home late that evening or that I was having too much fun without her. No, this was something quite different. After doing my best to calm her down, she was finally able to explain what caused her emotional outburst…she was pregnant.

Indeed that was "The big news heard around my world!" In a single moment, my life changed, and my future radically altered. Just hours before, I was chugging Southern Comfort on a ski slope, and now I was an expectant father. Abortion was out of the question for both of us. Therefore, it became an undeniable fact that I was to become a father within eight months.

Of course, there was only one option in my mind to consider, and that was to marry Kim. The fact was that I loved Kim but never intended to marry her. The news of her pregnancy, however, had changed all of that. Until then, I was biding my time, just waiting for an unforeseen circumstance to change my fate, and indeed fate did intervene. Would I have married Kim had she not become pregnant? The answer would have been a definitive "no." However, my ability to make that choice had now been taken away from me. Fate had called me in a direction I had never intended for myself, but I no longer had the freedom to make a course correction. There was a baby on the way who would need a father.

Many of my friends and family questioned just how this pregnancy could have happened. After all, Kim had been on birth control for several years without any such "accident" occurring. Speculation ran rampant that she had wanted to trap me permanently in the relationship. As for me, I never questioned her motive as, to me, it was completely irrelevant. The fact was she was pregnant regardless of how it had occurred, and there was only one choice left to me…marry her.

On February 16th, 1985, we were married in a relatively small ceremony. Kim's mother, Sandy, was aghast at the whole marriage idea. She hated me as she did most men, including her husband. Sandy was finally coerced not to wear black at our wedding as she made it clear to Kim that it was a day of mourning, *not* celebration. Her rudeness was palatable, and it extended beyond me to my family and friends as well. She even refused to acknowledge my parents when introduced to them on the day of the wedding. She simply turned her back and walked away, completely ignoring their extended hands of greeting, leaving her father to apologize for her disrespectful behavior.

The wedding reception was held at Kim's parent's home, and not one of my family or friends attended as they wanted no part of her mother's behavior any longer. All of them basically said, "Hey, I wish you the best, but I'm not going to be subjected to that nonsense any longer." Of course, I couldn't blame them, as I didn't even want to be there either, but obviously had no choice in the matter.

After our honeymoon weekend on the Oregon coast, Kim and I set up house in a small two-bedroom duplex. We began our lives as a married couple and waited for our new arrival, due in late August. We had been placed in a scenario in which we both were completely unprepared to deal with. Just months prior, I had been living with my parents, with my mother still doing my laundry. On the other hand, Kim was still struggling with her personal demons and was emotionally fragile as ever and now faced the additional burden of motherhood. What could go wrong…right? One thing was clear at the age of 23, I was way in over my head, and I most definitely knew it.

Awareness Born From Crumbling Rock

Rock Hudson

Rock Hudson was a prolific and well-loved movie star of the 50s and 60s. "The Rock" had looks, talent, and the adoration of women across the world. Hudson starred in dozens of movies in his three-decade career and was the "poster boy" for what would be considered a handsome debonaire movie star of that era.

Hudson rode his looks and talent to stardom and was one of the most sought-after actors during his peak. By the early 70s, however, his fame had faded due to poor scripts and ill-conceived movies that did poorly at the box office. Hudson then turned to tv and found a niche in "made for tv movies" and several television series, including the successful "McMillan & Wife."

Like many stars of his time, Rock indulged heavily in alcohol and tobacco. By the early '80s, his looks had abandoned him as well as his health, suffering a heart attack in 1981. The once irresistible man whom men wanted to be like, and women wanted to be with was clearly showing signs of wear and tear from his provocative lifestyle.

Ailing Rock Hudson

As it turned out, Rock Hudson had far bigger health issues of a much more dangerous nature than just his "hard living." On June 5th, 1984, Hudson was diagnosed with HIV, which just one year earlier had been determined to cause the disease AIDS.

There had been rumors and innuendo regarding the declining health of Hudson, but it was clear from his most recent appearances that he was ailing. Initially, his publicist had stated Hudson's deteriorating health was due to inoperable liver cancer. However, several days later, it was confirmed that he had, in fact, contracted AIDS.

The disease was a relatively new phenomenon, and it received minimal media coverage at the beginning of the 80s. The early cases centered around drug needle injection users and gay men but would eventually impact heterosexuals as well. HIV/AIDS would reach epidemic proportions by the mid-'90s, with over 40,000 deaths attributed to the virus. In the early 80's, however, it received little national attention until the announcement of Hudson's condition.

Although a well-kept secret in the Hollywood community, Hudsons' illness also exposed his private life and made public the fact that he was gay. This was stunning news to the general population as, for many, he would be the last celebrity anyone would consider to be a homosexual.

I was as stunned just as everyone else by the revelation that "The Rock" was a gay man. Hudson would die from the disease a few months later, but with his public pronouncement regarding his condition, AIDS was now receiving the media attention it deserved as a life-threatening disease.

Until the death of Rock Hudson, the general public paid little attention to AIDS. With the loss of such an icon as Hudson, Americans became keenly aware of this new "killer." Public discussion regarding the dangers and fatal nature of this disease became commonplace, with dialogue focusing on awareness, prevention, and of course, a cure. In a way he could have never imagined, Rock Hudson's death had served as an impetus to AIDS awareness. His untimely demise had brought the disease out of the shadows of the gay community and into mainstream society.

Sadly there would be several more well-known celebrities who would fall victim to this heinous disease in the early 90s. It would take the lives of two performers whose public images could not have been more disparate from each other; Robert Reed and Freddie Mercury. Both men died within six months of one another from complications related to AIDS/HIV, and their deaths only increased public concern about the fatal nature of this disease.

Robert Reed was well known as the tempered and compassionate father of six in the hit 70's television show "The Brady Bunch," and Freddie Mercury was the lead singer and frontman for one of the biggest rock bands of the 70s and 80s.

The "Brady Bunch," a television staple for those of my generation, had become an after-school viewing routine for many who grew up in the 70s. Reed's portrayal of "Mike Brady," the father who loved his adopted children as much as his own and who always provided the right advice at the right moment, was seen as an ideal "father figure." The fact that Reed had died of AIDS in addition to being a gay man was something none of us who had watched the show could have ever possibly imagined. Reed, like Rock Hudson, had kept his sexual orientation a secret from the general public.

Robert Reed

The flamboyant Freddie Mercury, on the other hand, had left no doubt regarding his sexual orientation. He was bold and unapologetic about his behavior on stage or in his private life. As

Freddie Mercury

the lead singer for "Queen," he became an international star and was unabashedly open about his diverse sexuality. Rumors about his health had started to circulate when Queen chose not to tour after the release of their album "The Miracle." It had always been standard practice for Queen, and most rock bands for that matter, to go on tour and support their new album. Soon questions from the media arose about why Queen was absent from the touring circuit. Although the band was aware Freddie was ill, they denied it to the public and made veiled excuses why the band chose not to tour.

Mercury's obvious physical deterioration in the months that followed, particularly his conspicuous weight loss, led many people to believe his frail physical condition was attributed to AIDS/HIV. Before the death of Rock Hudson, anything could have been attributed to Mercury's decline in health. However, now with increased public awareness of the disease, many were not surprised when the announcement was made the day before his death that he had contracted AIDS. Freddie Mercury was a rock 'n roll "original," and AIDS had taken one of its brightest and most talented stars. It would indeed take many more lives throughout the decade of the 90s as it reached epidemic proportions.

Eventually, treatment would be developed that would greatly diminish the death rate for those who contract the AIDS/HIV virus. Unfortunately, for two decades, it wreaked havoc across the world, destroying the lives of hundreds of thousands of people while also perpetuating an atmosphere of bigotry toward the gay community. It was indeed a dark cloud of death and fear that hung over the entire world during the last two decades of the 20th century.

The Soviet Union has a "Meltdown"

On April 26, 1986, the first "Level 7" nuclear accident in human history was recorded. "Level 7" is the most severe level of a nuclear mishap possible. It occurred at the Chernobyl Nuclear Power Plant near the city of Pripyat in the Soviet Union (now Ukraine). The accident occurred during a safety test, and as is almost always the case, human error caused the meltdown due to operator error and design flaws.

News of this event was indeed terrifying, and it placed great scrutiny on nuclear fusion as a safe energy source. Less than ten years earlier, the United States had also suffered its own nuclear accident resulting in a partial core meltdown at Three Mile Island in Pennsylvania. Chernobyl, however, was a much more severe scenario spreading radioactive contamination not only through Russia but also through a substantial portion of Europe. Radioactive material released from the meltdown has been estimated at four hundred times greater than both the Hiroshima and Nagasaki atomic bombings put together.

Chernobyl

Massive cleanup efforts were made, costing billions of dollars, and nearly a half million people participated in "cleansing" the area. The Soviet government believed it was critical, on a psychological level, to re-populate the area as quickly as possible. It believed it could minimize scrutiny over its nuclear energy program by quickly making the affected area habitable once again. The massive cost of the cleanup and the harm Chernobyl caused, not only through radioactive contamination, but also to the Soviet Union's pride and reputation, is considered one of the main contributors to the fall of the government, which would occur just three years after the incident.

It is estimated that nearly 350,000 people were displaced over the years due to the Chernobyl accident. Though the release of radioactive material was widespread, the degree of serious contamination was limited to a much smaller area. It has been estimated that the immediate area around the plant will be uninhabitable for as many as 20,000 years due to radioactive contamination.

Trojan Nuclear Power Plant

After the Three Mile Island partial meltdown in the United States, and certainly, after the Chernobyl disaster, public support for nuclear power began to wane. Even though the physics and theories behind nuclear energy argued that the safe application of this energy source was possible, both incidents proved that man himself could not be trusted. In both cases, it was the failure of man through complacency in safety protocol or poor design that caused the accidents.

I was intrigued but also concerned regarding nuclear power as an energy source. As a kid, my class took a field trip to the "Trojan Nuclear Power Plant." It was Oregon's only nuclear facility located just 45 northwest of Portland. We went to the Visitor Center designed to educate people on the safe application of nuclear power. The entire time I was there, though, I had an eery feeling of doom and pondered if I was going to get out of there alive.

After Chernobyl I became mostly opposed to the use of this energy source. Protests in Oregon demanding the permanent closure of the Trojan nuclear power plant also ramped up. Surprisingly each time a ballot measure was put forth to close the plant, it was soundly defeated by the voters. In 1992 after a number of cracks were discovered in the steam generator tubing, the operator of the power plant, (Portland General Electric), chose to shut down Trojan permanently. Trojan had met an untimely end to its controversial 16-year existence, never living up to expectations or promises made regarding its safety and productivity.

Meanwhile, Back at the Ranch...

In August of 1985, Kim gave birth to our son Nic. Looking back, it is clear neither of us was prepared for this new addition to our lives, but then again, who really ever is? Having a child changes everything permanently. There is no going back. Anyone who is a parent knows exactly what I mean. Though we were obviously unprepared, we were committed to raising our child to the best of our abilities.

Realizing Nic needed me to take care of him, a new sense of responsibility surged within me. I now had the duty and honor to ensure he was safe. I never really thought of anyone else but myself up to this point, but now, instead of worrying about my needs and desires, I was focused on my child's well-being. Nothing was more important to me than taking care of Nic, and suddenly, I was transformed from a selfish young adult to a caring and selfless parent.

I thought of Nic's future, what it would look like, and how I could contribute to his success later in life. I felt I was the leader of our small little family, which meant I had to plan for its future with every decision I made. There was no room for error, as was the case in the past when my poor choices only impacted me. My decisions now had to be well thought out, with my actions having purpose and clear direction.

Soon after Nic was born, Kim and I had the opportunity to purchase a small home in East Portland. Her father (Dave), a sensitive, caring, and spiritual man, was a person of many trades, including real estate. He genuinely cared about our family and wanted to set us up for success as early as possible. There was no way, on my retail clerk salary and Kim's wages as a secretary, we could afford to purchase a home, but somehow Dave had made it happen, and we soon found ourselves signing a home loan at 13 percent interest.

Hey, it was the 80s, and interest rates were very high, especially for a young couple with very little purchasing history.

Dave had made sure our family got off to a good start with his work in procuring a home for us, and he supported our marriage the best he could. From the moment I met Dave, I had no idea how he and Sandy could have ever been a couple. They were complete opposites. He was gentle and kind, and she was mean and mentally unstable. He loved his daughter, and he loved me with no strings attached. Sandy demanded that Kim be the person *she* wanted her to be and completely despised me.

It wasn't long after Kim, and I were married that Dave and Sandy separated and soon after divorced. One day after he had moved out of their home Kim and I were visiting her mother and two sisters. I was shocked to hear them brag about using Dave's credit cards to buy whatever they wanted, as he had yet to cancel the accounts. They were laughing about the hundreds of dollars they had spent under his name and encouraged Kim to do the same. This was just how mentally unstable and mean Sandy was, and I was appalled by the whole incident. As soon as Kim and I returned to our house, I called Dave and informed him of the deeds of his soon-to-be ex-wife. He immediately canceled his cards and saved himself from further financial damage.

It was no wonder Kim still carried the baggage of her youth. Her mother was a controlling diabolical woman who enjoyed nothing more than hurting others (in particular men). I eventually learned from Dave her own father had pondered placing Sandy into a mental institution on several occasions but ultimately had failed to do so. The whole situation was very sad, and unfortunately, my life, along with my wife and children, would be negatively impacted by Sandy for many years to follow.

It is hard for me to hold Kim responsible for all her outrageous behavior through the years, knowing the damage her mother had caused her. It was a never-ending barrage of insults, degradation, and emotional manipulation for which Kim had no ability to mitigate or defend herself. She was a victim of her mother's abuse as a child, and nothing had changed as an adult. The abuse was constant and pervasive in every aspect of her life. It was a dark cloud of wicked dysfunction which Kim could never shake, and it clearly demonstrates the impact we as parents have on those we bring into this world and the responsibility that comes with it.

How we treat our children will most likely set a permanent course for their future and quite possibly the future of their children as well. Sadly the cycle of dysfunction and abuse typically becomes multi-generational, and it is up to those who have suffered through this dysfunction to say, "No more... the abuse and dysfunction stop here." The cycle must be broken by those who have experienced it. They must find the strength to stop the spread by refusing to allow it to poison the next generation. Kim simply wasn't strong enough to break the cycle. No matter how badly she may have wanted it to end, it was just too much for her to overcome.

By the summer of 1987, both of us had enough of a failed relationship. I was tired of the constant verbal abuse and the occasional physical abuse. Meanwhile, Kim was tired of me failing her expectations of "making her happy." I had tried to eliminate any of my behavior that she claimed made her unhappy, causing her to behave with such irrationality and anger. However, every time I eliminated her definition of my "inappropriate behavior," an entirely new set of expectations would arise of things I needed to change about myself. It was an exercise in futility as no matter what I did to please her...well, it was never enough.

By 1987, I had maintained only a minimal relationship with my longtime friends as Kim would have none of it, and I would dearly pay if I chose to ignore her warnings. Anytime I attempted to spend time with my friends, no matter how infrequent it became, she would go into a drama-filled emotional meltdown. At times it would include her attempts at "self-harm," which entailed scratching her wrists as if she was attempting to cut them and bleed out. I missed my friends, but it was not worth the catastrophic events that would occur if I chose to spend time with them.

Divorce papers were filed that summer, and my dad helped me retain an attorney. I went into the divorce proceedings more than willing to end the marriage but with the full intention of retaining custody of my son. One thing I knew for certain, I could not let him live with his mother to be raised within her dysfunctional family circle. I had been planning for the inevitability of our separation for some time and had secretly tape-recorded several of Kim's tirades as proof that she was unfit to raise our son. I wanted this evidence to show to the court (if necessary) the emotional instability of Nic's mother and why he could not be allowed to live with her full-time.

Upon consultation with my attorney, I realized I was in a major bind as my belief regarding the justice system had been naive at best. When I explained to my attorney Kim's unstable nature and that I possessed the evidence to support my claim, she was not impressed. She asked me a simple question, "Is Kim a drug addict or a whore?" Well, Kim may have been an unstable mess, but she certainly possessed neither of those unsavory characteristics. When I responded "no" to the question, my attorney said, "I can take your money, and we can fight this battle, but you will lose your custody fight." I was devastated.

How could a half-crazed woman win a custody battle over a stable father? It made no sense to me whatsoever, and I was left pondering the serious question, "Do I save myself, or do I go back into the fray to protect my son?" Without my oversight to safeguard my son and provide some measure of normalcy in his life, what would become of him? How could I just walk away and leave Nic in an untenable situation, likely condemning him to a life of dysfunction and sadness?

Right or wrong, I made the decision to patch things up with Kim. It wasn't going to be easy, as her mother was now highly involved in ensuring Kim would never get back together with me. It would take time to try to piece back together a fractured relationship. Kim was now living with her mother, and Nic was subjected to chronic dysfunction on a daily basis. However, I needed to be thoughtful and patient in my approach to mend our relationship.

By early 1988 we both agreed to once again give the relationship another chance. I was hopeful that the six months of separation and our serious negotiations of what needed to change would be enough to set us on a course for success. The odds were certainly stacked against us, but it was worth a try to give our son the stability of a two-parent family, so we moved forward with our plan.

School is Out… Forever

Soon after our marriage, I determined it was necessary for me to give school once again a shot. It was true that I had bumbled and stumbled my way through college and had done poorly, but when the dust settled, I realized I was actually less than two years from getting my degree.

My work in the retail business had earned me a promotion to "assistant manager," but I was not happy with the job for a number of reasons, including the evening and weekend hours I was constantly forced to work. I could see no future in retail and desperately wanted out, but I had zero vocational skills to speak of other than operating a cash register. Conversely, I had accumulated over two years of college credit, and a professional career was likely waiting for me if I could just complete my education. It seemed to me that a degree was the quickest way to get out of retail and into a professional career, so I set out to finally accomplish something that had seemed unattainable just a few years prior.

With a new sense of purpose and diligence I had no idea I possessed, I went back to school to pursue a degree in Sociology. This time I had maturity and a sense of desperation on my side. I can't say I was a great student, but I can say I did what was needed to get through the academic requirements. It wasn't easy, as I still had to work almost 40 hours to help support the family. Kim was working full-time as well, so between us, we were able to make ends meet.

During that busy period of balancing school and work, a typical day would start with me dropping my son off at daycare by 8:00 am. I would then drive downtown Portland to attend classes at Portland State. After completing my classes at 12:30, I would drive home to change clothes and then drive 20 miles to my retail job. I would work until 11:00 PM and arrive back home at 11:30. Those were tiring days, but I also realized I had done it to myself with all those years of hanging with my friends and blowing off my classwork to party.

My last term at Portland State would be my most arduous and most successful. I took a large class load that final term because I did not want to spend any more time or money attending school. I endured a 21-hour class load coupled with 32 hours of work per week while garnering the best GPA of my entire college career.

It provided me with absolute proof that I could accomplish whatever I wanted to in life as long as I possessed the proper focus. That experience, and the confidence I garnered from it, would ultimately benefit me throughout my entire professional career. As it turned out, college, with all its twists and turns, had served me well in the end. In the years that would follow, I was offered on several different occasions to have my school paid for by my employer to obtain a master's degree. I always politely declined the offer as I had no desire ever to go back to school again.

By the spring of 1988, I had earned my degree, and Kim and I even seemed to be on an upswing in our relationship. We had been back together for nearly four months by then, and with my degree in hand, we both saw the potential for a brighter future. Late that summer, I landed a job at a brokerage firm near the Portland airport. It came with a hefty pay increase thanks to my new degree and my entrance into a professional career. All of this gave our family more positive momentum than we had ever experienced before…yes, things were indeed getting better for us. With a little luck, maybe… just maybe, we could make it all work.

The Actor and His Final Scene

It had been nearly eight years since Ronald Reagan had taken the reigns of leadership in the United States. Through that leadership, America had found itself in much better standing economically and geo-politically than it had seen in many years. Reagan's posture of "Peace through strength" and his implementation of "Supply-side Economics" had stabilized a reeling country.

Though the argument could be made that the gap between the "haves" and "have nots" had increased, the fact was that the American economy was in far better shape than it had been in a long time. The recession and stagflation issues which had plagued the country in the 70s were now in the rearview mirror, and an overall sense of optimism permeated the country. Sure, there were still economic concerns, including the stock market crash in 1987, where the markets fell over twenty percent in one day. However, most Americans were optimistic about their economic future.

The 1980s had begun with two recessions within three years, and by 1982, the unemployment rate had climbed to 10 percent. Meanwhile, the Gross National Product fell by 2.5 percent. American farmers, in particular, were struggling primarily due to the rise of oil prices in the 1970s. The cost of operating farming machinery, coupled with a reduced worldwide demand for farm products, left many families on the verge of bankruptcy and foreclosure.

Reagan certainly did not inherit a good economic situation when he became President in 1980, and during his first four years in office, there was little improvement. By the end of his second term in office, the American economy would rebound to score the largest peacetime expansion on record. In reality, much of this economic growth was due to government deficit spending. Under Reagan, the national debt almost tripled, and it appeared his economic policies had inordinately benefited the wealthy, with the middle class and certainly the poor seeing little improvement in their overall wealth.

One of the biggest contributors to the increase of America's debt during the Reagan administration was his push to expand defense funding massively. Under the "Reagan Doctrine," America would pour billions into the expansion of its defense systems, specifically in the area of technology. He would introduce the "Strategic Defense Initiative," more commonly known as "Stars Wars," with the goal (he claimed) of making the prospect of a nuclear attack obsolete. He proposed that the development of this defense system would be so technologically advanced that it would render ballistic nuclear missiles shot from the Soviet Union completely ineffective.

With the implementation of "Star Wars," the Department of Defense began to explore the utilization of developing technology to support the new Strategic Defense Initiative. Weapon concepts, including lasers, particle beam weaponry, and space-based missile systems, were all pursued as part of this new comprehensive defense system. In addition, highly developed computers would be implemented and utilized as command and control systems, accessing satellites around the world in a coordinated global approach to national defense.

"Star Wars" greatly concerned the Soviet Union as they deemed this new program a potential "game changer" in the balance of power between the two superpowers. The aggressiveness of Reagan's foreign policy, coupled with the potential development of this new space-based system, forced the Russians to expend far more money and resources than they could actually afford. The constant pressure Reagan applied to the Soviet Union ultimately would become one of the main contributors to the collapse of the Russian economy. Reagan had made it clear America could and would "outspend" the Soviets in the area of national defense, and through the creation of "Star Wars," he proved he was not bluffing.

Of course, there were some retractors to this aggressive stance Reagan had chosen as they believed it would only increase the chances of nuclear war. History has proven that Reagan was correct in his approach. In the end, the Soviet Union attempted to keep pace with the massive investment America was making in its national defense systems. Ultimately it went broke trying to match the United States, leaving its economy in shambles.

Reagan's second term in office was heavily weighted on his foreign policy endeavors, much of it towards the Soviet Union and curbing the growth of Communism throughout the world. He found himself immersed in a serious scandal during his second term attempting to arm the Contras of Nicaragua, which had been prohibited by law. The Contras were a rebel group fighting the Marxist Sandinista government, hoping to overthrow a government they felt had been oppressive to the growth of its people.

U.S. intelligence agencies had long feared the survival of the Sandinista government in Nicaragua could likely lead to a Marxist guerrilla movement in other Central American countries, including Mexico. Reagan also held this belief that "communistic style" regimes could spread further into the Western hemisphere if the Sandinista government were allowed to flourish. He was determined to provide aid to the contras despite the fact that Congress passed a law in 1982 prohibiting such activity.

Midway through Reagan's second term, it was discovered that between 1981 and 1986, administration officials secretly facilitated the sale of arms to Iran, violating the terms of the arms embargo on the country. The administration then diverted a portion of these proceeds to fund the Contra's fight against the Sandinista government. All of this was illegal activity and eventually was investigated by Congress. The results of the investigation did not implicate Reagan as having full knowledge of the extent of the nefarious activities and the multiple programs involved in the effort to aid the Contras.

Personally, I felt that the responsibility for the Iran-Contra scandal lay right in the lap of Reagan. My reasoning was simple, he was commander in chief, and anything that occurred during his watch was ultimately his responsibility. I was disappointed when news of this scandal hit the public airways, and although I had voted twice for Reagan, I wasn't certain I had made the correct choice the second time around. It seemed Reagan had lost something off of his fastball, and the focus he once had as President seemed to be fading. By the end of his second term, I was more than happy to see it end, and all of his charisma and leadership that had endeared him to me had dissipated by the time of his departure.

Several years later, however, with the fall of the Soviet Union, it became clear that Reagan's policies and strategies to address the cold war had successfully led to its peaceful end. Furthermore, as the decades passed, history would look upon the Reagan years as a time when America regained its domestic economic footing, re-established its stature in the global geopolitical theater, and re-ignited its sense of national pride.

The actor-turned-politician had successfully recalibrated two decades of American folly, failure, and disappointment into a new sense of optimism. He ushered in an era of conservative politics focusing on the application of less government through the deregulation of private industry and broad-based tax cuts. As Reagan said in his inaugural address, "Government is not the solution to our problem. Government is our problem." In his eight years as president, Reagan proved his conservative approach to limited government, coupled with his strong leadership, would serve the American people well, setting them on a course filled with a sense of optimism not seen in nearly three decades.

Meet the New Act... Same as the Old Act

In November 1988, George Bush was elected as the 41st President of the United States. He was the first incumbent Vice President to win a presidential election since Martin Van Buren in 1836. Bush easily defeated the Democratic candidate Michael Dukakis, Governor of Massachusetts, by a wide electoral and popular vote margin. It was the first time since the 1940s that a political party had won more than two consecutive elections and it has not happened again since.

Bush won the election by promising to continue the policies Reagan had made popular during the 80s. However, he also promised to lead a "kinder, gentler nation," as some moderates had felt Reagan's policies had been too harsh on impacting the less fortunate. With the results of the 1988 election, it became clear that "conservatism" had regained a foothold in American politics.

Bush, a Navy aviator, had flown missions in the Pacific Theater during World War II and had been a successful businessman after the war. He eventually became involved in politics in the 1960s when he was elected to the House of Representatives. He held many political positions through the years, including Chair of the Republican National Committee and Director of the CIA.

Bush ran against Ronald Reagan in the 1980 primaries for the Republican presidential nomination but lost the race only to be then chosen by Reagan to be his Vice Presidential running mate. Although there were times that Reagan took offense to the aggressive political attacks Bush had levied upon him during the primaries, he also realized Bush would draw the more moderate Republicans to support the ticket if he were chosen as Reagan's running mate.

George Bush

Bush had served Reagan and the country well during his eight-year tenure as Vice President. He was careful never to contradict or question Reagan's leadership or direction for the country. He understood his position as a quiet but consistent supporter of his charismatic President. He had patiently waited for his opportunity, which came at the end of Reagan's second term.

Bush quickly identified himself as a *different* style of leader than Reagan but also aligned himself with the successes Reagan had experienced during his presidency. He was also able to separate himself from Reagan in areas where some felt he had been uncaring towards those Americans who needed the most help projecting an image of empathy to those in need.

He promised to fight the rising crime issues that had been plaguing American cities throughout the 1980s. The past decade had seen an alarming increase in violent crime and homicides, and curbing this trend became a major talking point during the 1988 election cycle. Bush also promised to address the ever-increasing concern over drug addiction and homelessness in America.

In the end, it was the success of Ronald Reagan's administration that would catapult Bush into the White House. Reagan had left office with most Americans wanting more of the same. It was clear their lives had improved during the previous eight years and would likely continue to improve under the leadership of a conservative President. George Bush rode that wave of optimism and a sense of confidence in the conservative approach toward government to victory in 1988.

There's No Place Like Home

Due to lowering manufacturing costs and improved technology, the home computer became a viable purchasing option for families across America in the 80s. The personal computer or "PC" was no longer primarily limited to use in business or scientific settings as it actually became affordable and "understandable" to the layman. Prior to the 80s, "hobbyists" had mostly been the only people interested in acquiring a home computer. Access was typically limited through mail order or specialty electronic shops. However, it wasn't long before the "average person" realized its potential for application in the home in basic word processing, budgeting, and of course, gaming.

In the early 80s, home computers were primarily 8-bit systems having just enough power and memory to lure interested buyers into the world of technology at their fingertips. Aware of the budding and potentially huge market for PCs, a boom in manufacturing of these systems flooded the market with a wide array of choices offered in retail stores throughout the country.

At the time, I was working in the Photo Electronics department of a local retail store, and I remember being introduced to a new product from Timex marketed as the cheapest home computer on the market at just under $100. It was called the "TS1000" and, by today's standards, was extremely limited in its capability and use. However, it was exciting to see a device having capabilities far beyond a basic calculator.

It would not be long before Commodore would introduce the "Commodore 64" with far more memory and applications for use. Thousands of software titles were produced for use, from office productivity to video games. The cost of a Commodore 64 was just under $600, and it could be connected to the family tv or computer monitor.

I recall selling hundreds of these computers at the store where I worked. Occasionally we would run specials on the computer tied with software packages at reduced prices or free upon purchase of the computer. We would order palates loaded with Commodore 64s for these special sales and would sell all of them within days. To say the Commodore 64 had become a prolific seller in retail stores would be an understatement. It absolutely dominated the low-end computer market in the '80s. In fact, It has been listed in the Guinness World Records as the highest-selling single computer model of all time.

Commodore 64

Atari Game Console

Although the Commodore 64 had multiple applications, from my experience in selling them, the main reason families were purchasing the computer was for the gaming experience. Hundreds of titles were developed for strictly gaming purposes. Commodore was not the only gaming system available to consumers. The Atari 2600 and Mattel's Intellivision were strictly game consoles and were considerably cheaper than the Commodore 64. The Atari sold for just under $200, while Intellivision had a list price of just under $250.

Both the Atari and Intellivision consoles sold incredibly well and provided the user with an "arcade-like" game-playing experience ranging from target shooting style games to team sports-related games. Somewhere along the way, my friends and I pitched in money to purchase an Intellivision console, and we spent hours playing football, basketball, and baseball. It was incredibly fun and, at the time, seemed technologically advanced, but by today's standard, the graphics were actually pathetically simple.

Early Video Game Graphics

The decade of the 80s is known as the era that opened up the frontier of home computer use. From basic gaming systems such as Atari to more advanced computer-based systems like the Commodore 64, it was clear this new technology had entered the family home environment and would only continue to grow into a massive industry in the decades to follow. The gates had been opened to this technology for use by the average American, and households throughout the United States would never be the same again. Companies such as Apple and Microsoft would refine and expand the capabilities of the home computer while also simplifying its use.

The advent of the home computer absolutely revolutionized the way Americans live today. We had no idea at the time what an impact these basic computer systems would have on our future way of life. These pioneering systems of the 80s would eventually lead to our great dependence on this technology, simplifying our lives while at the same time complicating them in ways we could have never imagined.

The continued advancement of computer technology, including the advent of the home computer, would lead to a cultural and societal shift away from the age of "Industrialization" and into the "Information" age. It has been as dramatic a shift in how we live today as was our shift away from the agrarian society to the industrial age of the 19th century. Whether for better or worse, this technology has forever changed our country and the world permanently.

And the Wall Came Crumbling Down

On November 9th, 1989, Communist East Berlin city officials announced that East Berliners were free to cross the country's borders into West Germany at midnight. This historic announcement was followed by thousands of East and West Berliners flocking to the gates of the Berlin Wall, celebrating in wild fashion the end of nearly 45 years of cold war tension and forced separation between East and West Germany.

The origin of the decision to divide Germany was a direct result of the defeat of Nazi Germany, ending the European conflict of WWII. During peace negotiations in the spring of 1945, it was determined that Germany would be divided into four distinct "allied occupation zones." The western part of Germany went to the United States, Great Britain, and France, while the eastern section went to the Soviet Union. This division of Germany went into effect that June and would last for over 45 years.

Near the end of the war, thousands of Germans fled East Berlin in fear of the incoming Russian army and their well-deserved reputation for brutality. My mother and grandmother were part of this stream of war refugees fleeing East Berlin to escape Russian soldiers and the oppressive Soviet Government. Hiding under the cover of hay and blankets, they were smuggled out by French soldiers in a horse-drawn wagon. They managed to successfully cross through several Russian Army checkpoints along their way to freedom.

Not all made it out, though, and over the next decade, nearly three million refugees escaped into democratic West Germany and gained freedom. The Premier of the Soviet Union, Nikita Khrushchev, embarrassed and infuriated by this mass exodus out of communist East Germany (the Soviet Union being its puppet master), gave the East German government permission to close their borders and permanently stop the mass exodus to the west.

The Berlin Wall

In August of 1961, a makeshift wall was completed using barbed wire and concrete blocks. At its completion, the city of Berlin was separated into two sections, East and West, and would remain separated until late 1989. The cold war between the Soviet Union and the United States only became more heated with the construction of the wall, and tensions between the two countries continued to grow.

The wall not only divided the city of Berlin into two sections, but it also divided family members from each other. Those behind the wall in East Berlin were not allowed to cross into West Berlin for any reason. They, in essence, were prisoners held against their will. Over 170 people were killed attempting to cross over or beneath the wall.

By late 1989 East Germany was feeling immense pressure to dispose of the imposed restrictions levied upon its people and their ability to move freely between East and West Germany. The Soviet Union, under Mikhail Gorbachev, began to loosen control of its satellite countries due to extreme economic difficulties. Gorbachev had realized the cost of trying to keep pace with the United States, and their military build-up under President Reagan had brought the Soviet Union to the doorstep of complete economic collapse. The Soviet Union could no longer afford the cold war.

With other countries such as Poland and Hungary loosening their control over their citizens and Russia already beginning to reform many of its long-held practices, East Germany had little choice but to liberate its citizens, no longer restricting their freedom of movement from country to country.

The fall of the Berlin Wall was possibly the biggest international news up to that point in my life. I had been born just months before the construction of the wall and had lived my entire life under the dark cloud of the cold war. I had never known Germany as "one country." It had always been separated into two distinct countries, one representing freedom and the other representing oppression.

The Fall of the Berlin Wall

With the announcement of the fall of the Berlin Wall, it felt like the Cold War was nearing its end as the communist block of countries that had represented the Soviet Union's side of the Cold War was breaking apart from Soviet control and philosophy. It was a big moment in the 20th century as it was becoming clear that communism had failed in its attempt at world dominance.

Massive crowds celebrated the end of the division between the two cities. News reports coming from the wall showed thousands engaged in the celebration. Some individuals, armed with picks and hammers, dismantled small sections of the wall collecting small pieces of concrete representing the end of what once was and would never be again. Even bulldozers and cranes were used to take out large sections of the wall, as there was a strong desire to rid the city of this symbol of oppression as quickly as possible. The celebration was an amazing site to see as an estimated two million East Germans visited West Berlin that weekend for the first time in decades. It would be less than a year later that East and West Germany would finally be reunified after 45 years of separation.

Wagon Train to the Northern Plains

After my college graduation ceremony in June of 1988, I was more than ready to get out of the retail business and land a professional career-level job. Before that occurred, though, it was time to celebrate and relax after a tough year of balancing school, work, and family life. Summer was beginning, and my eye was on vacation and a road trip to explore more of America.

Kim's father, by this time, had already remarried, marrying his best friend's sister named Sharon. She was from South Dakota but had moved to Portland after her marriage to Dave. He had made sure to take her back to the Midwest on a regular basis to visit her family. They had made plans to do just that in June, and Dave inquired whether Kim and I would like to join them on their road trip.

I had already visited many areas of the country but had never been to the northern plains and was intrigued with the idea of a road trip to the Midwest. Kim and I had already discussed the possibility of taking a trip after I graduated, and we decided why not join Dave and Sharon in their sojourn to South Dakota. He had suggested we ride along with them in their van, but I declined as I wanted to bring our own car to exercise a bit of independence. So we caravanned across the country together like two wagon trains heading into the great frontier.

The trip was fantastic, and Kim and I both fell in love with the "laid back" friendly small-town experience we encountered in South Dakota. It seemed time slowed down in the Midwest especially compared to the West Coast tempo. People appeared honest and uncomplicated. They were comfortable with their lifestyle and sought nothing more than to maintain a pleasant existence. There were no traffic issues, crime, or anything else that resembled "city living." The better part of my life had been spent in city environments, either in Portland or Los Angeles, and I had never experienced the calm nature of rural existence. I found it intoxicating.

Upon returning home, Dave informed me he was determined to move to South Dakota to escape the throes of city living, and by the fall of that year, he and Sharon had packed up their belongings and moved. Both Kim and I were sad to see them go, and in a sense, we felt like we were left behind because we had also expressed the desire to escape Portland. Unlike Dave, though, we did not own a business we could just pick up and move to the Midwest. We needed to land jobs prior to any move we made, and we knew it would be difficult finding work in a small Midwest town.

In the meant time, I landed a job at a brokerage firm in Portland and began a career in an office setting. The work had nothing to do with the degree I had just earned, but for the most part, I didn't care. I just wanted out of retail. It wasn't long before I realized this type of work was not for me, and I soon began to hate my new career choice. I proceeded to limp through the next nine months at work, collecting a paycheck but desperate to get out.

During this same period, Kim's relationship with her mother had become more caustic, and she was feeling the emotional pinch of Sandy judging every move we made as a family. With Dave no longer around to counteract the emotional abuse dished out by her mother, Kim was feeling the full weight of her overbearing personality.

In May of 1989, Dave invited Kim and me out to the little farmhouse he and Sharon had recently purchased. It was situated on a hundred acres of fertile land, complete with all the farm amenities, including a barn and a stock pond. He convinced me over the phone that if we came out to visit, there would be opportunities for me to find a job. He told me about a boarding school located in a town nearby that served Native American children. I was intrigued by the possibility of pursuing a job related to what I had studied in college.

It would have to be a quick visit as we only had a week to make a 3000-mile roundtrip by car. We arrived in mid-May when spring had hit the Northern plains. The weather was beautiful, and the air was fresh and clean. We had a wonderful time on the farm, and Nic, who was now almost four, loved feeding the baby goats from a bottle. The whole visit to the farm was a taste of rural Camelot to us, and we hated to leave.

While there, I was also able to land an informal interview at the Native American boarding school in town. After the interview, I was informed that they were interested in me and would be in contact if something came up that matched my skill set. Kim and I left South Dakota a few days later with the hope that I might be called back for an interview.

Upon returning to Portland, Kim and I felt a sense of desperation to get out of the city. We had caught "the small town fever" and wanted to try our hands at simple rural living. In addition, I was completely tired of the rainy weather in Portland, which I had endured for decades. The bright sunshine and blue sky of South Dakota were imbedded in my brain, and I wanted to run as far away from the bleak rainy Portland weather as I could.

After a few weeks, I received the call Kim and I had desperately been hoping would occur. It was the Native American school, and they had asked me to come back for an interview to fill an open social worker position. They would fly me out on their own dime and would provide all accommodations. I happily accepted the invite and flew out in early June, hoping to land the job.

I honestly can't say I remember anything about the interview other than feeling I had done well. I was impressed with the school and the level of professionalism of the staff. They were all friendly and mostly young and energetic in their mission to serve Native American children. There was no doubt that after meeting with the staff and learning about the school's mission to serve children, I wanted to be a part of this important work.

Within a week, I heard back from the school, and they offered me the social worker job, which I accepted on the spot. I would be the conduit between the families who lived on the reservation and the children who attended our school. This meant there would be a great deal of travel to remote locations visiting families, and providing them with updates on their children. I was thrilled with the opportunity to utilize my degree in sociology for such an important endeavor.

For the first time in years, Kim and I were happy. We were escaping the city and the rain, but most importantly (at least to me), we were escaping the reach of her mother. Both Dave and I had privately discussed the importance of Kim putting distance between her and Sandy. It had been clear Kim had no hope of happiness as long as her mother was looking over her shoulder and imposing her will upon her. There was a real chance that by moving to South Dakota, Kim could heal and gain some emotional stability once again. Our broken relationship would also have a chance to completely mend as well. Optimism filled the air as we packed up our belongings in a U-Haul and moved to the Midwest.

We arrived on July 2nd, 1989, and late that summer, after selling our home in Portland, we purchased a mobile home that we placed on Dave and Sharon's property. It was an ideal setup as we sat less than a hundred yards from their farmhouse, and our view overlooked the stock pond and the rolling hills of their property. Life was good as the decade closed.

In a period of ten years, my life had changed considerably. I had gone from ringing in the decade of the 80's with my friends in Portland to celebrating the beginning of the 90's with my wife and child on a farm in South Dakota. I had grown from a boy into a man and faced the daunting proposition of soon leaving my twenties behind and saying goodbye forever to my youth. This was "real life" now, and there was no turning back. I was an adult with adult responsibilities. Life was moving on and taking me along with it regardless of how I felt about the whole matter.

The next decade would turn out to be the most pivotal of my life, and had I known what I was about to face, I might have very well run and hid. Life, however, does not allow you to glimpse into the future. It only allows for retrospection upon deeds already done. What I was about to face in the upcoming decade would permanently change the course of my life in a dramatic fashion, and no amount of reflection or retrospection could ever bring back what was lost during those ten years.

Part Four
(The 90s)

A New Beginning… Same Problems

The decade of the 90s began with the birth of our second child, another boy, whom we named Jordan. Kim and I had found some level of balance in our marriage, although it was far from ideal, it certainly had improved since our move to South Dakota. The calm influence of her father was the complete antithesis of her mother's influence, and with his guidance, Kim's emotions seemed to be under better control.

There was no escaping the damage her mother had already levied upon her, but there was hope it could be mitigated somewhat by her father's gentle approach. It was really the only chance Kim had to improve, as I was unable to provide her with the steadying hand she so badly needed. If anything, I was often the source of her frustrations, nothing I did seemed to make her happy. She was unable to realize she was in charge of her own happiness and still depended on me for a sense of fulfillment in her life. Sadly I had been an abject failure in my efforts to make her feel content, and often, I only seemed to exacerbate her feelings of unhappiness.

In any case, by the time of the birth of our second son, our marriage was in better shape than it had been for a very long time. The adaptation to a different lifestyle away from the city was an easy adjustment for both of us. We found ourselves thriving in this new environment, and for the first time, we made new friends together as a couple.

Kim eventually procured a job at the Indian School where I worked, and she had settled in quite nicely as an executive administrative assistant. As for me, my social worker job was both challenging and interesting. I also appeared to be impressing the "right people," making connections with those in high-level leadership positions from the onset of my employment. Looking back, I'm not sure what qualities they might have seen in me, but it appeared those in authority were drawn to me as much as I was to them. It wasn't long before I was more than just a "subordinate" but considered someone of value and insight. Again, what that value was, I really wasn't quite sure, but those in charge apparently recognized some intrinsic value in me, and I didn't argue with their assessment.

It was clear to me from the beginning that the school's leadership style was one I could excel under. They supported staff input, promoted creativity, and listened to the ideas of their employees. Management invested a great deal of faith in the youthful energy of its staff and trusted us with the implementation of the school's mission. They typically hired people in their twenties, recently out of college, and who still had idealism shining brightly in their eyes. Leadership looked for employees who believed they could "make a difference" in the lives of the children they served.

There were, of course, some serious questions regarding the mission of the school and its potential hypocrisy, but most of us chose to ignore these questions. Still, the fact remained that we were a boarding school that recruited children away from their families to be raised by strangers. That criticism, however, was a simple application of the facts and not the reality of how most of the kids arrived at our school. They were actually chosen through an application process initiated by the families. It was the parents who had serious concerns about raising their children on the reservation, where life was often hard and lacked resources. Many parents wanted their kids removed from reservation life and into a more stable environment. Frankly, for the most part, I agreed with their desire to place their children at our school.

Anyone who denies the level of alcoholism and dysfunction that can permeate reservation living is either lying to themselves or uninformed. I witnessed these issues on every reservation I worked throughout my career. It is a sad reminder of how badly Native Americans were treated in the previous two centuries and the long-term multi-generational harm it has caused to the indigenous people of this land.

Once the families applied for admittance into our school, my job was to help screen the applicants. I would travel to the reservations and conduct home visits in order to ascertain if the school was the right fit for the child. It was imperative that the services we offered not only met the child's needs but also they were a good fit for the culture established in our homes.

Our group home model was designed with the traditional "nuclear family" in mind, comprised of two houseparents, one male and one female. A home, on average, would house around eight to ten children, though it could vary in size depending on the ages of the children. Some kids thrived in this environment, while others could not adjust to a group home lifestyle.

It was my job to present the best candidates to the houseparents for review so they could make an informed decision as to what child was an appropriate fit for their home. An academic screening process was also part of the admittance procedure to ensure the school had the necessary resources to meet the academic needs of the child. It was my job also to present all of the academic information to the school as well.

There is no doubt it was challenging work but I enjoyed it very much, and for the first time in my life, I felt I was doing something important and worthwhile. This was a career I could be proud of, and although it didn't pay well, I didn't really care at the time as I felt I was finally "making a difference." It seemed that all of us who worked for the school shared the same feeling of pride, and we all brought positive energy to the job.

Between work going well and life on the farm being the right potion for our ailing marriage, Kim and I were feeling optimistic about our future. That being said, dark clouds always seemed to be lurking in the distance. One phone call from Kim's mother and our stability could easily fall apart. Sandy knew just how to push her buttons, and within minutes of talking to Kim, she could reduce her to tears. With mean and despicable motives in mind, Sandy could easily make Kim feel unworthy of her love or, for that matter, even God's love. Just one call from Sandy and Kim could lose all feelings of contentment and optimism. Those feelings would be replaced with resentment towards me for allegedly placing her in an untenable situation. Often after talking to her mother, Kim would transform into a bitter person, hating life and certainly me for failing her expectations.

No matter how hard Kim tried and regardless of how much support her father and I gave her, Sandy could crush her confidence in a single phone call. It was pathetic to watch Kim fold under the control of her mother, and I came to resent her weakness as much as I resented Sandy's cruelty towards her. It was dysfunction in the highest order, and everyone would pay who found themselves trapped within its wake.

A View Like None Other

On April 24th, 1990, the Hubble Telescope was deployed into space by the Space Shuttle "Discovery". The telescope, which had been in development for decades, was a momentous achievement in the pursuit of deep space exploration. The idea of a space-based telescope originated in the 1940s by astrophysicist Lyman Spitzer. He proposed there would be considerable benefits to having an observatory in space. He cited that significant improvement in viewing could be achieved in the absence of a planetary atmosphere that diffused clarity. Spitzer postulated that a space observatory could be built to circle the earth, providing a much more pristine view of the cosmos.

Throughout the decades that followed, many technological advancements were made that led to Hubble's launch in 1990. Congress approved funding for the project in 1977, and it was officially named the "Hubble Telescope" in 1983 after the astronomer Edwin Hubble who proved other galaxies in our universe were moving away from our own. Along with the development and implementation of the Space Shuttle program in the 1980s, the telescope now had the funding and the means to be launched into space.

Hubble Telescope

The deployment of the Hubble Telescope was delayed due to the Challenger Disaster in 1986, which led to the cessation of all Space Shuttle activities for nearly three years. Soon after the return of the Space Shuttle Program in 1989, Hubble was brought into space and deployed by Discovery. Decades of work in the development of the space observatory concept had been finally realized.

After deployment, a major flaw in the focusing mirror of the telescope was discovered. Although the "spherical aberration" was minuscule (just 1/50th the width of a strand of hair), it was enough

Image From Hubble

to blur photos coming from the telescope. This was a devastating blow to a project that had spent billions of dollars and decades in development. Considerable hype regarding the potential of this telescope had made the rounds in scientific journals and network news programs, but now it was being labeled as a national blunder of epic proportions. Hubble was to be the key to unlocking the universe and its many mysteries. Instead, it had been relegated to mockery and the butt of bad jokes.

Fortunately, in 1993 NASA was able to develop a solution to correct the blurriness created by the imperfection of the focusing mirror. A

Image From Hubble

crew of astronauts were sent into space to correct the problem by installing an instrument comprised of tiny mirrors, which served the role much like corrective eye glasses. This adjustment significantly sharpened the clarity of the lens, and Hubble began sending amazing pictures of our universe astonishing astronomers and laymen alike.

Through the use of the Hubble Telescope, scientists now have a much better idea of the age of our universe. Once estimated to be 10 to 20 billion years old, estimates now place its age at 13.8 billion years. Imagine just how long 13.8 billion years is. By any standards, it is almost inconceivable to imagine as there is little relativity to attach and contrast for that length of time. One could stipulate that

13.8 billion years might as well equal infinity due to the inconceivable nature of that length of time. Who really knows what infinity is and, for that matter, its relativity (if any) to our existence? In any case, we have embraced the Big Bang theory as the creation point of our physical universe, and through the use of Hubble, we have greatly improved our estimates of its creation point.

I have always been enamored by astronomy and all aspects of humankind's adventures into space. Beginning with the Apollo missions and continuing through to the deployment of the Hubble Telescope, I have found space exploration to be incredibly exciting. I was thrilled when Hubble was deployed into space and very disappointed to hear of its imperfections. Nonetheless, I was still interested in the images it relayed back to earth, no matter how imperfect they were. In the end, of course, NASA rectified the problem, and the images Hubble provided were nothing less than astounding, causing me to ponder our universe and its origin even more.

The fact is that the Hubble Telescope has fundamentally changed the way we perceive our universe. It has brought humankind closer to understanding the complex nature of its birth and ever expanding existence. We have learned more about galactic evolution, the nature of black holes, and the formation of stars through the use of Hubble than we had in all in all the previous centuries combined. The scientific knowledge acquired through the use of this space based telescope has truly changed our perception of the cosmos and humankind's place within its vast expanse.

Desert Storm

In August of 1990, trouble erupted in the Middle East. Iraq, which had been engaged in serious disputes with its neighbor, Kuwait, invaded the nation setting off a series of events that drew the United States directly into the conflict. Prior to the invasion, the Iraqi government had accused several Arab nations, including Kuwait, of engaging in unfair trade practices in the lucrative oil industry. In addition, Iraq's President, Saddam Hussein, accused Kuwait of siphoning crude oil from its oil fields. He also demanded that Kuwait and Saudi Arabia forgive 30 billion dollars of debt incurred during the Iraqi/Iran war, which had recently ended. All of these factors, coupled with Kuwait's refusal to meet Hussein's demands, led to irrevocable hostilities between the two nations.

On August 2nd, 1990, Iraq invaded Kuwait, easily blowing through its defensive forces and capturing Kuwait City within hours. Saddam Hussein immediately installed a provincial government and annexed the country. This gave Iraq control of 20 percent of the world's oil reserves and a substantial section of coastline on the Persian Gulf.

The United Nations quickly reacted and condemned the Iraqi aggression demanding they relinquish the captured territory. Within days its Security Council also imposed a worldwide ban on trade with Iraq. On August 9th, President Bush ordered the implementation of "Operation Desert Shield" to help protect Saudi Arabia from Iraqi aggression and to also prepare for a potential military offensive. He deployed hundreds of thousands of troops to the Persian Gulf area amounting to the largest deployment of American troops since WWII. In the meantime, Saddam Hussein amassed 300,000 troops in occupied Kuwait to defend the newly annexed territory.

In late November, the United Nations passed a resolution authorizing the use of force if Iraq did not withdraw from Kuwait by January 15th, 1991. Hussein refused to withdraw, which set the stage for war. By this time, coalition forces had grown to over 700,000 in the region, and the world waited for the deadline of January 15th to arrive.

These were tense times in America, and there was a sense that Iraq's highly respected Republican Guard forces would be a worthy adversary. Concerns ran rampant throughout America about the casualties that could be incurred if there was to be no peaceful resolution. It seemed the lines had been drawn, and America was drifting towards inevitable war.

I was very concerned at the prospect of our country engaging in direct conflict with Iraq. However, I was also aware of the inherent dangers of allowing Saddam Hussein to potentially run roughshod throughout the Middle East. The fifteen years of relative peace America had enjoyed since Vietnam appeared perilously close to ending. The mental scars I still carried from Vietnam had me on edge that this crisis could become another long, drawn-out conflict. A conflict that could end up costing the lives of many young Americans. It was true that at age 30, I was no longer at risk of being drafted, nonetheless, my trepidation concerning all the pain and anguish associated with war had me praying for a peaceful resolution.

With Hussein's refusal to withdraw from Kuwait by the January deadline, the coalition of countries opposed to Iraq's aggression initiated operation "Desert Storm." In the morning hours of January 17th, a major air offensive was put into action led by the United States. In what would become one of the biggest air offensives in military history, coalition forces constantly bombed Iraqi positions destroying its air defenses and crippling its air force. The Iraqi infrastructure and communication systems were left in shambles after 42 consecutive days of intense bombing.

The strategy to hit Iraqi positions hard with brutal air assaults in an effort to soften air and ground forces had worked exceptionally well. Perhaps most importantly, the bombings helped break the will of Iraqi forces long before a ground invasion was ordered. The air assault, which included over 100,000 sorties, greatly contributed to the success of the coalition ground offensive that would follow.

The air offensive was more effective than perhaps anyone had anticipated, and by late February, "Operation Saber" was initiated with the objective of liberating Kuwait. Within four days, the ground assault on Saddam Hussein's elite group of fighters, The Republican Guard, was easily defeated. President Bush declared a cease-fire on February 28th, effectively ending the Persian Gulf War.

Air Assault in Kuwait

In just seven weeks, Iraq had been beaten badly and in embarrassing fashion. Estimates of eight to ten thousand Iraqis were killed during the seven weeks of the war, in contrast to three hundred coalition casualties.

It was a dominant victory for the United States and the coalition forces. Iraq was forced to relinquish Kuwait, and it once again became a sovereign nation. Saddam Hussein also agreed to discard all weapons of mass destruction, including any biological, chemical, and nuclear weapons, in the possession of Iraq.

I clearly recall the day the Persian Gulf War began. There was a great deal of tension across the country with America's involvement in another war. Iraq appeared to be a formidable opponent, and the cost of engaging in a direct conflict was a major concern for many people. The question on everyone's mind was how much American blood would have to be spilled to secure victory in the Middle East. No one had any idea how long the war might last, and I was, of course, concerned that another "Vietnam" scenario could be on the horizon.

Perhaps one of the most emotional moments I experienced from this crisis did not come from the battle field at all. Just ten days after the war began, Whitney Houston performed the National Anthem at Super Bowl XXV. Her memorable performance was packed with emotion and filled with American pride. Later it would be disclosed that Houston had lip-synced the anthem. Nonetheless, her performance that evening is still widely considered the best in Super Bowl history. I recall being quite touched watching her perform our anthem with such passion. For me, it was a great example of the power of music, so clearly expressing the emotion of a country that was now at war. Anyone who watched Whitney Houston perform that evening, I'm sure, has never forgotten that moment. A sense of patriotism stirred deep in each one of us with her unforgettable rendition of the "Star Spangled Banner."

Whitney Houston

Cold War Put into the Deep Freeze

Though there were many factors contributing to the end of the Cold War, the cessation of hostilities between the Soviet Union and the United States ultimately was due to the fall of the Soviet government itself. The Cold War was actually *lost by the Soviets* and not just bargained into oblivion by the two super powers. Several catastrophic economic events shook the country in the 1980s, which ultimately led to its demise.

The Chernobyl Nuclear Power Plant disaster, the Afghanistan war, and Ronald Reagan's aggressive approach to the Cold War were all major factors contributing to the crippling of the Russian economy. The Chernobyl nuclear meltdown cost the Soviet Union billions of dollars in cleanup efforts, and the Russian/Afghan war became a serious financial drain as well. Perhaps the most damaging economic blow was due to Ronald Reagans' aggressive military defense spending in America. Early in his presidency Reagan made his philosophical opposition to communism very clear to his Soviet counterparts. He not only attacked Russia philosophically, but he also backed up his rhetoric through policies and geo-political practices referred to as the "Reagan Doctrine."

Reagan also provided financial and military aid to anti-communist governments and insurgencies throughout the world as part of this doctrine. He believed, as many previous Presidents had believed, the best way to win the Cold War was by stopping the spread of communism. This, of course, added an additional economic burden to the Soviet Union as they were forced to provide an increasing amount of financial and military aid to their satellite communist states to counteract the aid provided by America. In the end, these catastrophic financial scenarios, all condensed into one decade, took a serious toll on the Soviet Union's economy. They simply just could not afford the Cold War anymore.

Another serious issue facing the Soviet Union was its diminishing political influence in Eastern Europe. Over the decades, their sphere of power and control in Eastern Europe had eroded badly, the crushing blow coming with the demise of communist East Germany. The fall of the Berlin Wall in 1989 and the subsequent reunification of East and West Germany was a definitive moment highlighting the demise of the Soviet Union's powerful influence throughout the world.

In late December of 1991, the once mighty Soviet Union experienced a catastrophic collapse. The process had already begun the previous year with the Baltic Republics (Latvia, Lithuania, and Estonia) declaring separation from the Soviet Union. One by one, the republics of Russia declared independence from Moscow and reorganized as a Common Wealth of Independent States. In the end, only one republic, Kazakhstan, remained under the guise of the Soviet Union. The mighty Russian Bear had suffered a mortal wound, and the once super power was no more. The dark clouds of the Cold War had dissipated and when the skies cleared, it was the United States that was left standing.

For the first 30 years of my life, the threat of a nuclear holocaust had been a real concern for the world. From my early days in school, when we conducted bomb drills, the threat of nuclear war was just a part of life. We were taught that Russia was our enemy who wanted to destroy our way of life. This was just a matter of *fact* and one which we all accepted.

Occasionally, throughout the decades, there would be times when the prospect of nuclear war would increase and then decrease again. All Americans were very much aware of the threat the Soviet Union posed and were wary of what one wrong political move by either side might initiate.

When it was announced that the Soviet Union had collapsed, it was a strange moment indeed. The threat of a potential nuclear holocaust had become just a part of life, and I, like many others, had learned to live with it, giving little thought to the ramifications of such a catastrophic event. Upon hearing the news that the Cold War was over, I felt a huge sense of relief. This was quite a surprise to me as I would not have believed the good news would have had such an impact on me. The truth was that I had neatly compartmentalized the horror of nuclear war deep into the recesses of my mind. When the Cold War ended, it felt as if an incredible burden had been lifted off my shoulders. It was a burden for which I had no idea how badly it had weighed upon me until it was gone.

Hero's Are People Too...

My dad was a "tough guy," and I'm not just saying that because he was my father. Throughout the years, I had heard stories from family members of his toughness, and my own observations of him in action validated these claims. My uncles had shared stories of my father getting into fights as a kid and later while in the Navy. He would be the obligatory sailor at the bar looking for a fight while on shore leave, later returning to the ship with cuts on his face and raw knuckles. Sure, he lost sometimes, but by all accounts, he mostly won.

By his own admission, my father loved to fight, which I never understood as I wanted no part of fighting. I wasn't a coward by any stretch, but I also had no interest in putting my face in harm's way. I recall one time our family was enjoying a pleasant meal at a local restaurant when my father suddenly stood up and walked up to a man sitting in the booth behind us. To my surprise, he grabbed the man's shirt and said, "Get up, we are going outside." Before I could put my fork down, my father had already drug the man in the parking lot. My family watched aghast as he menacingly accosted the hapless man. I could hear him yelling through the thick glass window but could not make out the words though I'm certain he wasn't complimenting the man on his shoes.

A few tense moments passed, with all of us unsure of what would unfold next. My father, apparently satisfied with his intimidation tactics, calmly walked back into the restaurant and sat down to finish his meal. No punches were thrown, and when we asked him what occurred out in the parking lot, my father said something like, "He just needed a little attitude adjustment." I don't remember what precipitated this event or why he felt the need to take the man outside. I just remembered thinking my dad was "badass."

I recall one time as a teenager, I thought I was ready to challenge my father… that lasted for about five seconds. While on vacation, he had asked me to turn down my boom box at the hotel pool. I admittedly had the volume too loud for a public setting. Exercising a little teenage resistance, I responded with a flippant, "Maybe I will, Maybe I won't." In an instant, my father sprang out of his poolside chair with eyes ablaze. He took one step towards me and said, "What in the hell did you just say to me??" I think I turned that boom box off before he even finished the sentence and then went about cleaning the pee that was running down my legs with my towel.

Just kidding, of course, but I might as well peed my pants. I was terrified by the look he gave me, and I NEVER challenged him again. I wanted to live to be an adult. Mind you, he never laid a hand on me or my sisters (with the exception of an occasional spanking when we were young), but much like Clint Eastwood, one disapproving look from him could quell any thoughts of resistance.

My dad was the king of our house, and he ruled with a benevolent but firm hand. All of us, including my mom, played by his rules, and he would always have the final say on how our family unit functioned. My mom, nine years younger than my father, had, in a sense, been raised by him as they were married when she was just seventeen. She willingly deferred almost all decisions and trusted him implicitly to make choices in the best interest of her and her children. That's the way it was for many families of the mid-twentieth century, and I saw nothing wrong with it at the time and still don't. My parents were happily married for over 40 years, and that is proof enough for me.

My own marriage, unfortunately was nothing like my father's. I would do whatever was necessary to keep Kim from having emotional meltdowns and often catered to her demands just to avoid trouble. I'm sure it upset my father to see me cower to Kim's whims and emotional swings, but I often found myself in survival mode, just trying to avoid chaos in my family life. Looking back, I'm not sure I took the right approach, but youth sometimes is a double edge sword, with the absence of wisdom being one of its negative attributes.

In any case, it was clear my father's methodology had garnered far more success than my meager efforts in my own marriage. He led with confidence and a level of certainty that I greatly admired. Did he make mistakes? Of course, he did. Were there failures he had to endure along the way? No doubt. However, he had a strong belief in himself and his ability to lead. He had garnered success in his career as the President of several Credit Unions and also in his personal life. His strength resided in his belief in the power of the mind and how one is responsible for their own success or failures. He refused to play the role of victim, and anything that would befall him he owned as his own doing.

For three decades, I saw my father as damn near invincible, and he was not only my hero but someone I viewed almost as a superhero. He was an outstanding role model and a wise sage that I often came to for advice. His advice always seemed measured, and if I chose to follow, it almost always worked.

In 1985 he suffered a mild heart attack and was also diagnosed with colon cancer that had metastasized. Five years later, he was back at full strength and cancer free. He was just that type of guy, mentally and physically tough, but that would all change in 1991.

On a lazy August Sunday afternoon, I received a phone call from my mother. I could tell instantly that something was terribly wrong. She informed me that my father had suffered a massive heart attack that morning, and he had just come out of surgery. Her description of what had occurred, his condition, and his prognosis for recovery, was very disjointed and unclear, so I asked her to have the surgeon contact me. I don't recall how long I waited or whether I had spoken to my sister before the surgeon returned my call, but I do remember wishing I wasn't living 1500 miles away. I was in no position to provide support to my mother or sister and certainly feared I might never see my father again.

When the surgeon called, he provided the information I required regarding what had happened and my father's current condition. He made it clear to me that I needed to return home as soon as possible as there were no guarantees my father would live. He informed me that the next 48 hours were critical to his survival and, with cold candor, expressed a lack of confidence that he would survive.

Within hours I found myself driving early the next morning 140 miles to the airport in Sioux Falls. Throughout the entire drive, memories of my father filled my head. I had a difficult time reconciling the idea that there was a good chance I would never see him alive again. It was surreal and almost incomprehensible that I was on the verge of losing my father. He was my rock, my leader, and my strength. How would I carry on without him? Who would I turn to for guidance and wisdom, and who would take care of my mother? I simply had no answers to any of these questions as I boarded the plane to Denver.

Upon arriving in Denver, I immediately called my mother to find out whether my dad was, in fact, still alive. He was clinging to life as I boarded the connecting flight to Portland. I remember looking at the faces on the plane. Some were staring out the window, and others were chatting with each other. All of them, though, were completely oblivious to my distraught emotional state. They were just going about their busy travel day while I was praying my father would be alive when we landed in Portland.

I felt very disconnected and isolated as no one knew what I was going through. I'm sure those on the plane would have had compassion had they known, or perhaps others were suffering through a similar scenario. None of that mattered, however, with my dad clinging to life. The minutes ticked away slowly during that flight, and I couldn't help but think I might get there too late.

As it turned out, I wasn't too late. My father was still hanging on by the time I reached a phone at the Portland airport. I went directly from the airport to the hospital located downtown. My sister and mother were waiting for me in the lobby, and I have to say they both looked like hell. I may have had to travel halfway across the country, not knowing what was going on, but they were living every minute of it at ground zero.

I was updated on his current status, which hadn't changed since I left South Dakota. He was still in ICU and had stabilized somewhat but by no means was out of the woods. I was told the next 24 hours would likely determine his fate. I, of course, asked to see him and was told he was unconscious, but I could go in for a short visit. I was also warned to prepare myself for what I would see. I wasn't sure exactly what that meant other than he probably looked quite helpless lying in a hospital bed unconscious. What I didn't know, and was totally unprepared for, was just how bad he looked.

As I walked into the ICU room where my father lay, I was alarmed by all the gadgets and medical equipment that surrounded him. There was, of course, the obligatory heartbeat monitor beeping with every beat of my father's heart, but there was much more machinery around him that I had no clue of their functions.

There were two observations I made immediately, and both were very disconcerting to me. A large breathing tube had been placed in my father's mouth, which looked incredibly uncomfortable, and his face looked bloated, almost beyond recognition. In short... he looked awful. This once strong, handsome man had been reduced to a frail pathetic looking human being. I was aghast at what I saw, and part of me just wanted to run out of the ICU room and not stop until I was back in South Dakota. On that first visit, I didn't stay long…I just couldn't do it.

The next day my uncle flew in from Houston, and I warned him to be prepared for what he would see, but nothing could have prepared him for what his brother looked like. Upon us walking into the room, I suddenly felt something pulling on my right arm, dragging me towards the floor. It was my uncle who had grabbed me just before he passed out upon seeing his brother lying helpless in a hospital bed. My dad's appearance was *that bad*, but certainly, part of it was also the shock of seeing such a tough man reduced to a frail soul barely clinging to life.

That frail soul, however, survived the first 48 and then 72 hours and beyond. He somehow conquered the crisis, and his condition was improving. The surgeon and doctors all agreed he was stable enough to be released from ICU. He was conscious now and talking, but with some difficulty, as his throat was raw from having a breathing tube placed into it.

I inquired whether it would be okay if I stayed overnight with my father so my mom could finally go home and sleep in her own bed. The overnight stay was approved, and a lazy boy chair was even brought into the room for me to sleep in. I was pleased to be able to spend some private time with my dad, and though there wasn't a great deal of conversation between us, I know he appreciated me being there. It appeared the worst was finally over, but that would all change later that evening.

Sometime after midnight, I can't exactly say when, I was awakened by a storm of activity in my father's room. Nurses and doctors were scurrying about frantically, and as I gathered my senses, it was clear my dad was in some level of distress. Orders were barked out by someone in charge, and before I knew it, they were trying to regulate his heart beats with a defibrillator. Paddles were being placed on his chest, and the command "Clear!" echoed through the room. My father's chest convulsed upward as they attempted to shock his heart back into a slower rhythm. Then a very nervous young woman, with her hands shaking badly, administered something to him with a hypodermic needle. That was the last thing I remember seeing as I was quickly ushered out of the room and down the hallway.

The whole event was incredibly startling as I went from a sound sleep to suddenly watching people desperately trying to save my father's life. I staggered into the nearby waiting room, trying to comprehend what had just occurred while also coming to grips with the fact that this was likely the end for my father. Time slowed to a crawl as I waited for any news about his condition. In the mean time, I called my mother, informing her what had occurred but offering no guarantees of what she might face upon her arrival at the hospital.

Before my mother arrived, news came regarding my father's fate. The doctor and the priest slowly walked from his room down the long hallway and towards me. As they grew closer, I could see the tension and stress on their faces. It looked bad… really bad, but in that same moment, a sense of peace came over me. All my concerns were washed away in an instant.

I didn't need to hear from the priest or the doctor as I *already knew* my father had survived. There was no doubt in my mind that he was still breathing and a part of this world. I can't tell you how I knew this, but nonetheless, I did… it was like Deja Vu. Long before they reached me in the waiting room, I knew what they were going to tell me. I was informed that my father had been stabilized, but there was no guarantee he would last through the night. The doctor candidly told me he had a 50/50 chance of survival, stating that the next few hours were critical. The priest offered to stay to comfort my mother upon her arrival, and I was grateful for his support.

Tick… tick…tick the minutes dragged on as we waited for the critical two hour mark the doctor had spoken of to pass. With every passing minute, we were one step closer to the hope that my dad would live. Two hours became four and then six, and once again, my father somehow found a path back from the dead and to the living. He may have looked weak and frail, but it was clear the toughness had never left him. Hours turned into days, and days turned into several weeks, and eventually, I found myself flying back to South Dakota with the comfort of knowing my dad would live.

Unfortunately, there was a heavy cost to be paid for all of the heart damage he had incurred. He was diagnosed with congestive heart failure, and all indications were pointing to the fact that he would likely need an oxygen supplement to assist in his breathing. My father, the tough guy who was a pillar of strength, had been permanently damaged and would never be the same. It appeared he would be relegated to requiring assistance to conduct even limited daily activities. This prideful man would have to learn to accept his fate as unappealing as it might be… or would he?

Left Turn After a Right

For the first three years of his presidency, George Bush enjoyed excellent approval ratings and appeared to be on his way to a second term as President. In the fourth year, his ratings would drop significantly due to several factors that ultimately would have a major impact on the outcome of the 1992 Presidential race.

"GOP fatigue" was likely one of the reasons for Bush's lessoning popularity. Prior to the 1992 election, the White House had been occupied by the republican party for 20 out of the previous 24 years, which included 12 consecutive years. By the end of Bush's tenure, many Americans were seeking a fundamental change in practice and policy, moving away from the conservative approaches of Reagan and Bush. Most things in life are cyclical in nature, and the political world is no different. Many Americans were simply tired of the same old approach in governance and were looking for something different.

In addition, though Bush did receive incredibly high marks for his foreign policy endeavors, his approval rating regarding domestic issues had dropped significantly. Bush had promised never to raise taxes during his tenure but failed to keep that promise upsetting many conservatives within his own party. The country was also facing an economic swoon in 1992 and appeared to be heading towards a recession. These factors significantly impacted public support for his domestic policies, which bottomed out at 21% during his final year in office.

Perhaps the biggest obstacle Bush faced was stepping clear of the long shadow his predecessor had cast. Ronald Reagan was one of the most charismatic and successful presidents in recent memory, and anyone who has held a leadership position is aware of the difficulty in succeeding such a leader. Bush could never quite meet the standards established by Reagan. Though he tried to separate himself from his former boss, claiming he was a "kinder, gentler" version, he just simply had none of Reagan's charisma. His communication skills paled in comparison to Reagan, and frankly, he came across as downright boring compared to the former actor.

Making things worse, Bush was now facing a younger and more dynamic opponent in his run for re-election. Arkansas Governor and democrat Bill Clinton possessed the charisma and oratory skillset not unlike Reagan, both qualities Bush sadly lacked. Indeed it was a bad competitive match for Bush as he simply could not equal Clinton's ability to communicate and inspire the American public.

Bill Clinton

Clinton would win the 1992 election garnering 370 electoral votes, with Bush receiving 168. It was only the fourth time in American history that a sitting President would lose his bid for re-election. The sound defeat of Bush foretold a new era of liberal leadership was about to begin. Americans had made it clear they were looking for a different type of leader with a less conservative approach to domestic policy. Bush's precipitous fall from grace during his final year as President was now complete, and the republican strong hold on the White House had ended.

Clinton had campaigned strongly on the state of the economy, which had taken a downturn during Bush's final year. He successfully exploited the fact that Bush had broken his promise not to raise taxes and strongly supported the balanced budget amendment. His record in revamping the Arkansas school system was also a strong selling point during his campaign, as he also promoted school choice.

As for me, I was pleased to see new leadership in the White House. Like many Americans, I had grown tired of the conservative nature of the previous two administrations and believed more could be done to improve the condition of the least fortunate in our country. It felt as if the previous administrations had made the rich "richer" and the poor "poorer" and that social welfare programs needed to be enhanced. I had voted for Reagan twice but was never impressed by Bush and felt there would be no improvement in the social welfare arena under his leadership. I was, after all, in the social service business and had observed the hardship firsthand of those who could benefit from enhanced social programs. Whether Clinton would be able to address these domestic based issues successfully, I wasn't sure, but I knew Bush certainly was not the answer.

Smell's Like the Death of Rock 'n Roll

In the late 80s, a new form of rock music, "Grunge," was developing in the Pacific Northwest. The band that would bring this genre into the American consciousness and create a revolution in the music industry was "Nirvana". Formed in 1987, Nirvana and its front man Kurt Cobain burst onto the scene in 1991 with their hit song "Smells Like Teen Spirit". It was the first single released from their now certified diamond album "Nevermind," and it would change the face of popular music permanently.

The rock music I grew up listening to had changed considerably by the time the decade of the 90s rolled around. The 60s gave birth to legendary bands such as The Rolling Stones, The Who, Led Zeppelin, The Kinks, and the solo artistry of Bob Dylan. Of course, none had the impact of the Beatles, the most powerful musical force of the 20th century. The Beatles dominated the music industry while also immensely influencing popular culture until their demise in 1969. The new rock sound created by the "British Invasion" led by the Beatles continued its music industry dominance throughout the 70s. As Elvis Presley slowly faded into the abyss, The Rolling Stones, The Who, and Led Zeppelin carried the flag for rock 'n roll, producing one incredible album after another.

Songs containing political or spiritual themes (made popular in the decade of the 60s) decreased considerably by the late 70s. Themes celebrating excessive lifestyles and sexual promiscuity became the rock standard. Still, the music was powerful and creative, performed by talented musicians influenced greatly by the Beatles' musical mastery from the previous decade.

The 80s would be the decade rock 'n roll began to show cracks in its shell. Music was indeed changing, beginning to give way to solo artists such as Madonna and Whitney Houston. In addition, "New

Wave" rock had found a strong niche with the youth audience. This genre was not anchored to the traditional rock 'n roll formula of powerful down beats and guitar leads. Rather, it leaned on keyboards and synthesized drums. "Hip Hop," originally a form of music born in the dense urban areas of America, was also expanding its reach into mainstream America.

Another major issue contributing to the denigration of rock music was the advent of MTV. With the music video becoming a critical method in the marketing of bands, the image was often more important than substance. Rock bands became more focused on presentation and less focused on the quality of their music. Long sculptured hair, make up, and spandex pants became "the look" for rock bands of the eighties, and the era of "Hair Bands" was born.

Though still adept as musicians, rock bands of the eighties often chose flash over substance to sell records. The homespun earthy look of the 60s hippies had become obsolete, replaced by the plastic superficial look of the 80s hair bands. In addition, their music lacked the complexity of thought and was often penned with silly love songs and meaningless party anthems in mind. The rock 'n roll I had been raised on indeed was now a shadow of its former self. It had been weakened to the point where another form of music could replace it as a staple in the music industry.

Hair Bands of the 80s

As for me, I had already abandoned the contemporary rock scene after the death of John Lennon. Lost in the immense catalog of quality music created in the 60s, I completely ignored the hair band era and, for the most part, thought it was ridiculous. As is almost always the case, superficiality has a short shelf life, and the era of hair bands was quickly eradicated with the birth of grunge rock.

Nirvana

With Nirvana leading the way, grunge rock burst onto the scene in the early nineties with a style and presentation representing the antithesis of the hair bands of the 80s. The long sculptured hair and glittery outfits were replaced with an unassuming style comprised of t-shirts and jeans.

Grunge music was built on slow melodic verses followed by crashing power chords coupled with screaming aggressive vocals. Unlike its hair band predecessors, grunge lyrics also possessed a level of depth, often speaking of alienation and social rejection. This new form of rock swept over the country with amazing speed, exemplifying the thirst the listening public had for something more out of music than superficiality. In a blink of an eye, it had become the standard for rock music while also opening the door for other rock alternatives that would soon follow.

Grunge Rock, however, had one fatal flaw… it just wasn't that good. Sure, it was an improvement compared to hair band music, but only because it was a different sound with a different presentation. In fact, I would argue that grunge musicians were less talented than their hair band predecessors, often possessing a skill set just above the novice level. However, it was indeed a different approach to rock music, and the youth flocked to the new sound.

As for me, I was never impressed with grunge rock. From strictly a technical perspective, it appeared easily constructed, lacking very little complexity in its design. The music reminded me of an aspiring teenage rock band who never got any further than their parent's garage. Sure, it was raw, but the music felt uninspired and rudimentary. I labeled it as "quaalude music," songs seemed to drone on and on endlessly with minimal structural changes.

In addition, the lyrics often focused on feelings of victimization and helplessness, two subjects I had little interest in pursuing. This type of messaging was diametrically opposed to the type of lyrics I grew up listening to. Bands such as "The Who" also spoke of social isolation, but they wore it like a badge of honor, spitting back at those responsible for their plight. In other words, The Who would not complain about how the "the man" was sticking it to them. They told "the man" to go fuck himself. Grunge seemed to enjoy wallowing in its victimhood, lacking the intellectual capacity even to express feelings with any level of complexity.

Bottom line, it didn't matter what I thought of grunge as it became the rock music of choice for a large part of the decade. It began to fade as people eventually became bored with the music and its lack of variance in style and approach. It just droned on and on, never escaping its original format or evolving into something more complex. Hip Hop and the "entertainer" style of music took over the radio airways with the absence of something interesting or innovative coming out of the rock music world. Grunge had buried the rock music I knew with its un-inventive approach to the genre. The hair bands of the eighties may have placed rock on life support, but grunge put it in its grave.

The "Vegas Style" form of entertainment, made popular by Frank Sinatra and Sammy Davis Jr., had resurfaced with all new fresh faces but with the same formula, placing music in a minor role and the entertainer as the focus. Often the performer of these songs had not written the lyrics or the music.. in the purest sense, they were not "artists," but rather, they were performers singing someone else's song.

Hip-hop had also found a foothold in mainstream music as people who were turned off by grunge and could not identify with entertainers such as Mariah Carey and the Back Street Boys found a home in the lyrics and beat of hip-hop. To its credit, this genre did have some authenticity to it, and it delved into the trappings and dangers of urban living with candid clarity.

This urban based music style eventually reached the suburbs of America and ultimately supplanted rock music as the preferred form by the end of the decade.

For the first time in over four decades, rock had been relegated to a subordinate role in the music industry, one which it still occupies today. "Nirvana" had inadvertently placed a dagger in the heart of rock music, and the genre has never been able to recover from this fatal wound. The status it enjoyed as the king of the music industry had evaporated by the end of the nineties. The reign of rock'n roll had ended, possibly never to return. As Jim Morrison once wrote, "When the music is over… turn out the lights."

The Colonel and I

By the mid 90s, I was well on my way to establishing a career in the social service arena. My work, while employed at the Indian School, had been recognized and rewarded through several promotions. In 1994 I found myself in a position representing the school developing collaborative partnerships with Tribal entities throughout the state. I was assigned a new boss who, in the end, would teach me more about leadership and working effectively with people than any boss before. These were valuable lessons I would later apply throughout the rest of my career.

Bill Kilpatrick was a retired Army colonel who served in the Vietnam War. After he left the military, he returned to school, earning his master's degree in counseling. The Colonel possessed the classic "drill sergeant appearance. His hair was cut high and tight in a 50's style flat top. He had a "tough guy" physical stature with a barrel chest, thick neck, and big arms. His piercing blue eyes, I'm sure, had terrified many subordinates during his time in the military. With one look at the Colonel, no one was surprised to learn he had been a career soldier.

As a trained military man, he stressed structure and protocol in his work environment. He was direct and clear in his communications and expected the same in return from those who worked for him. The Colonel promoted the importance of candor and trust in the workplace and encouraged input from his staff without fear of retribution. I found him to be incredibly fair and one never to play head games with his employees. It was important to the Colonel that those who worked for him found success in their careers. He wanted all under his purview to thrive.

I liked him a great deal and respected him even more, and through the many hours we spent driving across the state together, I also realized what a gentle caring man he was. He had a big heart for the children we served, and it was clear this was not just a job to him but a passion to serve those with the greatest need.

One day, sensing my youthful arrogance, the Colonel sat me down for a talk. He told me he already knew he was smart, and it was clear that I was as well. He then asked me what value I saw in impressing others with my intellect. I pondered his question for a moment and said something like, "They need to respect me." He reminded me that a smart and confident man isn't worried about gaining the respect of others. He already assumes he has it. He stressed the importance of our approach with the tribal leaders we were soon to meet. He noted the justified suspicion and bias they may have towards white people proposing "plans" to them. History had proven that the "white man" could not be trusted, and there was no reason for the tribal leaders to buy into anything we proposed.

The colonel said the best way to get buy in from those you are pitching an idea to was for them to believe it was actually *their idea*. He told stories of how he would soften those he wanted to sell an idea to by proclaiming he was "just a dumb old farmer who didn't know much." The purpose of humbling himself to his audience was to disarm any defensive posture they may have brought to the meeting. He created an environment where those whom he was pitching the idea felt that *they* were the experts and that he was coming to them for advice. I observed him implement this strategy with tribal leaders, and it became clear that it was incredibly effective. He quickly put those at ease who may have had suspicions regarding our intentions. He was skillful in carefully guiding meeting participants towards embracing his ideas without them realizing what he had done.

Time and again, I watched him conclude a meeting getting exactly what he wanted while leaving tribal leaders feeling it was *them* who had developed the idea. We would shake hands and thank them for their insight and walk off agreeing to a plan he had designed to sell from the very beginning. His technique was masterful and hurt no one, as everyone, in the end, felt the result of the meeting was productive and collaborative.

In the decades that followed, (and at times leading a staff that numbered a hundred strong), I would use this strategy to garner support for my plans. I didn't need credit for the idea as I was only interested in results. Allowing my staff to believe *they* were the owners of the idea was often the best way to accomplish my objective. The fact is, people, will work harder for their own plan over another's plan every time. It's simply human nature to want your own ideas to succeed. As for needing my ego stroked and claiming ownership of my ideas, as the Colonel had said, a confident man already assumes he has the respect of those around him and doesn't require any further validation.

The Colonel and I spent a great deal of time together working on projects and promoting the programs our school offered to Native Americans. We learned a lot about each other during this time and became a good team having mutual respect for one another. One day, I can't remember how we arrived on the subject. We began discussing his time in Vietnam. He was Captain or perhaps a Major during his tour of duty. In any case, at one point, I asked him if he engaged in any direct conflict with the enemy, which in retrospect, was probably inappropriate to ask. However, I had an unhealthy relationship with the Vietnam war going as far back as when I was very young. It terrified me and had scarred my psyche, but I also could not look away from it.

To my surprise, the colonel's face turned an ashen color, and his hands began to shake. A strange, far away look washed over his eyes as he told me a story of how he had ordered a mortar strike on a Vietcong position believed to be cloaked under the guise of a civilian village. Half way through the retelling of this experience, he broke down and began to sob, tears flowing down his cheeks, whimpering as he explained that the alleged Vietcong position had actually been a civilian village. He looked at me as if it was terribly important that I believed him and explained he didn't know what he had done until they arrived at the village and saw the dead women and children.

I was completely surprised by the Colonel's emotional outburst. All I could think to do was to put my arm around his shoulders and assure him that I believed it was a mistake and could see how sorry he was for what had occurred. It was an unforgettable emotional moment I was not prepared to encounter. In a flash, I watched a confident and emotionally tough man fall to pieces, uncontrollably crying like a child. The war had found me again and shown its wicked face twenty years after it had ended, and for the Colonel, well it was clear… the war had never left him.

Through the months that followed, the Colonel and I continued to work well together as a team while garnering positive results in our outreach efforts. Sadly, all that goodwill and companionship would come to a crashing end due to my own youthful arrogance. His boss, Matt, was a good friend of mine, and we had developed a relationship that went well beyond work hours. Matt and I had traveled together to Minneapolis to attend a World Series game and also to South Bend, Indiana, to watch Notre Dame football. In fact, his wife and Kim were also friends, and we would often join them along with another couple, Dan and Nadine, playing cards watching movies, and having fun with the kids. I would ultimately use my friendship with Matt to usurp the Colonel's authority for my own personal gain.

I no longer recall the issue the Colonel and I were in disagreement over, but I do remember feeling absolutely "in the right." The colonel disagreed and would not bend in the least, eventually making it clear he was the boss, and the subject was closed. Unfortunately, I did not take "no" for an answer and would do the unthinkable by directly going over his head to his boss (my friend Matt) and convincing him to overrule the Colonel's decision.

I can't say for sure that my friendship with Matt was the difference in his decision to side with me, but my tactics felt sleazy and underhanded, to be certain. In any case, I marched into the Colonel's office along with Matt and puffed my chest out as Matt directed him to take the action I had recommended. The Colonel's face was filled with disappointment as he glanced over at me reflecting the pain of betrayal. I had dishonored him by breaking rank, going over his head to get my way.

He called me into his office soon after the incident and expressed his disappointment regarding my actions. To a military man who had invested so much time teaching me the finer points of leadership, my behavior was nothing less than treasonous. It wasn't long after that incident that I was placed under the direction of Matt, and though it was never confirmed, I believe the Colonel wanted no part of me after my betrayal.

To this day, I still feel ashamed of my actions and how I let a proud trusting man down. That being said, what would later transpire and the ethical crimes I would be guilty of committing made this betrayal look like a misdemeanor. In the world of ethics it was true I was guilty of stabbing the Colonel in the back, but I was soon to engage in behavior that would go far beyond the actions of a disobedient soldier.

The Juice is On the Loose

At the age of four, I became a fan of football. The reason for this was simple, my dad loved to watch football, and anything he loved to do, I did as well. From a very young age, I sat with my father and watched football games. He taught me the sport, and I grew to love everything about it, so it was no surprise that in 1968 I spent the limited funds I had to purchase a college football magazine. I carried that magazine with me everywhere and even took it to school for "show and tell," pointing out my favorite pictures to my classmates.

Inside the magazine, a young athlete named O.J. Simpson was featured. I still remember the photo of O.J. posing in front of a Trojan soldier statue located on the campus of the University of Southern California. The article went into depth about this star running back who played for Southern Cal. He was considered the best player in college football and was the favorite to win the highest honor in football, the Heisman Trophy.

OJ Simpson

From the first time I saw O.J. Simpsons' photo in that magazine, I was a big fan of this football star. He was a good looking young man with a big smile and natural charisma, and his talent on the field was undeniable. He was a combination of speed, grace, and power, and when he ran, there was no one else in football who was so elusive. He was something else to watch play, and to this day, I have seen very few players with his level of talent.

After a stellar college career, O.J. went into the NFL and rewrote the record the books as a running back for the Buffalo Bills. He was the first 2,000-yard rusher in NFL history, captured four rushing titles, and was selected to the Pro Bowl five times. He was inducted into the Pro Hall of Fame in 1985 and is widely considered one of the greatest running backs of all time.

Simpson as Hertz Spokesman

While still playing football in college, Simpson pursued a career in acting as well. He garnered guest staring roles on hit tv shows and later, while in the NFL, became the spokesperson for Hertz Rent a Car. His notoriety also earned him acting roles in movies, including the blockbuster hit "The Towering Inferno." After his retirement from football Simpson began a successful broadcasting career covering an array of sporting events for network tv. O.J. Simpson, or the "Juice" as many called him, was a fan favorite during his many years as an elite athlete and became a well loved American celebrity following his retirement from football.

All of that would change in 1994 when Simpson was charged with the gruesome murders of his estranged wife, Nicole Brown Simpson, and her friend Ronald Goldman. Both were stabbed to death outside her home, Nicole Brown Simpson's head nearly severed from her neck in the brutal assault. It already had been well documented by local authorities that the marriage between the two had been riddled with domestic issues, which eventually led to Nicole filing for divorce in 1992.

There had been eight recorded incidents of police involvement due to domestic violence calls, with O.J. being arrested on one occasion. After their separation, Nicole Brown made it clear she feared for her physical safety and would eventually claim she feared for her life as O.J. had threatened to kill her. Simpson, who fit the classic profile of a domestic abuser, was immediately considered a prime suspect in the murders.

After a positive DNA match connecting Simpson's blood to the blood found at the murder scene, two counts of first degree murder were filed against him. Previously, a bloody right hand glove had been found on the Simpson estate, determined to be the mate of the left glove found at the scene of the murders. With mounting forensic evidence, and a history of domestic violence perpetrated by Simpson, the District Attorney's office believed they had ample suspicion and evidence to charge him with the double homicide.

Upon notification of his imminent arrest, Simpson, through his attorney, Robert Shapiro, requested that he be allowed to turn himself into the police. This request was honored as the LAPD felt that due to his fame, Simpson was a very low flight risk. Over a thousand reporters flocked to the police station awaiting O.J.'s "perp walk," but he never arrived. LAPD then notified Shapiro that they would be arresting Simpson at his friend's home, Robert Kardashian, where he had stayed the previous night. When they arrived, it was discovered that Simpson and his friend Al Cowlings were no longer on the premises. Simpson, however, did leave behind a note which was interpreted to be a suicide note.

What occurred next was nothing short of bizarre as police began to search for Cowling's white Ford Bronco, believed to be hiding Simpson. Eventually, the vehicle was located heading north on Interstate 5, and when approached, Cowling yelled out the window, informing police that O.J. was lying in the back seat with a gun pointed at his head. Twenty police cars followed behind Cowling's bronco as he drove slowly on the interstate at 35 miles per hour. Helicopters from local news affiliates filled the airspace as they picked up the police radio calls and began an air pursuit of the Bronco, feeding the video of the low speed chase to a

The Chase

national audience. It is estimated that 95 million Americans watched the pursuit of Simpson that evening, in contrast, 90 million people watched the Super Bowl that year.

Eventually, Cowlings took Simpson back to his home, where he was allowed to enter his residence and remain inside while police continued to negotiate for a safe resolution to his surrender. There was fear throughout the evening that O.J. might commit suicide due to his distraught condition. The four hour saga finally ended when Shapiro arrived at his estate and brought Simpson out to surrender to police. LAPD found "$8,000 in cash, clothing, a passport, a loaded gun, family pictures, along with a disguise kit including a fake mustache and goatee.

As for me, my family had gone on a camping trip that evening with our friends Don and Nadine, and none of us had any idea what had occurred until we returned home. It was indeed a major surprise to discover "the Juice" had led a parade of police and helicopters across Los Angeles in a low speed chase. At that point, it appeared to me that O.J. was guilty of the murders because he had evaded the law, refused to surrender, and had brought along items that indicated a plan to flee from the authorities. There were so many questions needing answers, and I was hoping viable explanations existed that could exonerate Simpson from this unspeakable act of violence.

The subsequent trial of O.J. Simpson became "must watch tv" for millions of Americans. I had always been a fan of courtroom drama television and found myself engrossed in the spectacle as well. This was not a fictitious "Perry Mason" case. This was reality, including one of the most famous men in America as the defendant. Day after day, week after week, America watched with intrigue and fascination. The trial took on an almost a "soap opera" feel to it, with unknowns such as O.J.'s friend, Kato Kaelin, becoming national celebrities overnight.

The prosecution, led by Marcia Clark and Christopher Darden, had presented a mountain of forensic evidence pointing to Simpson as the killer that they meticulously laid out in their case. The "dream team" defense, which included Shapiro, Johnny Cochran, and F. Lee Bailey, built their case of "reasonable doubt" on accusations that the prosecution's case had been compromised, contaminated, and corrupted.

With Johnny Cochran leading the charge, the defense painted a compelling picture arguing that detectives assigned to the case were bigots and had planted evidence to secure a conviction of a black man. The defense successfully denigrated the character of several key witnesses for the prosecution while also pointing out poor investigative work involved in securing evidence, testing blood samples, and baseless "extrapolations of fact" that could not be proven.

One of the biggest moments in this monumental courtroom drama came when Simpson was asked to try on the bloody gloves, one which was found at the scene of the murders, the other found on his estate later that evening. The defense had claimed the bloody glove found at Simpsons' estate was taken from the murder scene and planted at his home by the detectives who were investigating the murder. In one of the most dramatic moments of the trial, Simpson went about trying to put on the gloves in question in the courtroom... they did not fit. This was a devastating moment for the prosecution as reasonable doubt must have seeped into the minds of the jurors watching O.J. struggling to put on the bloody gloves.

The Gloves

After nearly nine months of courtroom drama, a verdict was finally reached after only four hours of jury deliberation. It is estimated that over 100 million people worldwide either watched or listened to the verdict live. Many Americans put their daily lives on hold as the country waited with great anticipation to hear the disposition of the case. It is estimated that 480 million dollars of productivity was lost while the nation paused and waited for the verdict.

Considerable concern arose regarding the likelihood of riots if Simpson was found guilty. Local law enforcement was placed on heightened alert running twelve hour shifts to increase police presence in the streets. There was a clear division in opinion on whether Simpson was guilty of the murders; 75 percent of whites believed he was guilty, while 70 percent of blacks felt he was innocent. At 10:07 am on Tuesday, October 3, 1995, a moment where time almost seemed to stop for the nation, the verdict was issued, finding Simpson not guilty on all charges. The trial that had captured the fascination of millions of Americans for months had finally ended with O.J. Simpson leaving the courtroom a free man.

As for me, I was pleased with the verdict as I believed the defense had done a masterful job in casting "reasonable doubt" in the prosecution's case. Was there a mountain of evidence that pointed to Simpson as the perpetrator of these heinous crimes? Most certainly, however, the defense time and again successfully questioned the validity of the evidence and cleverly focused on the personal character of the investigators, painting them as bigots while also providing factual information to substantiate these claims.

Our justice system is appropriately weighed to provide the accused protection from "assumed guilt." It is the responsibility of the prosecution to *prove guilt. C*onversely, the defense is not required to *prove innocence.* In the end, I believe the defense had done enough to poke holes in the prosecution's case providing the jury with reasonable doubt to determine that the defendant may not be guilty.

Do I personally think O.J. Simpson murdered his wife and Ronald Goldman? Yes, I do. However, I also believe a compelling argument was made by the defense that put his guilt in doubt. The verdict was essentially correct based on the design of our justice system which states that the defendant charged with a crime is innocent until proven guilty. The prosecution, in my opinion, lost a winnable case due to questionable investigative methods, forensic evidence gaffs, and several critical strategic mistakes made during the trial, including the infamous request to have Simpson try on the bloody gloves. It should be noted that Simpson would later be found liable in the wrongful deaths of his wife and Ronald Goldman in civil suits (which carry a lower burden of proof). The plaintiffs were awarded over 33 million dollars in compensatory and punitive damages.

Good Times… Bad Times

By the mid-nineties, I was excelling in my career more than I could have ever imagined. In the previous decade, the same guy who chose to party over getting his school work done had somehow become a responsible, successful adult. How did this happen? Good question. I believe it was the values and expectations my parents had established for me at a young age. My mother and father both worked and took their jobs seriously. They believed they owed it to their employer to give their very best and modeled this behavior to their children. Their values and work ethic were always latent in me. It just took awhile for them to come to the surface.

I recall one profound moment when I made the mental decision to do all I could to elevate my career. One day I saw a friend and colleague of mine loading his children into a beat-up old van. We were about the same age, had very similar beliefs, and were both married with young children. As I drove by him and his young family, I saw my own face reflecting off the car window. It struck me, in that moment, that *his present* was *my future* if I didn't change course in my career. I wanted something else for my family than just barely "getting by." I felt I owed it to my wife and children to provide them with a better lifestyle than would ever be possible on a social worker's salary. I was proud of my job and the work I was doing, and I could think of nothing more admirable than serving Native American families. That being said, my family came first, and what I wanted for them could not be realized by doing social work for a living.

As fate would have it, soon after my stint with the Colonel, I received my big break. My friend Matt, who by this time had risen to a vice president position at the school, introduced me to the President. Matt told him I was the young leader he had been looking for, capable of handling some of his pet projects, including his favorite project…the high school program.

The high school program was considered the crown jewel of the Indian school. Graduation rates on the reservation were bleak, and the goal of this program was not only to improve these rates but also successfully integrate Native American students into the public school system. It was the ultimate "end game" for the Indian School, serving disadvantaged young children and guiding them through their elementary school years all the way to a high school diploma.

The program had two group homes, one for high school girls and the other for boys. Although student participation in the program was relatively small due to limits in group home capacity, the services provided were extensive. The President himself had invested many hours in ensuring the success of this program. Eventually, thanks to the efforts of Matt and my own growing reputation as a leader, I was promoted to the director of the High School Program.

Not long after my promotion, we began negotiations with a local university in an effort to establish a group home on its campus. The goal was to establish a college program for our recent high school graduates. If high school graduation rates were considered bleak for Native Americans, then participation in post-secondary education was almost unheard of. This was a great opportunity for our students to receive a free college education while still benefiting from the support services provided by our school.

In what seemed like a blink of an eye, I found myself near the top of our school's leadership group holding the position of Director of the College and High School Programs. Frankly, it was hard for me to believe how quickly I had risen within the organization, but I also knew I had put in the work and had proven to be a valuable asset.

In truth, without Matt's support and belief in me, I doubt I would have ever been given the opportunity. There is indeed validity in the statement, "It's not what you know… it's who you know."

I had never enjoyed a job as much as the one I found myself in as director of these two important programs…and I never would again. Looking back, I can say it was the pinnacle of my career, as I was so proud of the work I was doing and thrilled to be a part of this wonderful organization. The school was well-run, and its mission was honorable. It was filled with bright, compassionate people making a difference in the lives of children, and I was now one of its top leaders guiding the mission and principles of the organization.

Of course, my concerns regarding my inability to provide my family with an acceptable lifestyle had evaporated with my ascent into upper management. I was well paid for my work and suddenly found myself flush with money and able to leave the mobile home world behind and buy an actual house.

After several months of looking, Kim and I found a home in town that we both fell in love with. Sure, it needed some renovation work in the kitchen, but it also had a great deal of potential, including a large private backyard. We purchased the home in early summer, and over the next several months, we worked hard to complete the renovations and moved in that fall.

With all the new developments in our lifestyle and careers, it appeared Kim was happy for a brief moment. She had a successful husband, two beautiful children, a new home, and recently earned a promotion as administrative assistant to the President of our school. All signs were pointing in the right direction as our family gained positive momentum. Kim somehow had even talked me into attending Sunday church services on a regular basis, where I would eventually be asked to join its leadership group. Her dream life appeared to be unfolding right in front of her, and it was good to see her happy.

To most people, I'm sure it appeared we were a successful young couple who had life by the tail. Image was important to Kim, and in just six years, we had certainly created the image of the perfect young American family. The irresponsible man that once stared back at me in the mirror no longer existed as I had now taken on the persona of a successful modern-day family man. My transformation was indeed impressive, and I would have never believed it of myself, but there I was…the picture of responsibility. Unfortunately, Kim's deep-ceded insecurities still haunted her, and ultimately, they would resurface no matter how well things were going. It was just a matter of time before she would be looking for someone to blame for her inner pain.

Her mother, of course, made sure Kim did not forget I was responsible for her unhappiness. In the early years, while still a social worker, Sandy would often comment to Kim how much she pitied her daughter, forced to live such a meager lifestyle. Sandy would mock our life living in a trailer and would tell Kim she had hoped so much more for her daughter.

Now with me making good money, Sandy needed a new angle. She began complaining to her daughter I was never around, and my work seemed more important to me than my family. Since her claims of me being a poor provider were no longer applicable, she coyly now had Kim believing I was an absent, uncaring husband. She was a master at manipulating her daughter, twisting anything positive into a negative, and sadly there wasn't a damn thing I could do about it. Kim soon began to resent me for the time I spent at work and not at home, and it was all too predictable. Thanks to her mother's manipulation, she was always able to blame her unhappiness on my behavior, pointing an accusing finger at my actions regardless of my intent.

As if things weren't bad enough, Kim's behavior became aggressive again. She began to physically attack me on a consistent basis as her mood swings became more prominent. Whether it was throwing punches at me or throwing household items at my head, it was clear her behavior had become more unstable and dangerous. In addition, she began to engage in self-harm behavior again, scratching her wrists in a feigned effort to represent a suicide attempt.

One evening she went into the kitchen and took a knife out. She placed it against her stomach in samurai fashion, threatening to stab herself. I slowly approached her, calmly pleading for her to set the knife down on the counter. To my surprise, she took a step toward me, wildly lashing out with the knife and screaming for me to "Back off!" It was then I realized it wasn't just punches or thrown household items at my head that I needed to worry about. She was actually capable of truly harming me.

Often when these tirades began, I tried to immediately extricate myself from the situation by leaving the house before anyone got hurt. Kim would have none of it, though, and run to each door blocking the exit as I arrived. In essence, I was trapped unless I physically removed her from the area, which I had tried in the past, always resulting in a physical confrontation.

Unfortunately, her bad behavior also began to once again manifest itself in public as well. On one occasion, the mayor and his wife had invited us over for "game night," and for reasons I can no longer remember, Kim became incensed with me and threw a pair of dice right in my face. She stomped away from the dining room table, screaming profanities at me as the rest of us sat there speechless. To say it was an embarrassing, humiliating experience would be an understatement.

Another time during one of her tirades, I escaped the house out the front door only to be followed by her reigning punches down upon me in our front yard as our neighbors watched. The all-American family had brought domestic violence into our sleepy little neighborhood. The situation became untenable, and although our children were often witnesses to her violent behavior, Kim never raised a hand or threatened to hurt either of them. Aside from the madness she inflicted upon me, she loved her children and would never have physically harmed them.

The situation became so bad that I began trying to figure ways out of our marriage. I distinctly recall one summer day sitting in my yard, mentally going through what needed to be done to escape the hell I was in. I quickly surmised that, sadly, there was no way out. We had a mortgage, car payments, friends, good jobs, and, most of all, two children who needed us. I would have to abandon all of this if I was to leave the relationship. Everything we had built and worked so hard for would be left in shambles. It would mean starting completely over with nothing to show for all my efforts other than blatant failure. I just couldn't do it, and whether I liked it or not, I had to accept the fact I was trapped with no way out.

Just when it seemed my life had hit rock bottom…it got worse. I received a phone call from my father informing me that his cancer had returned. Somehow he had miraculously bounced back from the serious heart attack of several years ago and had been doing fine. Unlike all the prognostications predicting a radically different lifestyle for my father, he continued doing what he had always done, and though it may have been at a slower pace, he still mowed his yard, fixed his roof, and gardened. He had overcome what could have been and should have been a debilitating condition with relative ease, but hey, that was my dad; there was no quit in him.

At the beginning of the decade, he had been told he was "cancer free" and was considered a survivor of the colon cancer he fought in the mid-eighties. During his last checkup, it was discovered the cancer had returned, manifesting itself in the liver. This was, of course, terrible news, as liver cancer is often a deadly form of cancer. My father informed me it was inoperable, and his condition was likely terminal. How much time did he have? No one really knew, but we both were keenly aware that life expectancy for liver cancer patients was typically short.

I was devastated by the news and could find no relief from the terrible knowledge I was going to lose my father. A cold wave of fear washed over me as I realized I would be on my own without my dad to help me. I wasn't sure how I was going to make it without him. He had always been there, providing support and answers when I needed them most. All I could do was hope he could find a way to beat the odds again. I found some relief knowing my dad would be a "tough out" for cancer, or anything else for that matter. It was just in his nature to be a fighter.

By the midpoint of the decade, I had risen to new heights of success and experienced new lows of despair. I was faced with the staggering contradiction of both experiences happening at the same time. On one hand, I had reached the pinnacle of my career. On the other hand, failure and destruction were waiting patiently in the wings. One thing was certain, though, with the news of my father's terminal condition and a marriage ravaged by the disease of dysfunction, I had little hope for the future.

One Bill at a Time

Bill Clinton, at the time of his inaugural address, became the third youngest President in American history. This was a departure from the previous two Presidents, who at the conclusion of their terms in office, were 78 and 69, respectively. The former governor of Arkansas had risen to the highest office in the country at the age of 46. This young skilled communicator also embraced a political philosophy and domestic agenda much different than his predecessors.

After twelve consecutive years of conservative leadership, the disparity between the "haves" and "have nots" in America had only increased. Clinton's new vision for the future, in particular his domestic proposals, promised a more equal distribution of wealth and this resonated with many Americans. During his campaign, Clinton often spoke of the disparity of wealth and blamed Republican leadership for the increasing gap between the two socioeconomic groups. While in office, Clinton made good on his campaign promises, successfully signing into law several important bills addressing his domestic policy initiatives.

Some of the legislation passed during his tenure included the Family Medical Leave Act and the Violence Against Women Act. Clinton also signed welfare reform legislation, the Personal Responsibility and Work Opportunity Reconciliation Act of 1996 (PRWORA). PRWORA introduced TANF (Temporary Assistance to Needy Families) as a replacement for the old welfare system established in the 1960s. TANF would dramatically change the way the federal government and states would determine eligibility for needy families. It also introduced work requirements for its participants. Clinton also pushed hard for universal health care for Americans with his Health Care Reform Plan but ultimately failed to gain enough support from Congress. The inability to pass his Health

Care Reform Plan would be the biggest legislative failure of his administration.

Clinton, however, did find success in passing legislation related to gun control with the Omnibus Crime Bill that included a ten-year ban on assault weapons. He was also the first President to support gays in the military openly, and although he pressed hard to allow gays to serve, he eventually was forced to compromise. He implemented the "Don't Ask, Don't Tell" directive allowing gays to serve but only with the premise they did not disclose their sexual orientation. Clinton also selected openly gay people into administrative positions and is generally considered the first President to champion gay rights.

On the fiscal front, the Clinton administration pushed measures to reduce the federal budget deficit and also signed the North American Free Trade Agreement (NAFTA) that removed trade barriers between the United States, Canada, and Mexico. His fiscal policies helped push forward one of the most expansive economic growth periods in American history.

With the loss of both the House of Representatives and the Senate in the 1994 midterm election, Clinton was forced to compromise on his progressive agenda, which derailed some of his biggest initiatives, such as universal health care. All of this placed Clinton in a precarious position mid-way through his first term, seemingly destined to lose re-election in 1996. However, by late 1995, the economy was showing signs of strengthening, and the economic swoon of the early 90s had dissipated. With encouraging signs of economic growth, Americans became optimistic regarding their future. They saw the Clinton administration as a major impetus to the increased economic productivity the United States was enjoying.

Robert Dole challenged Bill Clinton for the office of president in the 1996 Presidential election. Dole, a senator from Kansas and a former WWll veteran, was a well-known Republican politician who had served in the Senate for over 25 years. As part of what many consider "The Greatest Generation" in American history, Dole attacked Clinton as a privileged, pampered "Baby Boomer." He argued what America needed was a mature President from the generation who had fought and lived through WWll. It was a weak argument that never gained much traction during the campaign because Dole's advancing age was actually a concern for many Americans.

One of Dole's biggest campaign promises was his commitment to cut the federal income tax by 15 percent across the board. Clinton countered, stating the Dole tax plan would increase the federal deficit by a large margin. He also claimed Dole would look to reduce the funding of popular social programs such as social security and medicare.

In the end, Clinton would win re-election, garnering 379 electoral votes to Dole's 159. It was the first time since Franklin Roosevelt a democrat, won consecutive terms in office. It was also the first time in American history a candidate won the presidential election without garnering the majority of the male vote.

As for me, I was pleased with the re-election result as I felt Clinton had successfully advanced policies that focused on important domestic issues. It also appeared the economy was on the upturn and gaining steam. Whether that was due to Clinton's economic policies was irrelevant, the incumbent typically is assigned the blame or the accolades of the current economic environment, and President Clinton was no different.

That being said, there is no doubt under the Clinton administration America experienced unparalleled economic growth. It would see its longest economic expansion in its history due largely in part to its fiscal policies and the booming computer/technology industry. Unemployment would reach 30-year lows, and the Federal Government would enjoy a budget surplus for the first time in more than a generation. Indeed under the Clinton administration, the U.S. would see an economic boom, unlike anything it had experienced in decades. However, all of these accomplishments, including many more during his administration, could not prevent his impeachment during his second term, the first impeachment of an American president in over a hundred years.

Love As a Wrecking Ball
Part One

To tell you the truth, after all these years totaling over a quarter of a century (in the words of Bob Dylan), "I can't even be sure if she was ever with me or I was ever with her." Attempting to reconcile all that occurred during an eleven-month whirlwind of activity is difficult to do. It was a period in my life so poignant that, to this day remains unparalleled in its emotional swings. Who is to blame for what transpired, I suppose, is a matter of perspective.

Buried beneath a mountain of emotion, the truth may lie somewhere, but I can only account for my own part in the dramatic play that was to unfold. The truth is, pointing fingers is never a means to an end and is nothing more than the suspension of personal accountability. That being said, I will own all I should, which amounts to everything, as without my participation, there would be no story to tell.

Physics speaks of the simple concept of "for every action, there is a reaction," but this is not just a physical phenomenon relegated to inanimate objects. We, as humans, respond in a similar fashion to stimuli, modifying our emotional states depending on the type of stimuli imposed upon us. How these emotional states will manifest themselves in this "cause and effect" world can often be complex in their nature. Layers upon layers of emotion intermingle, resulting in varied and often confusing behavioral responses.

The job of the psychiatrist, psychologist, counselor, or those of clergy is often to unravel this knot of confused emotions brought on by life experiences. What is entailed in these experiences and how they are perceived (based on our belief system) will bring about a cocktail of emotions and behavior. These emotions can be orderly and sensical but also can become confused and extremely complex based on the severity of the experience.

All that being said, I cannot be sure if my perception of the events I am to speak of is nothing more than "my truth" and may vary greatly from another's truth of the same events. This is my story, however, and I can only speak of these events from my perspective. Those who might disagree would have their reasons for doing so, and I am in no position to challenge their perspectives. In the end, I can no more validate or refute their claims as they can mine. As the old saying goes, "There are three sides to every story… yours, mine, and the truth." This is my side of the story.

I met Kari the day I visited the Indian School for the first time back in the spring of 1989. She worked as the school's personnel recruiter, and as I recall, she was the one who greeted me for my informal interview. It was clear from my interaction with her why she was chosen to be their job recruiter. She was incredibly affable, charming, and possessed a warm engaging smile. Kari also projected a youthful positive energy that I would later discover was one of the hallmarks of the organization as it cultivated this energy.

One of the characteristics I noticed about her from the onset was her curiosity which came across as a form of empathy and sincere interest. She genuinely appeared to care about your life, your dreams, and your ambitions. Now I'm not saying she didn't care about those things, but that's not what drove her to inquire about your life. She had an insatiable curiosity about *all things,* and she was skilled in satisfying this curiosity through a veil of empathy.

In her approach, she was so disarming that you would find yourself sharing things you would never have dreamed you would share with a stranger. She was a master at communication and would easily gain whatever information she required without you even realizing it. I recall driving back to Dave's house, pondering why I had discussed such personal things about myself during the interview. Not unlike when you drive away from a used car lot, and the thought slowly hits you, "Did I just get taken?" I felt I had shared too much about myself with Kari, possibly costing me a job opportunity.

She was not only a "charmer," she was also very bright. There was no doubt she was blessed with an intelligent mind, and though she was affable, one could since a strong aura of confidence about her. She had the perfect blend of feigned humility and outright confidence that drew the weak and strong-minded alike to her. She was an incredibly witty individual, the only person I have ever known able to surpass my own sense of wit. She was quick and clever in her delivery, and when she chose to, she could be quite cutting in her comments, and I totally dug that about her.

Another great thing about Kari was her choice of men. She had married Matt, whom I had befriended early on. Matt and I seemed to click from the very beginning having common interests in sports and life in general. We had attended sporting events together and often engaged in long discussions about the future of the school that we both worked for. He was already well established in a leadership role by the time I arrived, but it wasn't long before he would seek me out for my perspectives on the school's operation.

I believe Matt felt I was an "outsider" who had a fresh perspective. He understood the value of listening to different viewpoints not in line with the norm. He soon discovered I possessed a level of cleverness and insight that perhaps he lacked. This did not intimidate him as he realized his strengths resided in other areas of the business and saw value in my insight. It takes a confident person to recognize strengths in others, especially in areas where they themselves may lack. Matt was that type of person, and I immensely appreciated his willingness to allow me to shine without the fear of upstaging him. We became a good team and even better friends. He was a better man than I, and I'm sure he still is; any time spent with Matt would make me a better person. He was just that type of guy.

As time went on, Kim and I began to spend considerable time with Matt and Kari. Along with Dan and Nadine, the six of us would spend many a weekend doing fun family things together. All of us had children around the same age, and we just seemed to gel as a group. Nadine was incredibly funny, and along with Kari, they were the drivers of the activities and were often the source of energy within our group. They came up with fun ideas such as "prom night," where all of us dressed up and pretended we were back in high school with our dates. The bond that existed within our little group only grew stronger as the years went by, and Kim benefited from being around other women who modeled "having fun" over complaining about the injustices of life.

I thoroughly enjoyed the time we all spent together, and it still resides in my memory, always bringing a smile to my face upon reflection. The truth is I would never be involved in this type of relationship with "couples" again, and I never really tried knowing it was a unique group with dynamics that could never be duplicated.

It was during one of our weekend group gatherings, however, that the trouble began. It was so subtle I barely even noticed it at the time but looking back, it was when the fuse was lit, and once lit, it was just a matter of time before everything I loved would go up in flames. Kari and I were down in our basement, where Kim and I had set up a little party area for entertaining that evening. I had set up my stereo for dancing, and we had made some spiked punch that all of us had indulged in considerably. For some reason that I do not recall, I found myself alone with Kari down stares with Tom Petty blaring over the stereo. She had poured herself a drink and sauntered over to me. She was drunk and rather amorous, which I had not seen from her before. Sure, she could flirt, but before this moment, it was always harmless in its intent. She nuzzled up next to me, breaking the unwritten code of social distance, and I felt a little uncomfortable but played along and flirted back. What we talked about, I can't remember, but as we heard the others coming downstairs, she quickly kissed me on the cheek and walked away, pausing once to look back at me with a sly smile on her face.

I was surprised by her action, but I also knew she was intoxicated, and I wrote it off as a foolish flirtation that perhaps had crossed the line. Mind you, I wasn't bothered by her actions, and the next day, I found myself enjoying replaying the incident over and over in my head. Still, it really was "no big deal," and life went on for months without either of us ever talking about the incident and with her never making an advance such as that again. I had chalked it up to drunken flirtation that had been written off by both of us as meaningless.

In the meantime, my relationship with my wife continued to deteriorate. Bad days turned into bad weeks and months. I was feeling more desperate, with nowhere to turn and nowhere to run. I had confided to Kim's father my growing predicament, and I how as was feeling the situation was only getting worse. Dave encouraged me to stay the course and promised he would talk to his daughter regarding her increasing nastiness toward me. Dave indeed did try to get through to Kim, warning her "a man can only take so much," and she needed to soften her approach. Kim would have none of it; instead, she accused her father of "taking sides" and supporting me instead of his own daughter. Upon hearing the news of Dave's conversation with Kim, her mother, who was always circling above like a vulture, took the opportunity to impress upon Kim her father had betrayed her, and she had no one left to turn to other than her mother's undying love. Talk about throwing gasoline on a fire! Kim became convinced both of the men in her life were out to get her, and as usual, Sandy's rhetoric sent her into an emotional tailspin.

This had become our daily life now, filled often with antagonism and anger. Kim had become so unpredictable that within the same day, there could be radical shifts in her behavior. She could go from cuddling next to me on the couch in the morning to throwing a glass of water in my face in the afternoon, and by evening, her behavior could manifest into violence. In the meantime, our kids were forced to endure these unpredictable behaviors as much as I did. Their only blessing in the ordeal was the anger was rarely focused on them. Rather, they were helpless observers of the attacks launched against their father on a regular basis. The situation was becoming untenable, but then again, as far as I could see, there was no way out other than the destruction of all that we had built.

Enter the wrecking ball…

It was January of 1996 when I found myself in Kari's office answering "yes" to a question that I never dreamed I would be asked. I had made it part of my regular routine to stop by the personnel department and say hi to Kari. My office, after all, was just down the hall, and fresh coffee was always available in the personnel department. Often I would find myself standing in Kari's office with a styrofoam cup in hand, chatting with her about an array of subjects. Some were work-related, while some were not. Sometimes we would talk about my relationship with Kim as Kari feigned empathy to hide her curiosity about just what in the hell was going on inside the walls of our home. She had seen Kim misbehave on occasion and had heard stories from me as well as Don and Nadine, regarding her emotional outbursts.

I can no longer recall what led Kari to ask me if I would ever kiss another woman, but I clearly remember being a little surprised by her inquisition. I briefly pondered her question and responded with something like, "I might… it just depends on the situation." It was her follow-up question and my response that started the wrecking ball swinging. Immediately after my first response, she asked me, "Would you kiss me?" Before the echo of her words had vanished in the ether, I answered with a resolute "yes."

She smiled and said, "Well, maybe that's something we should try sometime." I agreed and told her I would like to try that as well. We made some uncomfortable small talk for a few minutes, and then I left her office with my face feeling flushed. I was totally surprised she had asked me about kissing her. However, I was more surprised with my answer. I felt a bolt of excitement jolt through my body, the kind which I had not felt in a very long time. I really didn't know what to make of what had just transpired, and I didn't spend time worrying about it. I was just glad it had happened, and I felt alive again for the first time in a long time. I went home that night thinking of nothing else of Kari and her question and how I would breach the subject the next day. Would she just play it off, claiming she was just joking, or would she up the anti and continue the discussion? I couldn't wait to find out, and not once did I feel guilty with my thoughts as I lay in bed with Kim that night.

The next day Kari confirmed she was not joking and, indeed, she was very interested in pursuing a kiss with me. She mentioned a recruiting trip she was making at the end of the month that would take her out of town for the entire day, and perhaps I could find a reason why I needed to go to the meeting. By this time, I was a director at the school and really didn't have to tell anyone what I was doing or where I was going, so I immediately told her I would go. Later I easily found a reason why it made sense for me to travel with Kari, and the trip was set for the end of the month.

The next several weeks went by very slowly as I waited for the big day. In the meantime, Kari and I grew emotionally closer as we both anticipated our moment together. I can't explain how almost overnight, everything had changed between us. We went from being friends to something much more, all because of her one question and my fateful answer. It was clear the genie was out of the bottle.

As fate would have it, the night before our trip, a storm blew into South Dakota, dropping six inches of snow across the plains. The next morning road conditions were poor, especially for a 140-mile journey on rural roads. Much to the disappointment of both Kari and me, the trip was canceled to be rescheduled for a later date. That night I lay in bed and fantasized about what might of happened had we gone through with our plan and wondered if the winds of fate had stepped in to stop us from pursuing a dangerous road.

The trip, however, was rescheduled for the week of Valentine's Day, and though I could have easily backed out… I didn't. I soon found myself driving with Kari to the University of South Dakota with only one thing on my mind, and it wasn't the meeting we were scheduled to attend. We chose to take the rural backroads, and along the way, we drove by a tavern located on the side of the highway. We both agreed we would stop there on our return home to consummate our clandestine "kiss." It was all set, and neither of us appeared to have cold feet, as the thought of aborting the plan was never discussed.

By the time we got back to the tavern, it was mid-afternoon. The lunch crowd had already dispersed, and only a few regulars sat at the bar counter. It was dark inside, but daylight spilled across the pool tables through the half-open blinds on the opposite end of the tavern. There was the usual clinking of glasses and casual talk at the counter with an occasional burst of laughter.

We sat at a small round table, only big enough to place our two beers on and a set of keys. I don't recall what we spoke about, but I remember being nervous, and by the time we had almost finished our second round of beers, I had resigned to the fact we both had been big talkers. The moment of truth had arrived, and it appeared neither of us was willing to back up the rhetoric we had engaged in for weeks. I was disappointed but not surprised, we had taken flirting to the cliff, but in the end, neither of us was willing to jump.

Our beers were finished, and I was about to suggest we leave when Kari said, "Well are you going to kiss me or not?" That was the green light I needed, and without hesitation, I leaned over the table and kissed her. It wasn't just a simple kiss. It was a long deep affectionate kiss filled with passion and emotion, and if the fuse of passion had been fluttering, threatening to go out, it now was burning brightly. With that kiss, any chance of changing course was over. Both of us were now immersed in a raging river of passion, one that would eventually drown us.

When I got home that night, I felt guilty for the first time. There was no doubt I had betrayed Kim, but I had also betrayed my good friend Matt. I made the commitment right then and there that this journey into immorality would end and go no further. That commitment lasted until Kari walked into my office the next day, closed the door, and we rushed into each other's arms. It was clear both of us had grown emotionally close to each other over the previous weeks, and this was not just a lustful sojourn. There was an undeniable affection for one another that went well beyond a "fling."

For the first time in a very long time, I felt love and affection from a woman without the madness of hate and resentment lurking in the shadows. Kari had none of the baggage Kim carried regarding me and my inability to make her happy. Kari was self-assured and confident. She needed no validation from me to make her happy. In the past, Kari had simply enjoyed our time together, but now I felt passion holding her in my arms, her chest swelling with each breath. We fell in love with "being in love" as it felt like the first time for both of us and soon, we found ourselves lost in the warm glow of physical intimacy.

Months went by, and as they passed, our love grew exponentially, and of course, as did our lies and deceit. Matt was an incredibly trusting person and never suspected foul play, and as far as Kim, she was too concerned about her own issues of inadequacy to notice anything different in me. Eventually, things did begin to change with us as I began to show complete apathy towards our relationship. I saw Kim now as a hindrance to what I actually wanted to pursue with Kari.

By mid-summer, Kim began to realize something was wrong as her manic behavior no longer drew my attention or efforts to quail her tirades. She would go about her self-harm tactics coupled with the obligatory screaming of insults towards me. Meanwhile, I just yawned and watched tv. She had lost me, and I was absolutely stupefied that she didn't understand why. Eventually, she would plead with me to go to a marriage counselor, and I complied, but only because I felt it would keep her from eventually sniffing out my misdeeds. We attended maybe three or four sessions together, resulting in no improvement in our relationship. In fact, it only cemented my position of wanting out of the marriage. One day I met privately with the marriage counselor, who first made it clear if I ever repeated what he was about to tell me, he would deny it. He told me Kim would never change her behavior and that unless I was willing to continue to tolerate her tirades and radical emotional swings, I should get out of the marriage as quickly as possible. Of course, my immediate thought was, "Tell me something I don't already know." However, his comment did validate what I already knew about Kim. It was over between us.

While Kim was fighting to save a broken marriage, my focus was on my desperate need to be with Kari. A big break came my way when Matt decided to attend summer school at Notre Dame to earn his master's degree. I, of course, wholeheartedly agreed with his decision when he asked me if I thought it was worth the investment in time and money. With Matt now out of the way, the only thing that stood between Kari and me was Kim, but in truth, even her presence couldn't stop me.

I recall one evening lying in bed next to Kim, desperately wanting to be with Kari. Matt was hundreds of miles away in South Bend, Indiana, and Kari was lying alone in her bed. I lay there almost in a cold sweat as I couldn't get her out of my mind, and in a bold and daring move, I decided I would sneak out of the house to see her. I slowly peeled off the covers and quietly slipped out of bed. I gathered my clothes and shoes as I kept one eye on Kim, being ever so careful not to wake her. In an effort that would have made James Bond proud, I snuck out of the house at around 1:00 AM and walked the two blocks to Kari's house.

I stayed with Kari for a passionate few hours and then made the trek back to my house. As I turned the corner and stepped onto my block, I paused and thought of what might be awaiting me. If Kim had awakened, she would surely know I was gone, and what would be my answer of why in the middle of the night would I go for a walk? It was certainly something I had never done before. For a moment, I felt like I was that young teenager again attempting to sneak back into my parent house after spending the evening roaming the neighborhood with my friends. As I approached the house, my trepidation faded as all the lights were still off. I successfully snuck back in and slid back into bed without Kim knowing. Such is the life of an infidel.

This would not be the first or the last time I would take such bold risks, but I was willing to do anything to be with Kari, and part of me was hoping to get caught. I had often spoken to Kari about leaving Matt, and in turn, I would leave Kim upon her request. She always talked about leaving her husband but never committed to anything. Eventually, this became a real issue for me as I wanted to end the disaster called my marriage and start over with Kari, but she was reluctant to leave Matt. The deceivers and cheaters had now created their own issues that began to eat away at their fairytale love story.

Love As a Wrecking Ball
Part Two

As the days grew closer to Matt's return home from school, I became more and more agitated. I no longer wanted to share Kari with her husband. As bizarre as that may sound, that's exactly how I felt. In an odd twist of fate, Matt asked me to pick him up at the airport in Sioux Falls at the completion of his summer school classes. I can't remember why Kari could not pick up Matt. In any case, I found myself driving to the airport, picking up a man I resented because he was married to the woman I loved. On the drive back home, he talked about his experience in South Bend, and I shared what had been going on at work. The weight of my sins hit me hard during that drive, as Matt had no idea how badly I was hurting him. I felt terrible for my actions but also was maddened with jealousy, knowing he would be in bed with "my girl" that night. I pitted and hated him as much as I pitied and hated myself.

With Matt back home limiting my access to Kari, I fell into a deep depression. There were days I could barely get out of bed, while other days, I found myself picking a fight with Kim to vent my anger and despair over my predicament. It was the pinnacle of irony that I was doing to Kim what she had done to me for years. I was actually blaming her for my predicament, which, of course, was ridiculous. In the end, by late August, I had moved out of our home due to irreconcilable differences between us. If I couldn't have Kari, I certainly wanted nothing to do with Kim. The wrecking ball had done its job well, as I had found my way out of an untenable relationship.

One day Matt came to me expressing concern regarding my failing marriage. He said he wanted to help in any way he could to get Kim and I get back together. I told him I didn't deserve his support or empathy, and he responded, "Don't be ridiculous. That is what friends are for." At the time, we only had one car between us, and Matt suggested it might be a good idea if I go visit my parents. He graciously offered his car to me for the trip and said I could use it as long as it was needed. I declined his offer feeling guilt wash over me. What was I doing to this guy? How could I be so disloyal to someone who had been such a good friend? What possible excuse could I ever have for behaving in such a disgraceful manner? Well, that much I could answer, it was his wife who had driven me to this decadent behavior. I wanted her and was willing to do anything to have her, including destroying Matt's life.

There is no need to go into detail regarding what transpired over the next few months but suffice it to say Kari and I were slowly being consumed by our own deceitful actions. Karma had wickedly turned on us as the foundation of our house of cards began to crumble. The wrecking ball was still working its magic, and it appeared nothing could stop it. Kari tried to end the relationship several times but always found herself running back into my arms. I would try to leave as well, but with the same results, always ending in failure. We both made sincere efforts to walk away from the monster we had created, each of us trying to escape the pain of misguided love. The truth was we were no better than the junkie who promises he'll quit but always go back to the needle. It was pathetic and weak, and the only time in my life I have ever been addicted to anything. I had become a slave to Kari's love and could not live without it, and although I felt immense guilt towards my friend Matt, I also hated him for standing in the way of the person I loved.

Somewhere during this period of time, Kari had informed Nadine of our affair. Nadine was a good friend, and we both trusted her not to share our infidelity. However, this was a major breach in secrecy as now someone else was aware of our relationship. In the end, the decision to tell Nadine would lead to the mercy killing of our love, which certainly earned the death penalty.

By early Winter, the situation between Kim and I had become unbearable. I had purchased a car as I was now living in an apartment and needed my own set of wheels. I spent the evenings alone in a vacant apartment while Kari sat in her house with her family. Matt was still completely in the dark about our affair, as was Kim. The one big difference, however, was my relationship with Kim had fallen apart while Kari maintained her's with Matt. I began to feel great resentment towards Kari because of this fact, and although she was an emotional wreck, on the surface, everything still appeared fine with her family.

Eventually, it came down to me issuing an ultimatum to Kari. I told her either she left Matt, or I would leave town for good. Of course, that meant leaving my children and my job, but I didn't see another way out of my predicament. It was time to force Kari's hand to choose either Matt or me, and whatever decision she made would still mean me leaving town. With her or without her, it was clear I had no future in this sleepy little South Dakota town.

Kari would not commit to leaving Matt, always providing excuses why it was not yet the right time. It was clear she wanted to maintain the affair while still keeping her family in tact. I eventually had enough of her delay tactics and went to Matt, informing him I wanted to resign but would need an additional three months of pay to make a new start. My boss, Matt, had the authority to approve my proposal. However, he refused. He stated he could not afford to lose me as I was an important piece to the success of the school. He encouraged me to continue to try and reconcile my differences with Kim and once again offered his support and assistance.

I was infuriated by his answer because it meant my threat to leave Kari now had no teeth. It would be nearly impossible for me to leave town without an additional three months of pay, so in essence, I was stuck. In addition, I was incredibly upset at Matt for poking a huge hole in my plan to force Kari's hand. My deranged mental state had me thinking, "Hey dude, I'm trying to end this affair one way or another, and all you are doing is ensuring it will continue. If that's what you want, then I'll keep screwing your wife." And that's exactly what I did.

The sad truth was the love between Kari and I which at one time had been so precious, was completely polluted. The raging river of passion had blown its banks and flooded the fields with a sulfurous stench that consumed everything. I was becoming more unpredictable in my behavior which greatly concerned Kari thinking I just might go to Matt and tell him the entire story.

In the meantime, Nadine had a front-row seat to the emotional demise of her close friend. Day after day and week after week, it went on and on until she could stand it no longer. Her friend was falling apart right in front of her, and she decided something radical needed to be done. She and Don secretly devised a plan to end the madness and hopefully save Kari's marriage in the process. Now it was true Don and Nadine were good friends with both our families, but when push came to shove, Kim and I were expendable Matt and Kari were not. Looking back, I hold no malice towards either of them for making the decision to destroy the wrecking ball… someone had to do it.

One night without warning, they went over to Matt and Kari's home and forced Kari to tell Matt about our affair. When they arrived, they took her aside and told her either she could tell him or they would, but it was going to be revealed that evening one way or the other. Of course, Matt sat dumbfounded when Kari informed him of our relationship. She downplayed the affair immensely as if it was just a one-time slip and nothing more, and Don and Nadine apparently supported the lie. Their goal, after all, was to save Matt and Kari's marriage, not destroy it. Kari painted a picture of her falling pray to my pursuits, and due to her deep empathy toward me and my failing marriage, she "got too close" to the situation and made a catastrophic mistake. In other words, *she* was the victim, and I was the perpetrator.

Of course, later that evening, Kim would find out about the affair through Matt, who wanted to get back at me by any means. The whole shit house was now going up in flames, and not even the local volunteer firemen could have put out the inferno. The year-long secret was now out in the open, with the only question left to be answered was just how much collateral damage would be incurred.

As an honorable infidel, I thought it only fair to share with Kim my side of the story, of course, leaving out many of the details which would make me look worse than I already appeared. The fact was "my truth," however, was far closer to reality than Kari's as she was trying to save her marriage, and mine had long ago expired. When Matt caught wind of my side of the story through Kim, he finally woke up from his stupor of denial. The cold hard reality was his wife had cheated on him not just once but often, and of course, he ended up blaming me for his wife's indiscretions.

Within a day after the mushroom cloud had settled in over our sleepy little town, Matt walked into my office and closed the door behind him. He was exceptionally composed as he asked me if I had time to talk. I nodded my head and offered him a chair. In one of the more surreal moments of my life, I sat across the desk from my boss and good friend, discussing my affair with his wife. After the initial pleasantries of "How could you be so disloyal to your wife and me?" Matt wanted more details regarding our affair. I had nothing to lose anymore, so I was willing to provide any information he requested, no matter how badly it hurt him. In my beaten down and angry mental state, I thought my life was an irreparable mess. Why shouldn't his be the same? Of course, he didn't deserve anything that had befallen him while I earned all the bad karma that could be sent my way. However, at that moment, I was more willing to let him hear the painful truth about his wife's affair with me.

He asked me how many times Kari and I had slept together which I replied there had been far too many times to remember the actual number. He then demanded to know all of the locations where we had engaged in sexual behavior. "Your office?".. "Yes." "Your home?".. "Yes." "My home?".. "Yes." "My bed?".. "Yes." " My office?".. "Now wait a minute Matt." I replied indignantly, "We *never* had sex in your office." And that was true; even an infidel has standards, I suppose. It would be safe to say though Matt was not impressed in the least with my sense of honor. He thanked me for my honesty and walked out of my office red-faced, mad.

About an hour later, Matt called me at my office. He made it clear he had left work, and this was a personal call and not one as my boss. Intermixed with an obscenity-laced tirade was the clear message he was going to "kick my ass," to which I responded, "Anytime, anywhere, anyplace." I informed him I would be more than happy to engage in a fight. However, I also made it clear regardless of whether he was able to kick my ass or not… I *would* hurt him. I then asked him to ponder how he would answer to the people at work regarding why his face was cut and bruised. There was silence on the other end of the phone and then a click as he hung up. I would speak to Matt only once more after that call. The day as I was packing my belongings into my car, he slowly drove by and yelled, "Get out of town!" I responded by flipping him off and telling him to "Go to hell." I would never speak to Matt again, and suffice it to say it was a sad ending to a once strong friendship.

The day after Matt visited me at my office, I was called into an impromptu meeting with the President of the school, the Director of Human Resources, along with the two other Vice Presidents who oversaw operations. Matt understandably had taken the day off and was not in attendance at what would be a quick and succinct meeting. The President accepted my proposal, procuring my resignation in lieu of three months' additional paid salary and the opportunity to say goodbye to my staff. I left the meeting unemployed for the first time in over fifteen years.

Meanwhile, back at the ranch, Kim had made it clear one of us would have to leave the area as news of the affair had spread like wildfire in our small town. I had known this to be a fact by all the glaring hateful looks I received from people who had once smiled and said hello to me. Kim said she would move back to Oregon immediately if I did not leave by the end of the month. I had no interest in seeing my children pulled out of school and moved halfway across the country as they had been through enough already. The choice was clear it would be me that would leave. I didn't even bother to inform the church board of directors I was resigning from my post with the church board, as they had already done that for me with the news of my infidelity spreading across the plains.

On January 27th, 1997, I left town. The day I departed, it was bitter cold, the temperature hovering around five degrees. I had planned to leave that morning, but getting everything wrapped up, including saying goodbye to the children, had taken longer than anticipated. I said goodbye to Dave and Sharon and thanked them for all of their support. Even though they were aware of everything I had done, they did not abandon me. Rather, they let me know I was always welcome in their home. I appreciated their support as they were just about the only people in a town of two thousand who would even speak to me. I had said goodbye to Don and Nadine several days earlier, and they expressed their sincere sadness about how things had turned out and wished me well in my future endeavors.

There was only one thing left to do now before I left town…say goodbye to Kari. I drove over to her house while Matt was at work with the intent to make the goodbye as painless as possible. We still loved each other, there was no doubt about it, but now there was also an emotional wedge driven between us that could not be overcome. The farewell would be a moment of clarity for both of us as we reflected on our actions and the harm we had caused to the innocent.

Perhaps for the first time, since all the madness began, we began thinking of others and not ourselves. It was clear that both of us were emotionally beaten and ridden with guilt. We were tired and defeated and simply were now seeking a merciful end to it all. I said my goodbye to Kari, looking deep into her eyes, and as we kissed for the last time, I was reminded of that first fateful kiss. The beginning and end of our love story had now merged into one; coming full circle with the parting of our lips. I walked away and did not look back. The wrecking ball had finally completed its mission. Everything in its midst was now in shambles…including our love.

I Want to Be Like Mike

As I have mentioned in previous chapters, there have been three times in my life I have witnessed "greatness" at a level above and beyond natural parameters. The first occurrence happened in the 1960s with the Beatles, the second in 1973 with Secretariat, and the third occurred during the decades of the 80s and 90s in the form of a basketball player.

His name is Micheal Jordan, and his level of talent and competitive desire in the sport of basketball remains unparalleled. I have witnessed many great athletes throughout my life, but I have never seen the combination of raw talent and fierce competitiveness at the level Jordan possessed. He was a unique athlete driven by the desire to be the very best, and his accomplishments were fueled by his incredible work ethic.

Jordan burst onto the scene as a freshman playing basketball at the University of North Carolina, hitting the game-winning shot in the 1981 National Championship game against Georgetown University. He spent two more years honing his craft at North Carolina, where he garnered first-team all-American in both his sophomore and junior years. At the conclusion of his junior year, Jordan was also named national player of the year.

After a brilliant college career, Jordan chose to leave school before his senior year to enter the NBA draft. He was selected third by the Chicago Bulls after Hakeem Olajuwon went to the Houston Rockets and Sam Bowie to the Portland Trailblazers. Growing up in Portland, I was a huge Trail Blazer fan, and the choice of Bowie over Jordan still haunts me to this day. ESPN has labeled the Blazer's decision to choose Bowie over Jordan as the worst draft pick in North American professional sports history.

Olajuwon became an outstanding player for the Houston Rockets, leading them to several NBA championships. He would also later be inducted into the Basketball Hall of Fame. Jordan's career speaks for itself. He is simply the greatest basketball player ever, while the often-injured Sam Bowie is a forgotten name except, of course, in Trail Blazer circles. The mere mention of his name reminds Blazer fans of what was and what could have been had the Trailblazers chosen differently.

During his rookie season with the Chicago Bulls, Jordan averaged 28 points per game and was voted as a starter in the NBA all-star game. He concluded the season by winning the "Rookie of the Year" award. Jordan, from the very beginning of his career, dazzled basketball fans throughout the country, but his team did not. Lacking a supporting cast, Jordan and the Bulls were not a good basketball team and were never considered a threat to the better teams in the league.

Micheal Jordan

The following year Jordan became a dominant force on both ends of the court, averaging 37 points a game and playing defense at a level rarely seen. He became the first player to record 200 steals and 100 blocked shots in a season. Still, with all of his efforts, his team could not advance in the playoffs and continued to be beaten easily. As great as he was becoming, basketball is a team sport, and Jordan needed a better-supporting cast of players around him. Even with a lack of talent surrounding him, Jordan scored 63 points against the Boston Celtics in a playoff game which still stands as a playoff scoring record.

In Jordan's fourth year in the NBA he once again led the league in scoring while also garnering defensive player of the year. In addition, he earned his first of five "Most Valuable Player" of the league awards. Although his team had significantly improved, the Bulls were beaten in the playoffs by their nemesis, the Detroit Pistons, and would lose two more playoff series to the Pistons until their breakthrough season of 1990-91.

After beating the Detroit Pistons in the conference finals, the Bulls went on to whip whip the formidable Los Angeles Lakers in five games in the NBA finals. Jordan and the Bulls had finally conquered the mountain, winning their first championship. He was voted MVP of the championship series, and the lore of Micheal Jordan began to permeate the country. He and the Bulls would go on to win two more consecutive titles, and then shockingly, Jordan retired from basketball to chase his dream of playing professional baseball.

Jordan Dunks

In October of 1993, Jordan announced his retirement from basketball and signed a baseball contract with Chicago White Sox. After playing for several of the White Sox's minor league clubs and struggling to compete at a level he expected of himself, Jordan made the decision to return to the NBA. After an 18-month hiatus from basketball, he returned to the Bulls mid-season, but they were beaten by the eventual champions, the Houston Rockets, in the playoffs.

In the next three seasons, Jordan would once again lead the Bulls to three consecutive titles playing some of the best basketball of his career. He delivered clutch performance after clutch performance, highlighted by his game-winning shot to clinch the Bulls' last championship against the Utah Jazz in 1998. Amazingly, Jordan and the Bulls had compiled six championships in eight years, winning every NBA final series they competed in throughout the decade. In January of 1999, Jordan retired only to return to the court once again, but this time playing for the Washington Wizards, a team he shared part ownership in and was also president of basketball operations.

Jordan would finally retire for good at the end of the 2002 season, receiving tributes in every arena he played during that final season. Perhaps the most touching of tributes was his return to his old home court in Chicago. He would be treated to an emotional standing ovation by his adoring fans, which lasted for over four minutes.

Gold Medal Winner

When it was all said and done, Micheal Jordan had become the undisputed greatest player in basketball history. His list of accolades is long and impressive: College basketball national champion, six-time NBA champion, six-time most valuable player in the NBA finals, five-time NBA most valuable player, two-time defensive player of the year, ten-time scoring leader, three-time steals leader, fourteen times all-star, three times most valuable player of the all-star game, ten-time NBA first team, nine times NBA defensive first team, and two-time Olympic gold medalist.

It is true Jordan was an amazing talent. However, many players bring an abundance of talent to their profession. What separated Jordan from all other sports professionals I have watched was his fierce competitiveness. His desire to win was so prevalent it was palatable, and it fueled his teammates, not necessarily because they were inspired by him. Rather, they feared his scorn if they did not live up to his expectations. He demanded and expected the highest effort from his teammates as he expected the same from himself. Nobody hated losing as much as Jordan. Therefore in the biggest moments and biggest games, he simply refused to lose.

The story of Jordan doesn't end with his greatness on the basketball court. He became a pop culture icon that, to this day, still resonates. It was not just his basketball prowess the world became enamored with. Jordan was a good-looking, charismatic, intelligent man whose smile could light up a room. He had all the makings of an American icon, and he performed in that role just as he had done on the basketball court, with outstanding success.

Perhaps his most well-known business endeavor is his relationship with Nike. Jordan had worn Converse basketball shoes during college and initially wanted to sign an endorsement deal with Adidas. At the time, Adidas had the largest market share of athletic shoes in the country, and Converse had been the shoe of choice for the biggest stars in the NBA. Nike was primarily known as a track shoe and had not gained much interest in the basketball market. That would all change when Nike landed the endorsement deal with Jordan. As they say, "the rest is history" as the "Air Jordan" brand was born, and Nike would become the largest athletic outfitter in the world.

As the spokesman for Nike, Jordan delivered for the shoe company far beyond their wildest expectations. The Nike "Air Jordan" brand is still a huge seller to this day. It is estimated Nike has paid Jordan 1.3 billion dollars for the use of his name and endorsement of their products, clearly making it the richest athlete endorsement deal in history.

After the partnership with Nike was cemented, Jordan's endorsement opportunities came as fast and furious as his slam dunks over opponents. He became the spokesperson for such major brands as Coke, Chevrolet, Gatorade, McDonald's, Ball Park Franks, Rayovac Batteries, Wheaties, Hanes, and MCI. He had become a familiar face across the world and as well known as anyone in the decade of the 90s. He would even star in the feature film "Space Jam," which became a huge success grossing over 250 million worldwide. Micheal Jordan had become a superstar.

Jordan's popularity didn't stop with endorsements or acting opportunities. As a pop icon, he also influenced fashion. Though there had been some notable actors who had chosen the shaved head look, most notably Yul Brynner and Telly Savalas, the style never took off as a fashion statement. After several years in the NBA, Jordan began to shave his head, and almost overnight, the look caught on like wildfire in basketball circles. Eventually, taking Jordan's lead, balding men across the country began to shave their heads in lieu of attempting to cover up their baldness. It was a look that took on a whole new level of "cool" because Jordan wore it so well. Eventually, men who possessed a full head of hair would still shave their heads to get the "Jordan" look. It is a fashion that, to this day still prominent in popular culture.

I recall the first time I saw Jordan play in person. I believe it was his rookie year, and my friend and I wanted to see this budding basketball star perform. Several minutes into the game, it was clear Jordan had something none of the other players possessed…and I'm not talking about irrefutable talent. Jordan's basketball shorts were extremely long and baggy. This was a complete departure from the style of shorts worn by men at the time. For decades men's shorts had been at mid-thigh level, but Jordan's shorts were almost to his knees! My friend and I could not stop laughing at Jordan and his shorts. He looked absolutely ridiculous in them, or so we thought. However, in the end, it was Jordan who had the last laugh as other players began to emulate his style, and before too long, it had seeped into the fashion world,

Jordan Resting Between Play

influencing men's shorts length across the world. The shorts you see men wear today are the result of Jordan's bold move to break the mold and wear longer shorts that at the time seemed ridiculous.

He would later disclose the reason he wore longer shorts, and to no one's surprise, it was centered around his desire to gain a competitive edge on the basketball court. He explained during gameplay, as he became exhausted, he needed something to grab onto during breaks. He would simply lean over and grab his shorts to gather his breath. He had actually requested the manufacture of the Chicago Bulls uniforms to make his shorts longer for this reason. So what initially was a uniform design to give Jordan a competitive edge would later become a men's fashion statement that still exists to this day.

Micheal Jordan was one of the biggest influencers of popular culture in my lifetime. His influence went well beyond the scope of his unquestioned greatness on the basketball court. He truly was an icon at the highest level, not only in America but the entire world. Much like the Beatles, whose influence swept across the world in the 1960s, Jordan's influence had a similar impact in the 1990s. Indeed it's fair to say there was a time when millions of people wanted to be just like Mike.

Only the Lonely

In late January 1997, I found myself once again returning to my parent's home with my tail between my legs. Sure, this was eighteen years later than the last time it occurred, but when it was all said and done, I was going back to live with my mom and dad. Unlike my return from college in 1979, when I had simply lost a portion of my pride, this time, I had lost *everything*.

As I drove through the cold night across the state of Nebraska, I had time to think about how much I had lost in such a short period of time. All my belongings were packed into the car, and there was no going back to my home in South Dakota. I was homeless, jobless, and no longer had a family. All of it had been left behind in a mushroom cloud of pain and loss. It was clear my long-standing conundrum of figuring a way out of a bad marriage had been solved, but the ramifications of doing so had been disastrous. At age 35, I was starting all over again. The small kingdom I had built in that sleepy little town in South Dakota was in flames now and had crumbled to the ground. As I drove through the darkness that evening, I came face to face with the reality of my situation.

It was indeed a long drive filled with contemplation and regret, and by early morning, I found myself at my parents' new home located in Colorado. I was physically and emotionally exhausted and slept a good portion of the next few days. When I awoke from my slumber, the realization of my situation hit me hard again. I really didn't know what my next steps were to be. Basic things like where I was going to live and what type of work I would be looking for were questions I just wasn't ready to face yet.

I was emotionally beaten down, and I spent several weeks simply trying to cope with my new life circumstances. I missed my kids terribly, and knowing they were no longer within my reach was difficult to accept. The fact was I could not return to visit them (at least not right away), as I would interrupt any normalcy they were trying to build without me. I called them regularly, but of course, that was not the same as being there. I missed Kari also and spent a great deal of time pondering the "what ifs" in our relationship. What if I could have convinced her to leave Matt? What if Nadine and Don had not forced her to tell Matt about our relationship? And, of course, what if I had never said yes to her question if I would kiss her? None of that mattered anymore, but nonetheless, I spent a great deal of time rehashing these thoughts knowing there was absolutely no resolution to any of them.

I also felt a great deal of guilt for what I had done to Matt. He was indeed a good friend and one I had betrayed for my own selfish desires. It was, without a doubt, the worst thing I had done to another human being, and I believed I deserved all of the bad karma that could be heaped upon me. As for Kim, I felt no guilt or regret for what I had done. In my mind, she had earned all of the pain and betrayal that beset her. Whether it was fair or not, I blamed her a great deal for all that occurred as it was her behavior towards me I believed led me to the path of infidelity. I was glad to be rid of her, though later, I would ponder getting back together in my desperate desire to rebuild the family I had destroyed.

For months I wandered around the West, burning up my savings and trying to recover from all I had been through. I spent a month at my parent's house, then with my uncle in Durango, and onto LA, spending time with Dieter and his wife. Eventually, I would land in Phoenix, joining my long-time friend who was also recovering from a failed marriage as well. We rented an apartment and began the effort to rebuild our lives by getting a new start in a completely new environment.

Unfortunately, it didn't matter where I went or who I spent time with, as there was a gaping hole of emptiness in my life I couldn't shake. Whether I was at the store, the mall, or the city park, the same scenario played out time and again. There were men my age everywhere, accompanied by their wives and children, who clearly had found a purpose in their lives. They were playing the role of husbands and fathers and responsible adults with jobs. I saw men going about their business, making money, and taking care of their families with a sense of self-worth. They all had something I had lost… an identity. I came face to face with the harsh reality I had lost myself. The things in life that defined me as a person had evaporated. There was nothing for me to cling to that defined who I was anymore. I was alone, and I was lost, no longer recognizing the person in the mirror. I truly felt like a "nobody" with nowhere to go and no idea what to do about my predicament. It was epic, it was awful, and it was where I found myself at age 35... just another lost soul.

No matter how hard I tried, I could not overcome the depression I found myself in. I watched my friend land a job and soon after landing a girlfriend as well. I would watch him get ready for work putting on his dress shirt and tie as I sat in my underwear unshaven, watching reruns of "Quantum Leap." He would return from a long day of work to get a change of clothes and then leave again to meet his girlfriend for dinner. Meanwhile, I still sat on the couch watching the replay of the rerun of "Quantum Leap" I had already watched earlier that morning.

To say I was living a pathetic life would be kind. My friend at times seemed to relish in my failure as much as his own newfound success. As I muddled in depression, it appeared he actually enjoyed watching me in my untenable predicament. The more I failed, the more he laughed at me, mocking my struggle to regain a long-lost sense of purpose.

Then one day, I thought to myself, "All this makes sense." I was paying penance for my prior infidelity and the pain I had caused to others. It was karma slapping me square in the face, knocking me to the ground. I deserved all that was happening to me, and whatever awaited me in the future, I would deserve it as well. I had given up fighting and accepted my pitiful fate as I just didn't care anymore.

I recall talking to my father over the phone during this period of despondency. He had no idea, or so I thought, just how bad off I was. He couldn't see me in my dirty clothes, unshaven face, and disheveled hair. I tried to keep him from knowing just how bad things were, attempting to sound optimistic even though that was far from the truth. My dad, however, knew me better than I thought, and he began to explain to me that it's easy for anyone to stand tall when things are going well for them. He pointed out the true character of a man is demonstrated when he is knocked down to the ground and whether he gets back up to fight again.

My dad, the tough guy who had been through so much, was still standing tall, landing punches at cancer and heart disease. There was no doubt he certainly knew a few things about getting up off the ground and fighting back. I couldn't disappoint him, I never could, and after that phone call, I made the decision to get up off the ground and fight until I got my life back in order.

My commitment to getting things turned around started with me leaving Phoenix. I had found no success in the several months I had spent there, and my friend had certainly provided little support. It was time for me to leave an environment that was unhealthy for me. I first checked with Kim to see what her plans were. Summer had arrived, and the kids were out of school. My plan was to get closer to my children, but I needed to confirm if Kim planned on staying in South Dakota or moving back to Oregon. She confirmed she was moving back to the west coast, closer to her mother and the rest of her family. It was then I began to look for jobs in Oregon immediately.

I made one last trip back to South Dakota to help Kim and the kids move. The house had been sold and all that was left was to get everyone relocated to Oregon. It was at this time I talked to Kim about getting back together again. Why, you might ask? Essentially it was out of desperation to get my kids back full-time and find some normalcy in my life. Kim also seemed intrigued by the idea regardless of just how bad it actually was. We drove the moving truck back to Oregon, but by the time we reached Idaho, I think we both realized there was no way we would ever make it as a couple. It was a foolish thought, but we both were lonely and desperate to find something to hang onto.

In the end, I would land a job with a tribe in Oregon managing the first Tribal TANF program in the nation. It was just a little over two hours away from where Kim and the boys had settled. The distance was far from ideal but certainly much better than the distance we had between us just months earlier. The job was interesting and challenging and provided me with the opportunity to manage and lead again. It gave me a sense of purpose and identity, which I had sorely missed.

Once I landed the job, the next step was to find a place to live. I soon went apartment shopping ending up at a property management office to inquire about several apartments in the area. I met a young woman who worked there named Janine, whom I found to be engaging and quite affable. She had a soft pretty face with sparkling brown eyes and a big beautiful smile, but most importantly, she had an aura of warmth about her. I left the office thinking she might just be someone I would like to date in the future.... just maybe. She did appear to be quite a bit younger than me, perhaps in her early twenties, but on the other hand, I had finally regained my confidence and so the age gap wasn't a concern.

The fact was, it was time to get on with my life just as my dad had urged me to do so. Kim and I had filed for divorce, and although my heart still hurt for Kari, it was over, and I needed to let her go. Little did I know though that this young beautiful woman, whom I had just met, I would fall in love with. Eventually, I did ask her out, and before long, I realized she was unlike any other woman I had dated.

There was no doubt I held some trepidation about involving myself in another serious relationship, but I also enjoyed her company a great deal and felt very much at ease with her. Janine was patient and understanding of my tainted feelings toward serious relationships. She never pushed or demanded anything of me. Instead, she patiently waited for my wounds to heal and for me to embrace her form of love.

Janine was mature well beyond her age of 23 and demonstrated a composer in our relationship I clearly lacked. As sad as it might be to admit, she may have been considerably younger than me, but she was certainly more mature. I eventually became comfortable with the thought she was nothing like my previous wife and was in complete control of her mental faculties. Perhaps *most importantly,* her mother was not an absolute "nut case" searching for ways to destroy her daughter's happiness at all costs. On the contrary, she was a quiet, well-educated, and compassionate person who loved her daughter. Hallelujah!!

Eventually, we would move in together, and although I still had no interest in marriage, I did have great interest in Janine. I loved her and wanted to spend all my free time with her. She had nursed my bruised soul back to health and given me hope for a bright future. For the first time in my life, I had found a woman I could lean on and completely trust… she would eventually become the rock in my life. I'm not sure why she chose to take a gamble on a two-time loser in love like me, but she must have seen something in me that still glimmered beneath all of my hurt and anger.

After the debacle in South Dakota, I found myself in the routine of living "day to day." I never thought of the future… not even a week ahead. My focus was just getting through each day, trying to survive and deal with my depression. That all changed in the fall of 1997 when I caught myself one day thinking about my plans for the next month! Big deal, right? Well, it actually was a big deal because it struck me in that moment, I had thought of nothing but getting through each day for a long time. It was then I realized I was finally healing and life was beginning to appear once again optimistic to me. Thanks to my dad, Janine, and my job, I had turned my bleak situation around in a span of about ten months.

Sure, there would still be bad days, especially struggling with the guilt of not being a full-time father. I helped assuage my guilt by telling myself Janine, and I could model for my boys what a positive relationship looked like. They had the opportunity to observe Janine and me treating each other with love and respect. There was no yelling or screaming, and there was no emotional crisis to constantly face. For the first time in their lives, they saw a happy couple living in harmony. Conversely, Kim would remarry less than two years later, only to go through a second divorce soon after. There was no hope for stability under Kim's roof that was painfully clear. I did the best I could to provide that stability, but being relegated to a part-time parent made it difficult.

The years of 1996/97 arguably were the most difficult in my life. I had brought down a living hell upon myself and also had dragged others into the fiery pit with me. There was nothing to be proud of during this period of time other than my refusal not to quit. It is true I was on the verge of quitting and may have well done so if not for my dad. He was the one person in my life I couldn't ever stand to disappoint, and he was pleased to see me rise from the ashes and rebuild my life. His approval alone was enough for me to claim the last two years weren't a total loss. I had shown him a toughness he had not seen in me before…I was a fighter just like him.

What the Hell Bill?

Just when it seemed things were going well for Bill Clinton, the roof caved in. Sure, his administration had some early struggles, but mid-way through his second term, the country was experiencing an economic renaissance. This was due in part to the booming computer industry, but it was also due to Clinton's effective economic policies. It appeared Clinton had found a positive rhythm to his presidency, and his approval ratings validated the American public saw his presidency as being, at the very least, moderately successful.

In what would become a historic turn of events, Clinton would find himself in the midst of one of the biggest presidential scandals in American history. By the fall of 1998, he would be under formal inquiry by the House of Representatives based primarily on the "Starr Report" prepared by independent counsel Kenneth Starr. The Starr report would expose an alleged sexual relationship between the President and a white house intern, Monica Lewinsky.

The trouble actually began in 1994 when Paula Jones filed a sexual harassment lawsuit against the president for actions that occurred while he was governor of Arkansas. One of the primary arguments for the Paula Jones case was there was an established pattern of behavior in how Clinton engaged with women. Their premise was simple if they could prove this sexualized behavior was part of an established pattern, then it would also be reasonable to assume Paula Jones' claim of sexual harassment could be validated.

In the meantime, unbeknownst to anyone, a friend of Monica Lewinsky had secretly been recording private conversations between the two. Within the recorded dialogue, Lewinsky divulged to her friend details of a sexual relationship between her and the president. This information was shared with Paul Jones' attorneys, who immediately added Lewinsky to their witness list.

At this point, according to Starr, Clinton began taking steps to conceal his relationship with Lewinsky, including asking her to conceal gifts he had given her and suggesting she file a false affidavit in an attempt to confuse the investigation.

Monica Lewinski

In January 1998, Clinton made a sworn deposition that he did not engage in a sexual relationship with Lewinsky. He would also publicly deny the relationship but later would admit that his relationship with her was "wrong and not appropriate." Eventually, the Paula Jones case was dropped due to her inability to show any damages. However, this did nothing to get the Republicans to back off their pursuit of Clinton. Armed with the "Starr Report" that concluded several serious violations had occurred, including perjury, obstruction of justice, and witness tampering, the Republicans authorized an impeachment inquiry in October 1998.

On December 19th, 1998, the House of Representatives voted for the impeachment of President Clinton on the charge of "high crimes and misdemeanors." The two articles of impeachment were specifically focused on the matters of lying under oath and obstruction of justice. Clinton, at the time, would be only the second president in American history to be impeached.

In what might be considered a bizarre turn of events, Clinton's approval rating spiked to 75% immediately after his impeachment. It appeared either the American public didn't care about his indiscretions, or they felt he was being unjustly attacked by his Republican counterparts. Whatever the case was for this unexpected boost in his approval, it was clear Americans were more interested in the positive work of his administration than his dubious infidelity.

As for me, I felt impeachment was the appropriate response to Clinton's misdeeds. I certainly was not one to be indignant regarding his sexual meanderings, as I had my own skeletons in the closet, but I was upset he tried to cover up his unsavory behavior. He had thrown Lewinsky under the bus and then lied to the American public instead of coming clean. Even I didn't do that!

I never looked at Clinton the same way after all of his indiscretions were made public. The least of my concern was his affair with Lewinsky. I was focused on the fact that he didn't own his behavior and that he painted Lewinsky as the "bad guy." He failed to demonstrate courage or accountability for his actions. He simply lied and tried to cover up his inappropriate behavior.

Clinton was the president who effectively "put the final nail in the coffin" regarding my mistrust of politicians. Prior to Clinton, I had no reason to believe any of them were capable of holding standards when it came to ethics or morality, but I suppose I still held out hope it was possible. After Clinton's indiscretions, I gave up expecting any politician to possess standards of ethical behavior. My rose-colored glasses have been trampled into pieces, and I am no longer surprised or disappointed in the character of any politician. I expect the worse, and they rarely disappoint me.

A Distant Ship's Smoke on the Horizon

It was in October of 1998 when I was told the news. I suppose I always knew that one day I would face mortality. It had always been there, waiting patiently on the distant horizon. Vietnam taught me that lesson at a very young age, death was real and those who were left behind dealt with an almost insurmountable sadness. Mortality, though, always seemed to tap others on the shoulder, rarely bothering people I knew or loved. Death is, of course, the nature of our existence and nothing to fear, as dying is as natural as being born, but still, at some level, we all fear the shadow of death, which follows us our entire lives.

Therefore when my dad called me and informed me he was giving up the fight against cancer, I realized death had finally come knocking at my door. My father had been such a game fighter, battling liver cancer to a standstill for years. I was shocked when he told me he was giving up the fight. I had almost come to believe my father could overcome anything, as he had proven the ability to do just that over the past decade. I couldn't understand why he would give up a fight he had been winning, and when I asked, he simply said, "I'm just tired of fighting it." The fighter had grown tired of fighting, quite the paradox, especially after going the distance with cancer. It appeared, however, the time had come for him to lay down his gloves and leave the ring.

I knew the moment he told me he was tired of fighting that it was over. It was his will and mental mastery which had brought him this far, without them, he was through. I began to cry when he broke the news to me, as it was clear I was going to lose him in the near future. My heart broke in that moment and has never really healed, but I had no time to mourn. He sharply responded to my tears, "Damn you... don't *you* do this to me. I don't need this shit from you... I'm getting it from your mother and I'm sure I will from your sisters and

I don't need it from you." Whenever my dad spoke to me in such a curt and direct manner, it always grabbed one hundred percent of my attention. I quickly snapped out of my self-pity and apologized.

He told me I needed to hold strong as he needed someone he could confide in to discuss all the financial ramifications of his death. He made it clear he could only find peace knowing my mother would be taken care of after his death and that responsibility would be entirely mine to carry out. I told my dad he would never see another emotional outburst from me again. He thanked me for my commitment, confident I would uphold my promise. I did my father proud, and though at times it was incredibly hard, I never broke down again after that call.

When I got off the phone, my head went spinning. I was just coming out of my own personal crisis only to be hit with this bombshell. Looking back, the imminent nature of knowing the end was near was hard for me to grasp. We didn't know exactly how long he had left, but he had told me he was looking into receiving hospice services which meant there was limited time available to him. I recall thinking my dad would certainly be dead within a year and how everything would forever change for my family. And the worst part… there was absolutely nothing I could do about it. I was completely helpless and relegated to just waiting for the end to come. I was filled with the "this will be the last time" blues. This will be the last Christmas present I will receive from my dad, this will be the last Super Bowl we will watch together, this will be the last Easter etc..

In early February, my father was still doing extremely well. He and I had even climbed up on the roof of his house to repair some loose shingles. I began to think my dad was doing it again… beating the odds. In fact, when his hospice nurse stopped by, I discussed with her that perhaps he should go off of hospice because it was clear he was beating back cancer once again. She gently smiled and said if he was still doing well in a month, perhaps we could consider it. The truth was I was clinging to a hope that no longer existed, and she knew it but let me live in denial a little longer.

By early April, when the whole family got together for Easter, it was clear my dad was going down for the count. There would be no more getting up off the mat to fight another round... he had nothing left to fight with. He had lost considerable weight and looked very frail. I had never seen my father look so weak, and it was hard to see him in such a beaten-down condition. If it hadn't been real before, it certainly was now... my dead was going to die and soon.

One day, while I was doing yard work at my parent's house, a hospice counselor stopped by. To my chagrin, the counselor gathered up my mother, sisters, and father, and they all sat in folding chairs in the garage with the door open. I passed by them often as I went back and forth, pushing the wheelbarrow dutifully, finishing the yard work my dad assigned me. The counselor hadn't asked me to join them, and I didn't volunteer. It wasn't long before I could hear the sobbing of my sisters and my mother as I passed the garage. Sadness welled up inside me. I kept focused on the yard work and ignored them the best I could.

As I passed by the open garage door again, I glanced over to see my dad crying. It was the only time I ever saw the man cry. It broke my heart seeing this scene unfold in front of me. Remembering the promise I made to my dad, I looked away and kept my head down, continuing the yard work. The counselor eventually left, never speaking a word to me, and to this day, I have no idea what my family discussed, nor have I ever asked my mother or sisters. I have successfully locked that memory deep in the recesses of my mind until the writing of this book.

After the Easter holiday, we all went our separate ways back to our own families and lives in Oregon. I waved to my father, standing at the front door for the last time. Three weeks later, he would die. We were all there at his bedside on the evening of April 29th as he took his last breath. The hospice nurse had prepared us for how death would take him. Sure enough, as if it was some recipe, he followed her description to the letter. When it was over, there was a huge sense of relief the end had finally come. We no longer had to wait for the arrival of the shadow of death. It was here now and had taken my father with it.

That evening I stepped outside as a rainstorm washed over the rooftop my father and I had recently repaired. I stood there in the shimmering light of the street lamp as the rain soaked my clothes. I just stared at my father's house as the rain cleansed my tired soul washing away the pain of the last several years. In a way, it was a new beginning... all that I had dealt with and faced was behind me now and the future, as uncertain as it was, would deal me an entirely new hand to play.

Several days later, we held a small private ceremony at the local church. Several relatives from my father's side flew in for the ceremony. I prepared a eulogy for my father, which I delivered to the small group that attended. It was a peaceful and quiet gathering and one that put closure to the final chapter of my dad's life.

That afternoon my mother called us over to the kitchen window, and we were all amazed at what we observed. The backyard was filled with blue birds... perhaps twenty or more who had come out of nowhere to land in the yard. It was the bird my mother and father would drive up into the foothills to catch a glimpse of as they were rarely seen in the valley where they lived. Nonetheless, here, in front of our eyes, a whole flock landed in our yard and nowhere else. The bluebirds stayed for several moments until they took flight and flew off into the horizon. We all took it as a message that my father had arrived on the "other side" and wanted us to know life continues after death.

It's been over twenty years since my father passed, but I still feel he is near me and almost within reach. It's like he is waiting just around the next corner, but when I arrive, he is not there. I've learned to live without his physical presence, but in a sense, his guidance is still with me. I can hear him in my head instructing and inspiring me to be the best man I can be. Those who have lost a parent know exactly what I mean. He continues to live in the dimension of the mind where all things spring to life and never die.

And So the Curtain Falls

I had almost completed forty years of my life as the new millennium approached. Four decades had passed into the ether, often without me noticing the breadth of time that had transpired. Of course, along the way, I learned many things that molded the person I had become by the end of the century. There was certainly no doubt I had learned some tough lessons, but then again, who would say anything different? Life is filled with the obligatory ups and downs that invariably include glorious victories and devastating defeats. To be alive is to be faced with this dualism. It is the nature of our existence, just as life and death are inexorably tied to one another.

From the beginning of my conscious awareness of the world around me, I felt blessed to be an American, and after almost four decades, this belief had only been cemented through my own observations of how others lived. The freedom and wealth we enjoyed in America were unparalleled compared to any other nation. I was proud to be an American as a child when I stood tall reciting the "Pledge of Allegiance," and I was still proud to be an American as I approached middle age.

Sure, through the years, I had watched politicians possessing corrupt souls lie and deceive the people they claimed to serve. I had observed them thoughtlessly destroy the lives of thousands as if they were nothing more than pieces on a game board. However, I had also watched the American people, with forgiving and kind hearts, rise above the stench of politics to help those in the greatest need. I had seen the "individual" accomplish feats of excellence while watching government accomplish feats of corruption and ineptitude. I learned by the age of forty that the less government involvement in the lives of its citizens, the healthier a nation will be.

On a personal level, I had spent nearly twenty years in a dysfunctional relationship that sadly stripped me of the potential to be truly happy. As they say, "It takes two to tango," and there is no doubt I contributed greatly to Kim's unhappiness as well. We were a bad match from the outset. Unfortunately, we stubbornly stayed the course of dysfunction for years, negatively impacting our children along the way.

Nothing had made me happier in life than finally being free of that relationship. I was certainly culpable in its failure and also for dragging others into its whirlwind of dysfunction. I carried that guilt and regret with me every day, but life cannot be lived, lamenting failures and past indiscretions. At some point, one has to move on and live in the present and by the close of the decade, I had made that transition. I was ready to leave the past and all its baggage behind and start anew.

Janine would be the woman I would begin this new life with. She was a wonderful person, and part of me wondered why she would even waste her time engaging with me. Janine was only twenty-three and had her entire life ahead of her. As for me, well, I was almost forty and had been beaten and battered by love. Nonetheless, Janine *was* interested in me, and I was smart enough to realize what had come my way. She would be in my future as I moved forward in life, or at least I hoped that would be the case.

As the decade closed, I had a new job, a new girlfriend, and a new home. I also faced life without the guiding hand of my father, as he was not destined to be part of the new century. What was to occur in the years that followed would be without my father to lean upon. I was on my own now and had taken over the responsibility as the patriarch of his family. I didn't want this new responsibility, but nonetheless, it was now mine to bear, and I was determined to do the best I could in an attempt to fill my father's shoes.

The new decade upon me would no doubt present new challenges as I entered a phase in my life like no other. In many ways, I was starting over again, but also I brought along with me decades of experience and perhaps even a dash of wisdom thrown in. Only time would tell if the choices I would soon make and the direction I would head would bear fruit for myself and my family. One thing was certain there would be a new cast of characters participating in the drama called my life.

I was optimistic I could find happiness and success with this new start given to me. It was my dad who, many years ago, had taught me, "You create your own reality," and I was determined to create a reality of prosperity and happiness. With Janine at my side, I was confident that together we could create a life filled with hope and peace, sharing our love between ourselves and amongst others. I had been given a second chance to do things right, and I was determined to make the most of the opportunity. As I sit here today, 23 years later, I can tell you, "Mission Accomplished." Thanks to the grace of God.

Part Five
The Truth as I See It…
Though I Could Be Wrong

How Different Could The Same Be?

My memories begin at around the age of four, and throughout the many years that followed (as recounted in this book), I encountered numerous profound experiences that shaped the person I am today. All of us as human beings share similar experiences, and yet we also lead lives that are uniquely our own.

The epoch we find ourselves occupying, with its own set of societal rules, will undoubtedly impact our contemporary beliefs and attitudes. However, each generation, or for that matter, each individual, also shares similar emotional and cognitive experiences regardless of their place and time in history.

Although my experiences are uniquely personal to me, there is no doubt experiences in my own life have produced similar emotions and cognitive thought processes. Due to multiple factors, including upbringing, socio-economic status, and geographical location, entirely different perspectives between individuals often arise. For example, we all know how to love and hate, and we have all felt the emotions of desperation and hope. However, how we deal with these emotions is often based on our personal attitudes, beliefs, and perspectives, which we have developed over the years.

So now the question must be asked, after recounting many of my observations and experiences in this book, what does all of it mean… if it means anything at all? Ultimately this book is nothing more than thoughts articulated through a particular medium from one mind to another. The observations and experiences shared in this book are certainly relevant to myself and perhaps to others who lived during this time period. The words and sentences I have strung together may have reached the reader by tapping into their memories or emotional affiliations of common experiences shared, but in the end, they are only words. The reader has breathed life into the sentences and paragraphs through the mental application of their own imagination based on their attitudes, beliefs, and perspectives.

Though many of my thoughts I have complete ownership over, there are also thoughts that belong to the collective consciousness of humanity. These are thoughts we share amongst ourselves, which help define our physical reality and make sense of the world around us. The nature of individuality demands that unique perspectives rise above collective thought, providing us with the sense of "I" or personal ego. We feel the bond of "togetherness" as species but also recognize that we are unique and unlike any other of our kind.

This uniqueness comes at a price in an inherent loneliness and distinct separation from all others. The personal ego must navigate its own course in the end, no matter how desperately one clings to others for guidance. This truth becomes painfully clear when we face mortality and, ultimately, our own death. We may live our lives amongst each other, sharing our thoughts, emotions, and experiences, but in the end, no one can die for us. It is something every individual must do on their own. It is the nature of our existence and the truth of our mortality.

Our existence can only be measured through relativity; what we perceive as non-existence also defines what existence means to us, including the fact that it must end. Everything in life, from the perspective of humanity, is built upon the concept of relativity. The moments and events recounted in this book may have seemed important or interesting to the reader, but only because there was some level of relativity the reader could attach to themselves from what was shared. In some cases, the events I described, which had a deep impact on me, may have had no impact on the reader whatsoever. From their perspective, little or no emotion was attached to the event because they could not find relevance in their lives to the subject matter presented.

So, in the end, our experiences, perceptions, and observations are uniquely our own. However, they are also often shared at many different levels, from as small as a nuclear family up to the size of world collective thought. It would not be a stretch to ascertain that although we are all unique, there is also a collective consciousness shared throughout humanity. We are one, and we are many in the same breath, like cells that comprise an organism. This unique relationship between the individual and the mass "collective" is where the purpose of our existence might possibly be found.

Just Think of It

Nothing in our world exists without thought, and thought exists by some existential means we cannot universally agree upon. Materialists would argue our reality begins and ends within the world we perceive around us. However, even materialists must concede that without thought, there is no world to perceive. They may argue that thought is simply generated by our brains, which is nothing more than a part of our physical world, but how would they explain thought as a physical entity unto itself?

Thought, after all, is invisible to all except to its creator, who may purposefully add as much color, action, resistance, and purpose to any aspect of their world through fanciful imagination and acquired beliefs they now perceive as fact. However, facts are ultimately in the eye of the beholder, and our physical reality has been created by a collective consciousness that is convinced of the physical nature of our world. Our five senses detect physical reality, but it is up to our minds to validate the messages our senses are sending to us. We then validate these interpretations amongst one another, establishing them as irrefutable facts.

"Facts are only accepted fiction," the author Jane Roberts once intimated. How true this statement is when all else is stripped away. What remains is pure thought. The mind is the creator of all we know, feel, and experience, and though it may appear we react to the physical world around us, we actually "think" the world around us. Though our own thoughts are often influenced by collective consciousness, we convince ourselves of a particular reality. We become lost in a delusional world that has been created from our own beliefs based on sensory perceptions and supported by others around us.

For most of my life, I have swung about like a tether ball in a strong wind, tied to a core belief but rarely finding a flow to my life. The contradictions that reality presents at times have bemused and confused me. The attitudes I have held also have changed as my circumstances and understanding of the nature of things have changed. Like many, I have been driven by the desire to attain happiness and fulfillment but never quite understood the methodology required to obtain such contentment. Such is life and our existence as a species. We are driven toward the goal of finding meaning in our lives but often get derailed by circumstances or by others who attempt to impose their own beliefs upon us. We are forced to believe a reality that, intuitively, we may feel is incorrect but have no ability to ascertain what is incorrect about it or why.

Through my endeavors in searching for "my truth," I have come to believe the world we exist in is nothing more than illusionary. This is not as crazy as it may seem, as scientific fact has already validated that physical reality is not actually as it appears. We abide by the rules of reality, as prescribed by our senses because what we touch, see, hear, and smell verifies it as such. The influence of collective consciousness then demands we adhere to the rules of materialistic existence, forming our beliefs regarding the reality of the world and leaving us rarely questioning why.

The complexity of reality and our existence can become overwhelming if one chooses to dive headlong into the question of "why?" A spontaneous reflection of "why?" to "why?" in a consistent linear pattern will topple the mind like the tipping of dominos. If there is a question derived from every answer, where will that ultimately take you? How far can one go asking "why" before they run into the wall of the unknown?

Either through apathy or the failure of our own intuition, we as a species have built a false nomenclature based on the inaccurate perception of the true nature of things. This is simple mathematics in play… if the answer we search for is itself in error, how can the equation ever be correct? However, that is exactly what we have done, substantiating a false reality at every turn, therefore, creating a preordained outcome through an error in collective thought.

As it was in the time of our first philosophers, the question "why" has chased illusionary answers from sincere seekers of truth. There were some who were able to conjugate a broader interpretation of existence and challenge the dimension of simple physical reality. Through the continued advancement of technology, answers to questions that once seemed un-answerable are now commonplace and beliefs we once held as "facts" have been disproved. The cause for this can often be assigned to flawed fundamental assumptions made either through bias, cognitive limitation, and, of course, sensory perception.

Consciousness itself presents a different set of rules as opposed to the unconscious state, where physical limitations do not apply. In a dream state, one can defy physics and the constraints of time… limitless possibilities with limitless variations. A different universe where it appears randomness collates with an infinite amount of scenarios and variations. One could argue the dream state is a creation of "abstract art" representing aspects of our conscious world.

Many species on this earth possess limited cognitive and visual perspectives of their existence, amounting to a distance of less than a meter. Whatever exists beyond that meter of clarity is a misty haze of non-existence. Spiders and ants do not nearly have the breath of clarity we possess. Beyond the distance of a meter, the mist of the "unknown" permeates everything into a sense of nothingness. We may pity the lowly spider for its limited view of existence, but we also share the same fate as him, as everything ultimately is defined by relativity. Could it not be argued that the astronaut who has traveled beyond our planet's atmosphere and into the stillness of space has not seen a different and more expanded view of existence? What of God's perspective of existence? The truth is our own self-centered and limited perspective of existence has tricked us into believing we know more than we actually do regarding the mysteries of life.

Mathematics and physical ingenuity may have brought humankind to the outer limits of space. However, at some point, it is reasonable to assume that one who travels to the boundaries of the unknown will ultimately encounter the unknown.

Our conscious mind has grasped the concepts of gravity and time and space, but it cannot grasp what it cannot conceive beyond the boundaries of its senses. There is an intuitive nature in us all that could prepare us for the unknown mysteries of life. However, it is constantly being dampened and repelled back into darkness by the overwhelming power of our senses and collective thought. Deep inside *what we want to believe* or perhaps intuitively *know to be true* is constantly being bombarded by our senses which perceive only physical reality. This casts a large shadow upon our intuitive nature if for no other reason, we often believe *what we see* more than *what we intuitively feel*. This contradiction created by the constraints which physical reality imposes upon us often confuses our intuitive nature and casts doubt upon the divine light inside each of us. This contradiction between the physical and the intuitive can greatly hamper our ability to discover "true reality."

Because of science, we now understand all is not as it seems in the physical world. It is common knowledge that everything around us is comprised of tiny atoms which form molecules that are the building blocks of all matter. The table we will lay this book upon is not solid and neither is the book itself though they both appear to be. If we were able to manipulate the molecular structure of our own bodies, we could put our hands right through the table in front of us. Of course, we cannot accomplish this task because our senses have convinced us it is impossible and that table, in fact, is solid.

The microscopic world I am describing comprises everything in existence, including us. A large redwood tree is ultimately nothing more than dancing molecules interacting with one another just as they are doing the same within our own bodies. The truth is the world we believe to be solid and comprised of objects we believe to be static, in fact, does not possess either of these characteristics.

Quantum Mechanics, a theory developed in the last century, proved without a doubt astounding "truths" that defied all common sense, including our understanding of physical reality. It would change our long-standing belief system regarding existence itself. As astounding as it may be to comprehend, our reality is not as "definite" as it appears. Quantum Mechanics proved that nothing exists until we conjure it up through observation. I will not go into the physics behind it but suffice to say it has been proven to be scientifically accurate.

So what does this mean? Well, to me, it means everything is created through "the mind" and that *We Create Our Own Reality.* We decide (through our beliefs) what is to be fact or fiction. Ralph Waldo Emerson once intimated that either we become enslaved to facts or, through illumination, we realize we are *in control* of facts. The creation of facts themselves is nothing more in the end than a mental exercise.

We (through our conscious and subconscious thoughts) focus primarily on all pertinent information that will support our beliefs, and then we neatly embed them into our psyche as "truths" regarding nature, society, and personal relationships. We roll along throughout life, gathering information to support these beliefs until, eventually, we become convinced they are facts. Of course, this would mean that our personal beliefs *can change* our reality. Through the act of retrospection, we can discover where our beliefs were formed and whether they are worth keeping, need modification, or are thrown out altogether.

All things begin and end with the mind. It is the key in creating a life filled with love and happiness. How we "think" will ultimately define how we will "live." Each of us has the power to define our existence through the creation of a set of beliefs that will provide us and others around us with a sense of happiness and fulfillment.

The Dimming Light of Religious Dogma

What is religious dogma? A concise definition would go something like this: "Those who refute any spiritual belief other than their own." Any of us who have spent time in churches have most likely been exposed to dogmatic beliefs. Those who subscribe to religious dogma carry little doubt that the religious belief system they embrace is *"the truth and the only truth."* Therefore, all other spiritual beliefs not in line with their own are built upon heretical pretenses.

Throughout my life, as I embarked on my own personal journey toward spiritual enlightenment, I consistently ran across dogmatic individuals and churches that carried a sense of self-righteousness in their teachings and beliefs. Whether it be Baptist, Mormon, Catholic, or Lutheran, it didn't matter as there was always a sense of "This is the truth" behind their message. There was little room left for any other interpretation of the gospel they worshiped other than their own. A sense of arrogance pervades these individuals and churches, which of course, carries a strong sense of irony, as it was Christ who had taught humbleness as being a virtue, and arrogance was to be condemned.

Nonetheless, time and time again, I heard the same thing from every denomination I visited, "This is the spiritual truth." I became extremely confused by all of these self-righteous claims. How could I know who was right? Someone had to be right, which of course, meant all others were wrong, but how to know which dogma to follow was indeed a perplexing proposition.

Some churches and their followers were more extreme than others, unequivocally condemning those who did not share their beliefs to hell. I recall one time listening to a sermon that basically implied my father and those like him who did not share the common Judea-Christian belief system were lost to hell for eternity. I was incredibly offended by this implication. My dad, who was beset by terminal cancer at the time, was going to hell because he didn't share the pastor's beliefs? He was marked as a condemned man because the self-righteousness rhetoric the pastor spewed from his lips was not part of my father's own spiritual doctrine. I don't think so.

In fact, it was my father who had introduced us to church at an early age and throughout my youth, we attended it periodically. Later, as I learned more about my dad's spiritual belief system, I realized there were some significant differences between the doctrines he followed and that of Christianity. One day I asked him about this contradiction. How could he attend church when he carried a belief system that was far different than what was being worshipped and taught? His answer was concise and easy for me to understand. He told me people go to church to worship God and any place that worships God is a place of spiritual levity. The details of how or what they worship were not nearly as important as their fundamental belief that a higher power exists. His answer resonated with me. It was the one thing religion had in common with my dad, the belief in God and the sense of humility that there was higher power well above and beyond the ignorance of our species.

Those who have embraced religious dogma have convinced themselves that their beliefs are simply an unbiased reflection of God's words. They have chosen to interpret their doctrine as they see fit through the guidance of their religious leaders and the support of fellow believers. They, in a sense, have become brainwashed into a rigid belief system that guides them in many aspects of their everyday lives. Without a dogma to lean upon, they feel like lost sheep searching for a herder to bring them back into the fold.

They are compelled to reject any other spiritual belief system as they have been taught to believe it is blasphemy to approach God by any method other than *their* means of worship. They will consider no other thought process, belief system, or spiritual overtures other than those they patently believe is *the word of God*, ironically words prescribed to them by mere mortals whom they deem as "authorities" on the subject. Questioning their belief system is tantamount to the treason of God, and they will not tolerate the spoken or written word of anyone who does not adhere to *their* strict and righteous interpretation of the word of God.

All of these attitudes, in my opinion, are guided by a simple-minded approach to a vastly more expansive subject. It is a pattern of thought based on naive and yet comprehendible concepts that are merely representations of our own meager understanding of the world around us. In the end, these simple concepts are reflected and re-arranged in a manner to create a God in our own image, and thus, in a sense, we worship ourselves through our own limited ability to describe the infinite.

The fact is none of us know "the truth," but there are many who claim they do. There is "faith," and then there is belligerent arrogance expounding righteous intuition above and beyond our capacity as human beings. We may believe in a particular spiritual or religious doctrine, but to proclaim it is the "absolute truth" is only to demonstrate one's ignorance and willingness to define the infiniteness of God through their own finite thinking.

History is replete with examples of those who have been persecuted for beliefs considered heretical at the time but later were verified as fact. Galileo, the famed astronomer and physicist of the 17th century, is a prime example of how religious dogma has been exposed in later years to be unjust and cruel to those who held an opposing belief.

Galileo supported the theory of "heliocentrism," which had been developed by the well-known astronomer of the 16th century

Nicolaus Copernicus. This theory stated that the sun was, in fact, the center of the universe and the earth revolved around it, which was in direct conflict with the religious dogma at the time that claimed the earth was the center of the universe.

The Catholic Church charged and tried Galileo for his blasphemy claiming his theory was heretical since it contradicted Holy Scripture. He was convicted of heresy and was confined to house arrest for the rest of his life. This example is subtle compared to the fate of others who were executed, burned at the stake, or exiled because of beliefs that opposed the contemporary dogma at the time.

I have no doubt if it were not for the moral and ethical restrictions our society has now placed on the act of undue persecution, including torture and murder, these offenses would still be propagated against the innocent by religious zealots. There are plenty of examples throughout the world where those who hold beliefs that contradict or offend the current dogma of society are tortured or killed due to nothing more than ignorance and fear created by ill-conceived belief systems.

Religious dogma cannot only be dangerous to those who oppose these beliefs it also hinders the spiritual growth of the individual in search of spiritual illumination. It often creates a nomenclature of strict adherence to a belief system filled with limiting constructs. Any expansion of thought regarding existential subject matter is quickly condemned as the work of "evil forces." How can spiritual illumination and growth occur under such constraints? Why would humankind ever attempt to explain aspects of infinity with such conviction and arrogance when infinity cannot be explained in finite terms? Is there ever any legitimate logic in expecting a finite being to explain infinity? All of this made me question the whole idea of religion and if any of these doctrines who professed they held the truth, based on God's words, were right about anything.

One day, as if all the tumblers had aligned and unlocked my mind to a clearer reality, it dawned on me that the truth could never be as narrow-minded and scripted as many religious doctrines appear to be. It was then I realized there was no "right answer" to all of these existential questions I was looking for. No religious dogma was better than the other or, for that matter, worse than the other. It was never about religion, as I had once believed, it had always been about the individual and the unique spiritual journey we must all make by ourselves.

I came to realize all of us are on our own path toward a higher divinity and God. There is not just one righteous path but many that ultimately conjoin in the end. Spiritual illumination can come in many forms, from Christianity to the ancient ways of sages from the Orient or India as well as countless other sources. There is no limitation to the enlightenment of the soul but the ignorance and prejudice of a mind which is unable to comprehend the limitless possibilities of an infinite being. Too often, we fall into the trap of anthropomorphic thinking that, by its very nature, it is filled with error due to the imperfection of its source.

I hold no other truths but my own, knowing that, in the end, those truths are based on conjecture and faith. Our species needs hope and relies on faith to assuage the reality regarding our mortal fate. Our consciousness has brought an astounding truth with its creation of self-awareness. We are mortal beings with a physical end to our reality. Death is a partner for life until it extinguishes life itself, and all that remains is dust. However, for many, there is something greater that goes beyond the limitation of these mortal bones. There is a sense, though almost a mystic recollection, of something else from which the fountain of life springs from. It is something ethereal and nebulous that tugs at our conscious minds but resides in our unconscious state.

There is a yearning for truth to life's mysteries out of a desire for self-preservation and hope of eternal life. We also sense something is hidden from us, perhaps its content being divine enlightenment, that remains just out of our reach. It is almost as if we could find home if only we knew what direction to head. There is an inherent feeling that "something else" exists beyond our comprehension that is the purveyor of all we know and all we will ever know. We intuitively understand this to be true as we see it represented in the physical world around us and in the numerous examples demonstrating an order to the randomness surrounding our existence.

Our finite existence falls within a greater concentric circle of infinity, thus creating a paradox between life and death and time and space. All of these aspects of existence are coalescing at once in the same instant without limitation and beyond any modality of measurement. It is the convergence of the finite river (which comprises our existence) with the infinite God-driven ocean where illumination lies in wait.

There is not just one "righteous path" leading to mystic truths or soulful revelations, as religious dogma may have you believe. A single path to an infinite source makes as much sense as having one access to a vast ocean. Infinity swallows everything in its wake, and God *is infinity* absorbing everything into his "oneness," encompassing all.

When You Are Swimming in a Sewer, it's Hard Not To Be Covered in Shit

I addressed my opinions regarding politicians in my allegory presented in Part Two of this book. That being said, if this section is dedicated to "truths as I see them," I would be remiss in not addressing the issue of "people in power" in further detail.

There is something dark and ugly connected to those with power over others. We have all observed at one time or another when people have abused their power and hurt those unable to defend themselves. History is filled with examples of this type of behavior and the carnage left in its wake. All of us have some level of power we exercise every day, from control over our choices to the often-forgotten control over much of nature. However, this level of control is typically very limited in scope, having little or no impact on the masses within a society.

A politician's power is much different, often possessing the ability to impact large groups of people. This level of power carries with it massive responsibility to serve the needs of others over oneself. Sadly, somewhere along the line, politicians have forgotten this most solemn tenant of leadership. It would appear the sewer of corruption and the narcissism they bathe themselves in contaminates not only their minds but, indeed, their souls. Corruption can only breed more corruption amounting to more lies, deceit, and thievery. This appears to be the cornerstone of political practice amongst many politicians who have sworn to serve their constituents. How did these people become callous monsters who abuse the fundamental aspects of moral conduct? What happened within their souls that led them to this path of darkness? Well, it is a question worth dissecting in order to get to the truth behind this certain breed of person.

The first thing to consider is what type of personality is attracted to politics in the first place. Often it is a personality type that has a desire to lead rather than follow. We all understand the importance of leaders, and we also know without followers, there would be no leaders. The duality of our existence once again is demonstrated in the symbiotic relationship between these two types of personalities.

The importance of leaders is at the core of the social structures we create. We require the duality that exists between leaders and followers to create a society built upon order and reasoning. Neither can exist without the other. Christ was a leader, but so was Napoleon and Hitler. Not all leaders are good and not all of them are bad. However, it would seem that the more power a leader garners, the more they become disconnected from the people they are designated to lead.

Christ understood that a humble leader could bring his followers into the light of true divinity, while Hitler used his power to control and manipulate those around him. Both eventually would meet their demise. However, one rose above the constraints of physical reality, demonstrating the unyielding power of divinity, while the other would simply turn to dust. This lesson should never be forgotten, but time and again, it is by those who wield the sword of power and control.

Politicians may be the pinnacle of corrupted power, but corruption can exist on many levels. I began my career as a humble social worker who only wanted to improve the lives of those less fortunate. There was something pure in my heart, and my intentions were sincere. I made little money, but my heart was filled with the desire to serve others over everything else. However, the more I focused on my family and myself, the less I focused on my original purpose to help those in need. Eventually, my desire to help those in need morphed into demanding higher and higher financial compensation for my efforts. I was still willing to help people, but only if I was paid well enough in the process. The humble satisfaction of serving others was gone, now replaced with selfish intent to get as much as I could out of the work I was providing. I could have been stacking rocks as long as I was paid well enough.

By the end of my career, I was overseeing a rather large social service operation, and for many years, I remained well-connected to my staff. But power has its way of seducing those who bare it to eventually believe they are smarter and more important than those they lead. Somewhere along the line, I became bloated and pompous, forgetting exactly what had made me a good leader who was able to inspire others. Over time, while in a position of leadership, I had sadly forgotten what had attracted me to serve in the first place.

My job had become one of focusing my efforts on the control and distribution of financial and human resources. I was no longer visiting Native American families on the reservation. That was left to staff members who I didn't even know their names. I no longer had the time or desire to work with "those people" anymore. Again I can't even tell you when I became this callous person, but I had become cold and cynical, only concerned about impressing my boss and getting my yearly salary increase.

Around six months after I retired, upon many nights lying awake retracing my career, it dawned on me what type of leader I had become. The cold reality I was forced to accept was that the lure of power eventually did corrupt my thinking and blinded me to the person I had become. I would have never believed it of myself thirty years prior, but I had become distorted by my own perception of self-importance. Now if it can happen to me (someone who politicians would consider a "nobody"), imagine what can happen to people with *real* political power. What are the chances they can maintain a humble nature in the sewer they swim in? Corruption of the mind and the soul would appear almost inevitable.

One only needs to look at the current leader of our country to recognize that he simply operates on political instinct and nothing more. He is the owner of a vacant mind and tarnished soul, spewing lies and half-truths, all in an effort to maximize his power and control. There is literally no interest in the profound honor of servitude to his country or a desire to lead with a greater purpose. Those feelings were lost long ago as he cheated, betrayed, and trampled over others during his long political career. The fact is, honest self-reflection of his unsavory deeds would require the act of his own self-condemnation, but his soul is likely too far gone to feel the need ever to seek redemption.

He has convinced himself of his own preposterous stature as a superior human being, unaware of his ameba-like spiritual evolution. He abrogates all responsibility for his actions pointing his boney finger at others and accusing them of perpetrating his misdeeds. Any sense of dignity or honor that might have ever graced his consciousness has long been obliterated by the weight of his own unethical behavior. All that matters now to this Cretan, who has been consumed by corruption, is his wealth, his image, and his power. He will lie without a conscience, he will hurt without remorse, and he will destroy without regret.

To be fair, this poor example of a human being is just one of the thousands who operate with the same blind narcissistic intent within our political sphere. They have resided in the White House before, and they will reside there again. They are in the halls of Congress and in state legislatures and city councils. Anywhere where there is a nexus of power, there will be those lusting to suckle at the breast of self-adoration.

So now we've established the personality type of those who seek power, but what is the solution to mitigate their destructive behavior? Unfortunately, for this question, I have no answer. As social beings, our very nature is to congregate in mass. We need leaders to organize and establish rules of societal operation. Without societal rules, there would be disorder and chaos; therefore, the need for leadership is clear. As we have already established, though, those with the desire to lead are often the least qualified to do so. It is an irrefutable fact that nature abhors a vacuum and in the absence of a leader, someone will step up to fill the void whether they are qualified to lead or not. Therefore a "leaderless" commune-type environment could never survive for very long though naive idealists would have you believe differently.

So how do we function or even dare to thrive under the leadership of crooks, thieves, and liars abound? First, it must be noted we already continue to function regardless of corrupted leadership because many of us still abide by a set of ethical standards and moral tenants. We don't just feign adherence to these standards; we live our lives by them. We behave with dignity and honor whether someone is watching us or not. It is in our nature to "do the right thing" as we have not been corrupted by power, money, or self-adoration. This is where our hope lies: Within each one of us.

We must tap into our spiritual essence, whether through God or nature or some other worthy natural attribute. We must seek inspiration where divinity resides and avoid the darkness that power, money, lust, and greed attract. It is ultimately our choice, as no one can ever take this choice away from us. *We choose* what path to follow, and *we decide* where to seek our inspiration and moral guidance. We can make a difference in this world one individual at a time by turning to the light of divinity we all intuitively know exists. This light may take on a multitude of forms and experiences, but within each one of us, we can find our path toward spiritual illumination.

We must not be deterred by the lures of society that often interfere and distract us from our mission to seek goodness over decadence. Humankind has created an existence filled with meaningless distractions having nothing to do with our core need to seek divinity. Our lives are bombarded by manufactured illusions comprised of empty promises leading to pointless self-gratification. Sadly, in the waning moments of life on this earth, many will realize they were sold an illusion of which they became mindlessly obedient to its lure. The truth behind our existence has never included obedience to superficial manifestations created by an imperfect species. It is a lie that, if propagated, will only lead us further from our pursuit of the divine nature of our existence.

Propinquity Where Have You Gone?

Propinquity is defined as "The state of being close to someone or something." In general terms, this definition speaks to the concept of "proximity." In other words, one might conclude propinquity to be the proximation of people and events relative to one's own locality. Why is this important? Well, it speaks to "relativity," which is one of the guiding constructs in our perception of the world around us. Propinquity speaks to relativity, and relativity defines our individuality.

As discussed in previous chapters, relativity also exists in the world of dualism, and dualism provides us with the necessary contrast to validate our existence. Again, how would we know what day is without the contrast of night? How would we know what life is without death? This dualistic nature of existence is how we define ourselves in relation to the physical world around us.

Propinquity, in the end, is just another "compare and contrast" exercise defining the world we live in from the one we do not. The world we perceive to exist in will no doubt radically change based on the breadth of the lens we view it from. Imagine the difference in perspective between the astronaut viewing our world from space and the physicist who studies life at the sub-atomic level. Both are viewing our physical world but from far different perspectives drawing radically different conclusions.

Think of how your own home and its immediate surroundings appear to you standing on its roof. Now think of how that same setting would appear flying in an airplane above. What has changed? In the truest sense, nothing, however, our relative position or proximity of observation no doubt has changed our perspective on what we see. Standing on the roof, our observation is ruled by propinquity. Everything near us is in focus, including awareness of the interrelation between all things within the immediate area. From the airplane, however, the detail and clarity of this interrelated bond between all things living and inanimate have been completely lost, giving way to a different contextual reality appearing nothing like the rooftop view.

Why does any of this matter? Well, whether it is recognized or not, propinquity is incredibly important to our overall happiness. As propinquity dissipates due to our ever-expanding world, so does our happiness. All of us live in a bubble within a bubble within another bubble etc. Of course, the first bubble is our sense of "I," our recognition of our own individuality which is represented by our inner voice. This awareness slowly expands out to our immediate family, closest friends, work environment, neighborhood, and, eventually, our local community.

Like the ripples created by throwing a stone into a pond, propinquity expands outward. The impact point where the stone hits the water is the base from where it begins, and as the rings expand outward, so does our awareness of the world around us. The ripples closest to the impact point are more intense than those expanding outward into open water, just as our closest relationships carry more intensity than our cursory encounters.

This "wave-like" behavior, as physics has proven, is simply part of our natural world that extends well into the cosmos. Just as the "Big Bang" theoretically was the beginning point of our universe, our own birth is an example of this same theory. From the point of birth and as we continue to age, our awareness is much like the ever-expanding universe. Our minds are in a constant state of expansion, collecting thoughts and experiences, forming our attitudes and beliefs. Broader awareness brings with it a multitude of varying experiences that ultimately dictate how we perceive the world around us.

Recall how the spider and ant possess an extremely limited view of the world around them, perhaps just mere inches. Beyond this limited scope is a mist of nothingness... the unknown. Due to the vast amount of variables that exist, i.e., socio-economic status, geographic location, etc., all of us also have limits in our perception of the world around us. These variables ultimately restrict or expand our boundaries of awareness, modifying our experiences as well as influencing our beliefs and attitudes.

However, what would happen if the boundaries of propinquity become muddled and confused? What if the ripples in the pond expanding outward are disrupted by another stone thrown into the pond? What happens to the waves created by the first stone thrown? Obviously, their natural path will be disrupted by the second stone entering the water, causing the direction to change. Ripples that were expanding in a natural concentric circle from the point of their creation are now scattered and redirected in a confused manner from their original natural flow.

We have seen this phenomenon within our own lives, and on a much grander scale, we have seen it impact all of humanity. Before the advent of electronic technology, the ripples in the pond were limited to the scope of the first stone thrown. Imagine a world where long-distance communication and the transference of information could only be made through the kinetic act of physical travel, i.e., by foot or by horseback.

This system of communication existed for thousands of years until the late 19th century with the advent of the telegraph. For thousands of years, people existed within the limits of propinquity, its boundaries defined by distance or geographical obstructions such as rivers or mountains. People were engaged in life within their own villages, and what lay beyond was of no consequence to their existence. Life happened in the "here and now," and much like the spider or ant, what occurred beyond this limited scope of awareness was a mist of the unknown. It was inconsequential and irrelevant and, therefore, of no concern to the village dwellers.

As the expanses of our awareness grew through technology, our lives became more complicated. Information has always been a double edge sword. More information creates more awareness and more awareness will always complicate our thought processes. In the simple world of duality, black is black, and white is white. The contrast between the two is obvious and simple to discern. However, the more information introduced into our lives creates "the grey," and this is where confusion and disorder are bred. I'm not saying life should be led by the simple rules of basic duality. However, one cannot disagree with the premise that information does create "the grey," ultimately complicating our lives.

Imagine seven unfortunate souls shipwrecked on a deserted island in the south pacific. Sound familiar? Now imagine these castaways are from diverse socio-economic backgrounds. Some have lived urban lifestyles, while others have lived rural. Some are highly educated others are not. Values and ethics may also be quite diverse. What is likely to occur in such a small but diverse group of individuals? The natural tendency is for them to find commonalities amongst themselves. They will certainly be able to connect the dots regarding similar experiences they share. All of them are victims of a shipwreck, isolated from the rest of the world and fighting for survival. They will build upon these commonalities to develop a social system that is amenable and acceptable to all. The group is small enough that differences can be overcome, and much like a loosely knit family, a sense of unity will develop. Most importantly, a desire to survive will bond all of them together.

In this metaphor, this is the entry point of the stone being thrown into the pond. Due to the small number of castaways and the imposed geographic isolation, the ripples created by the stone expand and dissipate in an orderly and predictable wave-like fashion. Propinquity is king under these circumstances, as no other outside forces are impacting the natural order of their interrelated existence, the ripples of water function as they should, the intensity of the waves dissipating as they expand away from the creation point.

What if the castaways possessed a radio delivering information from the outside world? How would this change the balance of the little society they created? We have all observed how the flow of information into this uncharted island affected its inhabitants. Often it was this flow of information that created chaos and disrupted the natural order which had been established by the castaways.

Within their own small group, they had found a rhythm to their existence and a purpose based on common goals. The introduction of an additional variable (outside information) equates to the second stone being thrown into the pond. The established order they had developed is now disrupted. The inhabitants of the island would have no doubt continued to survive without information flowing in from the outside. This additional information did nothing to improve the castaway's situation, and it only created more issues for them to address. Information changes our lives by introducing a multitude of variables into our consciousness. These variables, in the spirit of duality, have positive and negative impacts on our psyche. In the case of the castaways, news from the radio often created mistrust and conflict within the group. The information rarely benefited the inhabitants of the island, and rather, it disrupted the natural flow of life they had grown accustomed to.

It is often postulated that the more educated the person is, the less happy they become. The expansion of our awareness through the influx of information comes at a cost. The intrinsic value of propinquity becomes diminished, disrupting our emotional security and our ability to maintain happiness in our lives.

Look no further than my own story to see an example of where information disrupted and changed my life permanently. Images and sounds from the family television set brought the Vietnam War into my living room, invading the most intimate level of my own propinquity. The ripples of awareness naturally emanating and controlled within the security of my family home had been disrupted by the knowledge of war thousands of miles away.

All I had known was peace, safety, and security until Vietnam entered my consciousness. My young mind, not yet prepared for this ugly side of life, was introduced far too early to concepts of violence, pain, and suffering. This untimely exposure disrupted the natural progression of my understanding of the outside world and its correlation to my own existence.

The impressions of war entered into my scope of awareness far too early and damaged my psyche. Though other children must face the horrors of war and perhaps have always known of it, this need not have been my fate as the war was nowhere near my doorstep. It was an unwanted guest that should have never been allowed to enter my realm of propinquity.

The reality is that we cannot go about living our lives with our heads in the sand. Society moves much too quickly to ignore all that is occurring around us. However, the importance lies within the regulation and timing of information that is allowed to enter our world. Our propinquity must be protected and nurtured if we are to maintain a healthy balance in our lives. What occurs within our inner circle and the balance we have developed within our scope of awareness, which defines our purpose cannot be disrupted. Information that is secondary to our immediate experience, or in other words, our daily lives, cannot become the dominant force. Information should be a supplement with its dosage closely monitored.

Where is this all leading? It is leading to my concern regarding where we all find ourselves immersed today, the "Information Age." During my lifetime, I have observed the shift in our society from the industrial age to the information age. It indeed has been a unique opportunity to have observed the birth of a new societal era, an opportunity very few generations are given.

Before the 19th century and the age of industrialization, humankind had been agrarian-based for thousands of years. The industrial revolution, a time of dynamic growth, introduced a mechanized world to humanity, bringing great change to all aspects of living. Industrialization created massive amounts of wealth, prosperity, and opportunity for millions. Conversely, it also contributed to many new harmful scenarios, from urban hell holes to the threat of nuclear holocaust.

All new eras come with a list of benefits to humankind, or they would not be embraced and advanced. However, the side effects of these new "ages" and the issues they bring are often unseen or ignored until it is too late, and they become embedded within the newly established culture.

With the dawning of the information age, an entire set of issues, originally not identified 30 years ago, have now become blatantly clear. I have built the foundation of my argument with the premise of the importance of propinquity. The information age has gutted propinquity, impacting anyone within reach of a cellular phone or computer. I have outlined how the abundance of information can disrupt the established order within our immediate surroundings. I have discussed how the natural order of expanding awareness is replaced with chaos and disorder when too much information is accessible too quickly. Education of the mind is no longer earned. It is provided instantaneously without discipline of thought and with no concern for the consequences.

One can find any answer they desire via the internet and one can find affirmation for any idea through social media. By this, I mean anyone can find an answer that fits their narrative, but it is not necessarily the correct answer. This is incredibly dangerous as lies are easily propagated and interpreted as "truths." Therefore, anyone can find affirmation for their narrative regardless of how dangerous or immoral it may be.

The internet and social media are the grandest experiment in brainwashing ever created and its effectiveness is unparalleled in human history. Without discipline and guidance in the dissemination of vast amounts of information, true comprehension cannot exist. In its place, disorder, and confusion will reign supreme. If our entire reality becomes one subjective interpretation, easily swinging from one side of the pendulum to the other, the stability duality provides will also fade into the grey.

The threat of overexposure to extraneous information is particularly dangerous to developing minds. Access to an abundance of information without proper oversight can leave the young to drift into an ocean of self-doubt. Whatever values or beliefs established during their youth still require nurturing, not divisive messaging delivered by outside sources. The internet and social media have invaded the precious propinquity inherent within a family setting, stealing the minds of the young from those who truly care about them.

I can only imagine how difficult it is for children of the current generation to balance the multitude of opinions and the crush of information in a healthy, productive manner. The innumerable choices offered to youth, who often lack the cognitive ability to make good decisions consistently, can result in an emotional overload, leading to questioning their own values. The result of this self-doubt promotes insecurity and depression.

The massive influence of the internet, coupled with social media, has created a society where people are literally addicted to their cellular phones. Everywhere you look, people are mindlessly gazing at the device held in their hands. Whether they are at the store, gym, their child's school event, or even driving their cars, people cannot break away from the allure of the phone. Sadly, people are not even aware or perhaps don't care. They are held in bondage to an electronic device. It is mass dependency, the likes I have never seen, and there appears to be no answer. People have lost their dignity and self-control to the cellular phone. They have allowed this device to control much of their lives, behaving as if they cannot exist without it in their hand.

What is the answer to this mass addiction? Again, it starts with each individual making the decision to say "no more." It begins with the desire to establish and nurture one's own propinquity. We must first focus on the development and protection of our own immediate interpersonal environment, as it is the key to our happiness. The outside voice that is social media must be reduced to a whisper instead of a roar. It is up to each of us to decide to walk away from this enslavement and condemn it for what it is… mind control.

A commitment must be made to be no longer seduced by outside forces that deem to control our beliefs and actions. We are responsible for our own behavior and the choices we make. We must choose to honor and listen to our inner voice and ignore the static emanating from the world of social media. Any addiction can be beaten through the power of the mind. However, the mind must first be committed to fighting the battle with tenacity and resiliency. This is indeed a battle worth fighting. What is at stake is the health of our own inner sanctum and, in the broader scope, the health of our society.

There Once Was a Note…

Upon reading my story covering four decades, it should come as no surprise that I have a strong interest in music. For each decade covered in my book, I shared my observations and feelings about the popular music being created at that time. I also discussed the evolvement and, in my opinion, the eventual de-evolvement of popular music. Throughout my life, like many others, I'm sure, music provided me with a soundtrack to my life. We all know how it feels to hear a song from the past and be instantly taken back to a time when we were younger. Music is a memory maker and, much like other forms of art, can transcend time when at its very best.

I have always loved music, and it has been a part of my life for as long as I can remember. By the time I reached my late teens, I had ideations like many of becoming a rock star. My friends and I used to drink and play air guitar late into the night listening to the classic rock bands of the 70s. I tried on several occasions to pick up a guitar and learn to play, but I had neither the aptitude nor the required motivation to make it happen. I wanted to play guitar and be in a band garnering the adoration of beautiful young women, but like most things in my life back in the day, I just couldn't muster the discipline to make it happen.

At the age of forty, I would once again try to pick up a guitar and learn to play. My motivation, however, was far different from the days of my late teens. It was clear that at age forty, my life's long past time of playing team basketball had ended. I no longer had the physical ability to play at the level I was accustomed to and was being beaten by younger players with far less talent but had the attributes of youth on their side. My pride would not allow me to compete against "older players".

\] If I could no longer hold my own against the best basketball players I wanted nothing to do with the game. It was with great sadness that I turned in my basketball shoes and walked away from the sport. I distinctly recall walking off the basketball court after a particularly sub-standard effort on my part, knowing I had reached the end. I left the team that evening and never returned.

The next day I went to the local pawn shop and purchased a used electric guitar. I needed a new challenge now that my basketball days were over and I felt it was finally time to make a sincere effort to learn to play. I immediately signed up for guitar lessons but attended only one lesson as I realized there was no way I was going to learn to play through someone else's instructions. It would have to be done on my terms and in my own way.

I quickly ran into the difficulty of attempting to learn. My fingers hurt as the strings cut into their tips at times, causing them to bleed. It took weeks for me to build up callouses so I could play without pain. In addition, my fingers could not form in the proper position to play chords. I felt completely uncoordinated and my frustration grew. I also had no concept of music theory whatsoever. It was like I was trying to learn a new language without having any concept of its alphabet.

The one thing that kept me going was an article I had read about George Harrison (former Beatle) and his journey in mastering the guitar. Apparently, Harrison was not born with a natural talent for music like his colleagues Lennon and McCartney. He had to work twice as hard to become proficient in playing. He never gave up though he just put his head down and worked at it. Now I knew I would never be in the same universe as Harrison as a guitarist, but his story motivated me in the sense that if I worked hard enough, I could learn to play at a rudimentary level.

After several years of hard work attempting to learn the instrument, I finally reached the level of "acceptability" in my guitar playing. Eventually, I would form a rock band along with other aspiring musicians naming it "Final Theory." We performed live, including at several music festivals. We wrote our own music resisting the temptation to do cover songs. In the end, we were good but nowhere near great. I was clearly the weak link in a band that, aside from myself, possessed considerable talent. I was never good enough to be any more than a hobbyist, and I knew it.

We recorded some songs and talked about making a push to get to the next level of popularity, but like most aspiring bands, all those dreams fell to the wayside in the end. Still, I enjoyed being in a rock band and performing live, and I had successfully accomplished my long-standing dream of being a guitarist in a rock band. To this day, I rank this accomplishment equal to earning my college degree.

Music, to me, has always been more than just "ear candy." I have always considered it the most profound and intimate form of art. Its variability in sensory perception is unmatched by any other art form, and it is not static in its presentation. There is a sonic resonance to this form of art that not only can be heard but also felt. Poetry can inspire the soul with thoughts of passionate insight, but often times music includes the written word as well. Through music, thoughts of the poet can be embellished with the addition of sonic impressions that produce a physical response to accompany the spoken word.

Making music is a universal human trait going far back into our distant past. The original age of the creation of music is unknown, but it is estimated it likely began during the "stone age," when humans initially began to devise tools for use. Suffice to say music is part of the human equation and has been around since the earliest of civilizations. It is undoubtedly part of the fabric of our existence created by the mind, as everything ultimately is in the end.

Those who are musically gifted actually dream of making original music or have music come to them in a conscious state, seemingly out of nowhere. They simply just hear it as if it was their inner voice talking to them. Like magic, they are graced with beautiful tonal sounds that seemingly are created out of thin air. There is something transcendental about music that cannot be fully explained. It can be felt, and it can be shared, but there is something ethereal surrounding music and its effect on people's behavior and emotions.

Of course, science is always the first place to look for answers to the mysteries of our world. What does science have to say regarding the impact music has on our lives? From a strictly physical perspective, our response and reaction to music comes from the brain through the release of dopamine. Dopamine is a neurotransmitter that enhances pleasure impacting many aspects of physical and mental living. It can have positive and negative implications ranging from feelings of happiness to addictive unhealthy behavior. Without delving into the depths of neuroscience, it is safe to say music triggers these neurotransmitters causing the human body and mind to respond and react in a multitude of ways, including the reduction of anxiety, blood pressure, and pain. It can also improve sleep, overall awareness, memory, and mood.

We have all experienced the power of music on our bodies and mind. We have sulked during a sad song that brings back memories of lost love. We have also regained the feelings of being a child listening to songs we recall hearing in our youth, and who hasn't found themselves unconsciously tapping their feet or moving their body to the rhythm of a beat we find pleasurable? Music has that level of power and influence in our lives.

There can be no doubt that music has been and will continue to be an important part of the human equation and the overall health of our species. This summation is strictly from the perspective of the physical reality we all find ourselves immersed in but what of the spiritual aspect of our existence? What part does music play in the reverence and enlightenment of our spiritual side?

The history of music as a spiritual device goes back to the age of the creation of the art form. It is worth delving into the cause-and-effect relationship between music and our own spirituality. The deeply intertwined relationship between the two may hold secrets to our own divinity or, at the very least, our awareness of a divine being. Historically speaking, it appears spirituality and music have been tied together since perhaps the inception of both phenomena into the human psyche.

The original meditative trances humans engaged in thousands upon thousands of years ago were simply intuitive efforts to connect with a divine source. Often this meditative practice was accompanied by chanting in a rhythmic tonal infliction of the voice utilizing rudimentary notes varying in spatiality and length. This semi-conscious chanting married the sounds of the physical world with the metaphysical state of the spiritual world, thus bridging the gap between the two different realities and enhancing the spiritual experience.

One can therefore extrapolate music and spiritually feed off of one another. Can moments of deep spiritual reverence be responsible for the creation of inspiring music? Absolutely. Can tonal vibrations brought to clarity through our senses and then deciphered through brain activity create an environment conducive to spiritual illumination? No doubt.

Love, as discussed prior in this book, also possesses strong transcendental characteristics. Love cannot be "seen," but acts of love can be observed. Love is not a physical condition. You cannot look at a human body and surmise, "This person is in love." However, one can feel the love emanating from within themself and project this "feeling" onto someone else. Music is very similar in the manner in which it works. Strictly speaking, music cannot be seen; it is simply a collection of sound waves emanating outward from its source. However, music can be "felt" through our senses as well as "felt" within ourselves. You cannot beat someone to death with music or love, but it is possible to drive them to new levels of emotional depth with its power.

Much like love, music's transcendental qualities can make it a great source of joy for us. As a derivative from a divine source that is infinite (God), music can also be perceived with dark unsavory intent. For every light, there is darkness, and for every action, there is a reaction. Music and love are not insulated from this dualism. If God is EVERYTHING, then he must rule over EVERYTHING. He has given us the gift of free will and the opportunity to walk toward the light or the dark. One path leads to spiritual illumination the other path takes us further away from recognizing our true self in relation to God. One path provides enlightenment and spiritual growth. The other path is the retardation of the spiritual evolutionary process.

As we all know, love has driven people to perpetuate violent acts upon others. Music can also impact the mental state of individuals and their desire to commit violent acts. No one needs to look any further than the Manson Family (covered in part one of this book) to recognize the spell music can have on people. Manson and his followers believed Beatle's music was sending a message that fit into their belief system. Manson became enamored by the lyrics and chose a dark and violent interpretation of the music to inspire his followers. Ultimately this misguided "brainwashing" led to unspeakable acts of violence. Make no mistake, there is indeed power in music as it can raise people to new heights of spirituality or embellish the dark harmful thoughts of an unhealthy psyche.

Whether you are a big listener of music or enjoy it in smaller doses, there is the undeniable truth it permeates the human condition. One can be in a remote area of the Australian Outback or in downtown Manhattan and music will be found. Its ubiquitous nature cannot be denied, and its transcendental qualities offer a multitude of applications enhancing lives throughout the world.

Pete Townshend, the main composer for the rock band "The Who," developed an intriguing idea many years ago regarding the nature of music. His thought was brilliant in its simplicity... what if the meaning of life was held within one note? It is indeed an interesting idea that he pursued in his song "Pure and Easy." "There once was a note pure and easy playing so free like a breath rippling by. The note is eternal. I hear it… it sees me. Forever we blend forever we die." Townshend put forward the idea that music is eternal and attached to a higher source of divinity. Personally, I believe this to be the case, but whether you support his hypothesis or not, it is a compelling idea.

As I close out on this journey we have taken together, I will leave you with some of the songs that through my life have touched me in one manner or another. Below is the title of each song. I will also include my favorite verses as well. Perhaps you will find in these verses something worth pondering… perhaps not. In any case, they have become part of the soundtrack of my life, providing me with insight and inspiration over the years, and I am honored to now share them with you.

Senorita With A Necklace of Tears…. Paul Simon

"I was born before my father and my children before me, and we are born and born again like the waves of the sea. That's the way it's always been, and that's how I want it to be."

Drowse…. Queen

"Thinking it right… doing it wrong. It's easier from an armchair."

Get Together…. The Young Bloods

"We are but a moment's sunlight fading in the grass."

Sea Refuses No River…. Pete Townshend

"The sea refuses no river. Remember that when a beggar buys a round."

The Show Must Go On…. Pink Floyd

"There must be some mistake. I didn't mean to let them take away my soul. Am I too old? Is it too late?"

Five to One…. The Doors

"Your ballroom days are over, baby… night is drawing near. Shadows of the evening crawl across the years."

Brainwashed…. The Kinks

"You've got a job and a house and your kids and a car. Yeah, you're conditioned to be what they want you to be and happy to be where you are… yes you are. Get down on your knees."

Any Road…. George Harrison

"And if you don't know where you're going, any road will take you there."

Won't Get Fooled Again…. The Who

"Meet the new boss… same as the old boss."

The End…. The Beatles

"And in the end, the love you take is equal to the love you make."

May the rest of your life be filled with love, joy, and of course, enlightenment.

**James Artemus can be contacted at:
artemusjames19@gmail.com**

Made in the USA
Monee, IL
27 December 2023

e0c9ce8a-f819-4289-9dec-3bd66daeea4aR02